The Music of the Close

 # the Music
of the Close

The Final Scenes
of Shakespeare's Tragedies

WALTER C. FOREMAN, Jr.

THE UNIVERSITY PRESS OF KENTUCKY

*For my mother
and father*

Foreman, Walter C   1943-
    The music of the close.

    Includes bibliographical references and index.
    1. Shakespeare, William, 1564-1616—Tragedies.
    2. Shakespeare, William, 1564-1616—Technique.
    3. Death in literature. I. Title.
    PR2983.F63   822.3'3   77-75484
    ISBN 0-8131-1366-0

A statewide cooperative scholarly publishing agency
serving Berea College, Centre College of Kentucky,
Eastern Kentucky University, The Filson Club,
Georgetown College, Kentucky Historical Society,
Kentucky State University, Morehead State University,
Murray State University, Northern Kentucky University,
Transylvania University, University of Kentucky,
University of Louisville, and Western Kentucky University.

Editorial and Sales Offices: Lexington, Kentucky 40506

Contents

 # Preface

THIS book will end with an allusion to Antony's vision of the rich, ever-changing spectacle of clouds in the evening sky:

> Sometime we see a cloud that's dragonish;
> A vapor sometime like a bear or lion,
> A towered citadel, a pendant rock,
> A forked mountain, or blue promontory
> With trees upon't that nod unto the world
> And mock our eyes with air. Thou hast seen these signs;
> They are black Vesper's pageants. . . .
> That which is now a horse, even with a thought
> The rack dislimns, and makes it indistinct
> As water is in water.
>
> (*AC* IV.xiv.2–11)

Antony's problem here—trying to establish a shape for himself and his world—is something like the problem of writing about Shakespeare's tragedies, those magnificent spectacles, magnificent illusions, of the coming of night. Literally, of course, the text which we contemplate is, for all its annoying or fascinating problems, relatively stable, but the Shakespearean tragic sky itself seems so rich and ever-changing that the shapes we impose on it are never adequate and our books can never really be finished. Thus the present book, instead of meekly allowing itself to be revised into its "original" shape, kept trying to become the next book. A publication, then, is but a momentary shape, a pause along the way in our vision of the show. Not that this situation is in the least to be lamented, for there is a great beauty in that changing sky, a beauty that Antony was not then in a mood to appreciate. But if we continue to accept its richness and variety of shape, its beauty in the fullest sense, we will hopefully find that what is really changing, growing in response to the beauty we find there, is ourselves.

In writing a book on Shakespeare's tragedies there is not only the problem of relating to the text but also the problem of relating to earlier criticism. One realizes, at a time like this, one's debt to what has been written before, a debt so vast that one is no longer sure to whom some of it is owed. I of course refer carefully to such specific debts as I am aware of. But there is also the debt, at least equally large, to Shakespearean criticism that has passed through my consciousness long ago and left its ideas somewhere beyond my explicit awareness but ready to come forward to pose as my own. Shakespearean criticism is a collective activity of being concerned about Shakespeare, finding him important in one's life, profiting from the record left by others who have felt this concern and this sense of importance, and, finally, writing about the plays. It is in the hope of contributing in a small way to this activity, of saying something somewhere here that will become part of someone else's assimilated but valuable mental debris that I go forward. I go forward in that hope, and with the explicit awareness of something Anthony Burgess said one night in a television interview with Dick Cavett in 1971, while I was just beginning this project. Contrasting Shakespeare with Woodrow Wilson as a subject of scholarship, Burgess said that because there were already so many books on Shakespeare, there was always room for one more. Burgess was justifying *his* book on Shakespeare, but, with due credit, I can steal his justification for my own.

For the purposes of this study, I take as "Shakespeare's tragedies" the following thirteen plays: *Titus Andronicus, Richard III, Romeo and Juliet, Richard II, Julius Caesar, Hamlet, Troilus and Cressida, Othello, King Lear, Macbeth, Timon of Athens, Antony and Cleopatra,* and *Coriolanus.* One might question, for one reason or another, the inclusion of *Richard III, Richard II,* or *Troilus and Cressida.* I hope that the first two chapters will show why it is useful to consider them with the rest of the plays in this group. I have left out plays like 3 *Henry VI* and *Henry VIII* (which are curiously similar to each other in structure) because

Preface

in them the "tragedies" are too local, the tragic effect too diffuse. The deaths of York and Warwick, for instance, have at least as much impact as the death of Henry VI. Our real interest, with *3 Henry VI,* is in the rise of Richard—as if the play were really a Part 1 of *Richard III.*

I cite and quote Shakespeare from *The Pelican Shakespeare* (gen. ed. Alfred Harbage [Baltimore: Penguin, 1956–67]). Occasionally I restore a quarto or Folio reading; the only significant such change is at *Hamlet* V.ii.211–13, where I follow Q2: "Since no man of aught he leaves, knows what is't to leave betimes, let be."

What I take as "the final scenes" varies from play to play. When I say "scene," I normally have in mind the conventional usage; that is, a "scene" is a section of the play bounded by complete changes of onstage personnel and designated by lower-case Roman numerals. I also observe, however, the convention by which a section of *Hamlet* III.i is "the nunnery scene" or a section of *Antony and Cleopatra* V.ii is "the Seleucus scene." But in any case, a precise definition is of little importance here since my purpose is not to look at *the* final scene, one scene and only one, of each play. With some plays I will be looking primarily at one scene, while in other plays I will be looking at a group of them. One must be flexible about this because Shakespeare is. For example, what takes one scene in *Othello* (the hero facing the consequences of his "fatal" murder) takes four acts in *Macbeth.* Obviously it would be absurd to consider the last four acts of *Macbeth* as its "final scenes," but at the same time what I think one would consider its concluding phase (roughly V.ii–viii) includes a number of "scenes" in the conventional sense, while the concluding phase of *Othello* is V.ii alone.

The exploration of this kind of structural variety will be as important in my study as the search for similarities. In the examples from *Othello* and *Macbeth* given here, for instance, the differences in form are significant not only for their reflection on the different paths by which the heroes realize their guilt but also for what they suggest about the relation of the hero to his world. By Act V Macbeth is in conflict with the rest of humanity, as it were, so Shakespeare keeps switching us back and forth from a short "scene" with Macbeth to a short "scene" with the opposing armies. (Actually the number of such switches is not adequately suggested by the traditional scene numbers. If a "scene" is marked by a complete change of personnel, V.vii could be three "scenes" and V.viii two.) In *Othello*, on the other hand, the principal conflict is within the hero. The rest of the world doesn't oppose him. Thus Shakespeare keeps Othello onstage throughout the final phase of the action, which is one long scene. Because Shakespeare varies his methods like this, experimenting with tragic form, there is no point in setting up a mechanical definition of "final scenes."

Earlier in this preface I indicated my sense of inadequacy in the presence of both Shakespeare and those who have written about him. And now I face an inadequacy of a different sort when I turn to acknowledge the people who have helped me in the course of this project. In the first place, one simply cannot mention all those teachers, students, and friends who have helped in one way or another, at one time or another. But even with people whom I can thank by name, that thanks is inadequate to the kind of debt owed to those who have tried to make both the book and its author better than we were and better, alas, than we are.

My oldest debt in writing this book is to my father, Walter C. Foreman, Sr., of Oregon State University, who first read and discussed Shakespeare with me years ago and whose thinking about the plays has strongly influenced my own (which of course doesn't make him guilty of my excesses). He also once suggested, for another occasion than the present one, that I might write about death scenes in Shakespeare. That topic was too ambitious for the occasion, but in the present book I have, in a sense, finally taken it up, even if it turns out to be too ambitious for *any* occasion.

At the University of Washington I was fortunate enough to have the experience of a seminar on Shakespeare's tragedies with Brents Stirling, fortunate to have the benefit of his example as a teacher and scholar of Shakespeare, which leaves me with even less excuse for my own lapses. He gave me generous encouragement for some work that turns out to have been the practical beginning of this project. To William Matchett I am indebted for sharing his knowledge of Shakespeare and for some written commentary he took the time to make for me when this book was a dissertation. To the director of that dissertation, Roger Sale, I am grateful not only for the advice, encouragement, and criticism he gave me but also for the tolerant patience he showed when his student made some rather presumptuous demands. I have written the chapter on *King Lear* for him. It is an attempt not only to thank him but also to be a little more specific about what I meant one evening ten years ago in a seminar on the text of the play when I mumbled somewhat vaguely that *King Lear* was "a spectacle." No, indeed not like *Henry VI!*

At the University of Washington and the University of Kentucky and beyond I have valued the encouragement, the intelligence, and the friendship of Kenneth J. Semon. The book has profited from our discussions of Shakespeare over these years, and in fact it would most likely not exist at all without his demand, sometimes gentle, sometimes fierce, always kind, that I get on with it.

For typing various parts of this work, in one version or another, I am grateful to Valerie Burke, Dianne Butler, and especially Caroline Semon, who, in addition, once typed the whole thing very quickly in a fine display of patience, stamina, and care. There are far fewer errors in my quotations and citations of Shakespeare than there would otherwise have been because in checking them I have had the aid of Leslie Boxer, though I am sure my own part in the process has managed to keep some errors hidden even from her sharp eyes.

I also wish to thank the Graduate School of the University of Kentucky, which has supported work on this book through its program of Summer Faculty Research Fellowships.

My greatest thanks, in this as in so much, are expressed, inadequately as ever, in the dedication to my parents. Among everything I have to thank them for, one moment will need to stand for all—a moment one sunny afternoon in August many years ago when they had brought their then young son to Ashland, Oregon, to see some plays at the Oregon Shakespearean Festival. There, from the hillside above the outdoor theater, he looked

Preface

down into the bowl for the first time at the Festival's Elizabethan stage and saw a rehearsal of what must have been, given
the arrangement of banners, halberds, swords, and bodies, the
last scene of *Hamlet*. It is as good a moment as any to take as
the first scene of this book.

1

tragic death
and dull survival

We that are young shall never see so much.

A DYING man, early in one of Shakespeare's tragedies, tells us that "the tongues of dying men / Enforce attention like deep harmony":

> He that no more must say is listened more
> Than they whom youth and ease have taught to glose.
> More are men's ends marked than their lives before.
> The setting sun, and music at the close,
> As the last taste of sweets, is sweetest last,
> Writ in remembrance more than things long past.
> (*R2* II.i.5–6, 9–14)

It is to the harmony of the tragic close in Shakespeare that I wish to devote my attention in this book. I will attend to the words not only of the men who die but also of the men who survive them, and not only to the harmony of words in the final scenes, but also to the harmony of dramatic structure, to the often painful music of the shapes the characters seem to create for their lives, the shapes that Shakespeare has created for them, through them—his various music of the close.

Hamlet, King Lear, and *Antony and Cleopatra* are, I think, Shakespeare's most complex and fascinating variations on the tragic ending, but in each of the tragedies he gives disaster a unique form, its own "deep harmony." Because of this variety, it

seems clear enough that Shakespeare experimented consciously
with tragic form: when he repeats, he also changes, and changes
more than superficially. As he extends and explores the possibilities of tragic form, he creates dramatic worlds which mirror
the possibilities of our own; in bringing us to the boundaries of
his art he brings us to the boundaries of human experience.

2

Death, at least, is common to the endings of Shakespeare's
tragedies. However different the particular forms disaster takes
in these plays, there is always death—death of the central figures, the tragic individuals, and often of others whose lives were
closely bound up with the lives of the central figures.

"Death is a fearful thing," says Claudio and elaborates in the
famous lines which worked so powerfully on Samuel Johnson's
imagination as to suggest unbearably the presence of death:[1]

> . . . to die, and go we know not where,
> To lie in cold obstruction and to rot,
> This sensible warm motion to become
> A kneaded clod; and the delighted spirit
> To bathe in fiery floods, or to reside
> In thrilling region of thick-ribbed ice,
> To be imprisoned in the viewless winds
> And blown with restless violence round about
> The pendant world; or to be worse than worst
> Of those that lawless and incertain thought
> Imagine howling, 'tis too horrible.
> The weariest and most loathed worldly life
> That age, ache, penury, and imprisonment
> Can lay on nature is a paradise
> To what we fear of death.
>   (*MM* III.i.116, 118–32)

Though *Measure for Measure* is not a tragedy, it was written
in a period when Shakespeare's imagination tended to express
itself in tragic forms, and it shares with many of the tragedies a
world in which individual desires apparently can never fit
naturally, or without coercion, into society's rules. Yet this fear-

ful image of death is not the obsession one finds in a tragic hero. The kind of suffering imagined by Claudio is more likely to characterize the tragic hero's life than his anticipation of death. It is true that Hamlet is concerned that one's sense of "The undiscovered country, from whose bourn / No traveller returns" interferes with one's impulse to act; but Hamlet also sees death as an end to life's torture, and one of the things Hamlet must do (and does) before assuming his tragic destiny is to exorcise his fears about experience after death. When the final scene comes, Hamlet is "ready" for death. "The readiness is all." Almost all of Shakespeare's tragic figures are ready, in one way or another, and show none of the panic that is so painfully present in Claudio's speech.

In fact, most of the tragic characters eventually long for death, desire it, seek it, either as a rest from suffering or as the only thing consistent with their integrity, with their sense of the value of their own lives. There are the suicides—Romeo and Juliet, Brutus, Othello, Antony and Cleopatra, and, in effect, Timon. There is Titus, who, living only for revenge, sets in motion a chain of events he can hardly hope to survive. There is Coriolanus, who accepts his death when he spares Rome. There is Troilus, who looks forward eagerly to death, though in the ironic world of his play he hasn't yet brought it off. There are Richard II, Hamlet, and Macbeth, who look toward death as relief from a disappointing world, though they all die like lions thrusting forth their paws. There is Richard III, who, though he experiences some panic after his prebattle dream, dies like the rest of these men and women, preferring to maintain his integrity by facing death instead of running away (he wants the horse in order that he may fight, not escape). Finally, there is Lear, essentially alone in this group as in his own play, in that he gives virtually no thought to his own death, one way or the other. He neither avoids it nor seeks it. Death catches Lear by surprise as it does no other tragic figure, so much so that he never even realizes that he is dying. He is the only one, in fact, who can be said to die of "natural causes," a phrase that is hardly casual when we remember Lear's own search into "cause in nature," down to the cause—the reason—for Cordelia's death. But like the rest, Lear is ready, or, in the terms of his play, "ripe."

3

Claudio's speech on death expresses, rather, the feeling of those who stay alive to populate the world and keep society going. (Indeed, his impulse to populate the world is what gets him into a situation where he must contemplate death.) If Claudio had been killed, he would not have been tragic, only pitiful, like the equally panicky George in *Richard III*. In the tragedies, the character who perhaps comes closest to Claudio in sentiment (though he has a good deal more nerve) is that very untragic figure Edgar. "O, our lives' sweetness," he says, "That we the pain of death would hourly die / Rather than die at once" (*Lr* V.iii.185–87), a remark which has little to do with the experience of Gloucester, which he is describing, but aptly characterizes Edgar's own kind of endurance in the face of adversity.

Edgar is an example of the kind of man who does not die at the end of a Shakespearean tragedy and who becomes instead the center of a new community, the reestablished order in which tragic figures have no place. An interest in the fate of the community is, like death, common to the ends of all the tragedies. In fact, Shakespeare places the fate of the central figure against the fate of the community in a way that characterizes the particular tragic world of each play. Shakespeare doesn't show us the same kind of world over and over again in his tragedies. Things can go wrong in many ways, and this relation of individual fate to communal fate suggests from play to play the particularities of his various tragic visions. Thus it is important to note the values embodied in the new, surviving order.

3

A Shakespearean play is in general a process of going from one order to another (the first sometimes shown, sometimes only implied), and this process itself always involves a good deal of disorder. That this is true is hardly surprising, since conflict is the basis of drama. But the nature of the disorder varies from play to play. If we ignore for the moment the complexities, ambivalences, and impurities that make Shakespearean drama so rich, we can divide the plays into groups according to whether the disorder is mainly creative or mainly destructive. The former is comic disorder; the latter is tragic.

The disorder of a given play is normally produced by characters who are felt to be the center of energy in the play, characters whose activity breaks down the conditions prevailing at the beginning. It is important to distinguish here between the disorder that we see in the course of the play (and this disorder is what I'm talking about here) and some "given" disorder that may be part of the play's premise. Thus it may be Duke Frederick and to a lesser degree Oliver who originally upset the order of things, but in the dramatic structure of *As You Like It* the centers of energy and of the dramatic disorder are Rosalind and, to a lesser degree, Orlando. The same distinction can be made in a tragedy: Claudius may be originally responsible for the rotten disorder in the state of Denmark, but what we see and hear in the course of the play is the energy of Hamlet breaking up the "order" that Claudius and others have tried to establish.

This center of disordering energy needn't lie primarily in a single character, particularly when love is involved. There are Romeo and Juliet, Antony and Cleopatra, Lysander and Hermia and Demetrius and Helena, and so forth. And in *Troilus and Cressida* there is perhaps no center at all. In *The Winter's Tale* the center shifts and diversifies after the first half, which is dominated by Leontes. In *Othello,* Iago is the center at first but by the end of Act III he has managed to bring the tremendous energy of Othello into the disordering process, and Othello's energy supersedes his.[2]

I am interested here in what characterizes the kinds of energy that carry the tragedies to their final scenes, and for this purpose it is useful to distinguish broadly between comic disorder and tragic disorder. Comic disorder—the sort, for instance, of which Antipholus of Syracuse, Portia (of *The Merchant of Venice*), Rosalind, Viola, and Prospero are centers—is ultimately and especially creative disorder. It breaks down an original order that should not be maintained, an original order that is unproductive, unnatural, deadly, and stifling to the best tendencies of human nature and of the best characters in the play. And, most important, the creative energy that leads everyone into the disorder also leads the way out of it into a final order that embodies this energy and thus includes the best elements of the play's dramatic world. At the end of a play structured by comic energy we tend to have a sense of a productive community being established and a sense that what lies ahead for this community is health, growth, fertility, and a free harmony among its members—a harmony that has been achieved by the energy of the best in the community, not a harmony imposed on it by survivors of the dramatic process.[3] Often (in *A Midsummer Night's Dream, As You Like It,* and *The Tempest,* for instance) we even have the feeling that the community is a harmonious part of a superhuman order.

Tragic disorder, on the other hand, is essentially destructive in its effect. The order that tragic energy breaks down may or may not be worth keeping. In *Othello* and *Macbeth,* for instance, it apparently is worth keeping, while in *Romeo and Juliet* and *Hamlet* it is presumably not. Structurally, the value of the original order is not so important a question in tragedy as it is in comedy. But the order must be there, in one way or another, and the center of energy in the play breaks it down. As in comedy, the disorder finally issues in a new order, but in tragedy the new order does not embody the central energy, the tragic, destructive energy. The new community in tragedy excludes the best, either wiping it out or profiting by its self-destruction. (This exclusion is made easier by the fact that the central energy in tragedy is more likely than in comedy to be confined to one or two characters.) We often feel that the new order is imposed rather than achieved. We often have a sense of a community that is *merely* ordered, a community that is strong, stable, efficient, well administered, even bureaucratic. This new community, lacking the energy of the central figures, the tragic figures, seems to be thoroughly human. The final harmony is usually not part of a larger, superhuman harmony. If anything has been superhuman in the world, it has died out along with the tragic energy and those individual men and women who embodied it.

It is in the disorder that the tragedies test the limits of human experience, so that by analyzing the disorder we get a sense of the scope of the tragic energy and, as far as the endings are concerned, a sense of the human possibilities we have lost in losing the tragic hero. In the course of the plays, disorder may

6

be stirred up on one or more of the following six levels, listed in order of increasing breadth: mental, sexual, familial, political or military, elemental or cosmic, and metaphysical. (This scheme is one way of describing the various levels of human experience on which disorder occurs; the division could be made in other ways.)[4] These levels tend to be analogous or even congruent to each other. For example, sexual disorder in *Antony and Cleopatra* is seen as being also political. In *Hamlet* sexual disorder is also both mental and familial. Metaphorically, and by extension, it is also metaphysical.

Our sense of the "profundity" of any one of the tragedies depends on which and how many of these disorders are powerfully and extensively confronted. *Hamlet* and *King Lear* are generally accounted the greatest of Shakespeare's tragedies because, although they are very different in structure and tone, in both of them the situation blows up so thoroughly on so many levels. *Macbeth* is not far behind these two in its range, but we normally think of *Othello*—superbly powerful and painful as it is—as less profound because the elemental and metaphysical disorders, and even the political, are more narrowly circumscribed. There is no need here to go from play to play asking what disorders are stirred up in each case. Enough has been said to suggest how the range of disorder produced in the middle of a play shapes our sense of the human significance of the tragic death.

A Shakespearean tragedy, then, shows us the production of disorder on at least one of these planes, and in the final scenes— the area of the plays with which I am particularly concerned— this disorder, or complex of disorders, issues in a disaster (one or more deaths) and a new order. It is typical of Shakespeare to make the disaster or, especially, the new order in some way ironic. For one thing, the new order is likely to involve fewer levels, except in theory. We generally don't *feel* them in the order as we do in the disorder. There's no sexual disorder in Fortinbras's Denmark, but then there's no evident sexual order either. This failure to exist on several planes is one of the things that makes the new orders in the tragedies seem comparatively dull and bounded. The new world is not so rich as the one that has died out.

Shakespeare repeatedly sees the ironic nature of the new

Death and Survival

order as one of the things that makes the world tragic, a kind of posthumous cruelty, a final twisting of the knife, though we are the ones who are alive to feel it. While Romeo and Juliet are alive, Montague and Capulet, partly through traditional malice and partly through carelessness, allow a situation to continue which prevents the lovers from being together, except one time in secret; but once Romeo and Juliet lie together in death, the fathers are eager to let them lie together publicly forever, in monumental gold. Dead, they may be married, and world-famous. In *Julius Caesar* the new order, the venal rule of Antony and Octavius with its hints of the emergence of a new and more subtle Caesar, is precisely the sort of thing Brutus was trying to avoid by the act which allowed it to come into being. Brutus's republican virtue hastened the end of the republic. In *Timon* we see the triumph of a reasonable sort of order, neither perfectly good nor perfectly bad but on the whole as decent an arrangement as one might expect, an order that is just the sort of mixed state, reflecting a "mixed" human nature, that Timon could never accept, an order that is the antithesis of his either-or world. "Dead / Is noble Timon," says Alcibiades:

> Bring me into your city,
> And I will use the olive with my sword,
> Make war breed peace, make peace stint war, make each
> Prescribe to other, as each other's leech.
>
> (V.iv.79–84)

Ironically, Alcibiades achieved this order, this mixed affair, partly in Timon's name.

Richard II is unique among these plays in that it is the beginning of a historical series and explicitly looks forward to a continuation. Here we already see the new order in charge for two acts, and in subsequent plays we will see it work out its own destiny. Thus in *Richard II* it is finally the living Bolingbroke more than the dead Richard who is the victim of the irony at the end. We won't see the new order in action this way in any of the other tragedies, including *Richard III*, which ends the series. (The closest we come to an exception is the relation of *Antony and Cleopatra* to *Julius Caesar;* but though the complicating in-

8

troduction of Cleopatra in the Roman plays may be compared to the introduction of Falstaff in the English, the concerns of *Antony and Cleopatra* are much different from those of *Julius Caesar,* and the earlier Roman play does not explicitly look beyond its own action the way *Richard II* does.)

Hamlet, Othello, King Lear, and *Antony and Cleopatra* provide some of the most interesting examples of this ironic relationship between the new order and the disaster. I will consider the endings of these plays in detail in later chapters.

4

Since the new order is so important to the structure of final scenes, being in a sense the background against which the tragic hero dies, we should look in a little more detail at the variety of things Shakespeare does with it as a formal device. The new orders, the worlds that go on without the energy of the tragic figures, vary in their natures, in the processes by which they come into being, and in their relationships to the designs or desires of the tragic figures.

Sometimes the process that leads to the establishment of the new order is directly opposed to the process generated by the energy of the tragic hero, in which case the drive to establish the new order produces the immediate occasion for the tragic death. This happens in *Richard III, Richard II, Julius Caesar, Macbeth, Antony and Cleopatra,* and *Coriolanus.* In these cases, there is a character (or with *Julius Caesar* and *Macbeth,* two) who from at least the middle of the play on can be said to be the hero's antagonist(s). The defeat of the hero and the establishment of the new order are the direct result of the conflict between the heroes and the men who rule the new world.

In *King Lear, Timon,* and *Titus Andronicus,* the process that eventually establishes the new order ironically moves in the same general direction as the process generated by the tragic energy, even to the extent of being carried out at least partly in the hero's name. But Lear is past any comfort the victory of Albany and Edgar could give him, Timon has no interest in sharing the benefits of Alcibiades' conquest, and by the time Lucius takes over, Titus is dead.

In *Hamlet* the new order is causally incidental to the defeat and death of the tragic hero. Fortinbras's accidental assumption of power is, however, ironically parallel to the process initiated by the tragic hero (revenging a murdered father) and, for that reason, potentially antagonistic to the hero's desires. As it is, Hamlet, in the interests of a stable state, gives his dying support to Fortinbras's new order.

Sometimes the new order is really the old order, without the tragic figures, as in *Romeo and Juliet* and *Othello;* and in one case, *Troilus and Cressida,* the new order is really the old order, *with* the tragic figures, more or less. *Troilus and Cressida* is such an odd, ironic dramatic structure that I will save it for special treatment in the next section, observing here only that the old order and the firmly established new order are virtually the same —a chaos of wars and lechery, Greek and Trojan, the only change being that because of death in battle and venereal disease the number of participants seems to be dwindling. In *Romeo and Juliet* the prevailing order in Verona is antagonistic to the desires of the tragic figures, but to a large extent unconsciously so; because of the secrecy in which Romeo and Juliet carried on their love, the prevailing order never really knew what it was doing. Though the world does not change hands, there may be a new order at the end to the extent that the Montagues and the Capulets, such as are left, recognize their guilt and promise to change; but, as I noted in the previous section, the change is ironic, more depressing than hopeful, perhaps pointless. In *Othello* the new order is *precisely* the old order, with Lodovico representing the Duke of Venice. The prevailing order was neither antagonistic to the hero's desires nor aware of them. The irony here is that, so far as we can tell, the tragedy had no effect on the state other than to make it sad.

Because the new order is so often felt to be merely political, lacking any positive sense of order on other planes, perhaps the most common form for the process that leads to the new order is a movement to stabilize the state by consolidating or acquiring political power or by rescuing the state from irresponsible rulers or from chaos. There is, of course, no need for this kind of activity in either *Romeo and Juliet* or *Othello,* which is another way of saying that these are the most "domestic" of the tragedies. But in the other plays, the drive for a new political order puts forward a group of men who are, at least formally, winners of the play's conflicts, and they become the center of the final community from which the tragic figures are excluded. Because our sense of the value of that community in comparison with the value of the lost heroes depends partly on the motives of the men who are at its center, we shall look for a moment at the attitudes they have toward their enterprise.

We might begin by listing them, since we are temporarily giving the plays a new, unusual set of heroes: Lucius Andronicus, Richmond, Bolingbroke, Antony and Octavius (in *Julius Caesar*), Fortinbras, Albany and Edgar, Malcolm (with Macduff), Alcibiades, Octavius again (in *Antony and Cleopatra*), and Tullus Aufidius.

There are a number of motives operating in this group, and various combinations of motives. (After the early plays, with Lucius and Richmond, Shakespeare always sees his political winners in a complex, if not ironic, light.) Richmond and Malcolm clearly see themselves as rescuers of the state from a dangerous ruler and from moral and organic chaos. Bolingbroke also has this image of himself, maintaining the need for a responsible ruler to replace the self-indulgent Richard. But Bolingbroke's case is more complex because Richard II, unlike Richard III and Macbeth, came to the throne legitimately and also cannot be conveniently characterized as a devil. Thus Bolingbroke finds himself in the paradoxical position of having to break the law to protect the law. It is a paradox that haunts him to his death. Bolingbroke's case is also more complex than Richmond's or Malcolm's because Richard is alive for two acts after losing his power, as a kind of accusation of Bolingbroke's "responsible" act. Again this suggests the irony of Bolingbroke's "stabilization," especially when coupled with the prophecies of future strife made by Richard and by Carlisle. Bolingbroke can't have peace with Richard alive or with Richard dead, an irony Shakespeare emphasizes in the final scene. (As I noted earlier, Shakespeare carefully places *Richard II* in a historical process which extends beyond the play's own dramatic structure.) Lucius Andronicus steps into a political vacuum to take charge after a chaotic final scene has wiped almost everybody else out (there are just enough people left to choose him as emperor). So does Fortinbras, who has the additional advantage of neither having to wipe anyone out himself nor having any emotional ties to those who are dead.

But another motive operates in these men, particularly when we associate Macduff with Malcolm—the motive of revenge. Though it operates more strongly in some than in others, there's at least a touch of the revenge motive in all the stabilizers. Lucius and Fortinbras are particularly interesting in that they are in effect successful, surviving revengers in plays where the central character was a revenger who could accomplish his end only at the cost of his life.

In the entire group of winners, Aufidius is the closest to being a villain. He is the least attractive, and his methods are the vilest. His use of a gang is reminiscent of Achilles. His motives are the least justifiable, though Shakespeare makes it clear that he is already well on the way to justifying them to the Volscian lords, who though they seem to be reasonable men, will apparently feel that they can use his military strength. (I suppose that is one sign of their common sense.)

Another motive that appears in this group and contributes to the shapes of the final scenes is simple acquisitiveness, or the will to power. All of them have it except Albany, who is only too eager to give his power and responsibility away. Acquisitiveness is underplayed in Lucius and Richmond, again a reflection of the relatively simple moral world of these early tragedies. Nor do Edgar and Malcolm-Macduff seem terribly eager for political power for its own sake, but the rest do. Bolingbroke and Fortinbras are great opportunists.[5] So is Antony in *Julius Caesar;* but Octavius appears ready to overtake him, and in *Antony and Cleopatra* he does, becoming "the universal landlord." Alcibiades leads an obvious war of conquest and revenge (not without moral justification, however); so does Coriolanus, with whom Plutarch compares Alcibiades, but Aufidius outdoes Coriolanus and thereby becomes the most powerful military man in the world.

Most of the winners like to see themselves as *responsible* men, who act as they do to bring moral as well as political order to the state. The "rescuers" clearly act responsibly, especially Bolingbroke, for it is his principal moral advantage over Richard. Octavius belongs here too, because he sees himself as the responsible leader of the Roman state in contrast to Antony, who lives a life of hedonistic self-indulgence in Alexandria.

It is interesting to consider Brutus and Cassius with this group, because one might say that they wished to be the winners in a *Tragedy of Julius Caesar* in which Caesar really was the tragic center. And their motives would be the ones we have been discussing. They would rescue the Roman state from the tyranny of Caesar and thus be responsible, in contrast to a self-willed Caesar and a hedonistic Antony. We can distinguish between them, too. Brutus has no revenge motive; Cassius has. Brutus is not acquisitive; Cassius has "an itching palm" (IV.iii.10) and can be "never at heart's ease / Whiles [he] behold[s] a greater than [himself]" (I.ii.208-9). Brutus has a sense of tradition; Cassius only plays on it. But Antony understands their motives, and the Roman mob's motives, well enough to defeat Brutus and Cassius, and they, not Caesar, become the centers of the tragedy. As a result their motives, especially Cassius's, begin to appear more complex, for tragic figures are more complex, in Shakespeare at least, than winners.[6]

5

Three plays may seem to be exceptions to what I have said about the tragedies' always ending with tragic death and a new order and to what I have said about the absence in the "new order" of a comprehensive positive sense of order. In *Troilus and Cressida* there seems to be no new order and perhaps no tragic death; and in *Richard III* and *Macbeth* the new orders are associated with a superhuman order and seem to represent more than simply political stability coupled with the absence of the more exotic disorders produced by the tragic heroes. (It is a curious additional distinction of these three plays that they are the only plays in which the tragic figures die in military combat.)[7] If these plays are not absolute exceptions to what I said in the previous sections, they are at least cases where some qualification is needed.

Actually, there is a good deal of controversy over whether or not *Troilus and Cressida* should even be considered a tragedy.

In terms of what I have been saying, there is certainly plenty of destructive disorder in *Troilus and Cressida* and little evidence of creative disorder. But the play has no clear center of energy, and the ending, instead of establishing a new community, implies the imminent destruction of any that might be left:

> Sit, gods, upon your thrones, and smile at Troy.
> I say, at once let your brief plagues be mercy,
> And linger not our sure destructions on.
>
> (V.x.7–9)

Troilus, who speaks these lines, is perhaps the character closest to being a center of energy or a tragic hero.[8] But Troilus, like Timon, mechanically replaces one inadequate idealistic view of the world by another inadequate idealistic view which is worse than the first. His maturity is a matter of giving up lechery and addicting himself solely to wars. In these things he may be similar to other Shakespearean tragic heroes, but unlike them, he cannot find his consummation in death. Disaster only toys with Troilus. We do not see that final engagement with death that is so important in establishing the other tragic heroes in Shakespeare.

A character who does die in *Troilus and Cressida,* and probably the play's only other possibility for a tragic hero in the ordinary sense, is Hector. But Hector seems finally too absurd to be a hero. He gives up his noble, impressive, even courageous good sense for the sake of his honor (in the Trojan council of II.ii) and then shows us how petty a thing his honor really is by chasing a cowardly Greek simply to get his armor. He never realizes, even at the end, the contradictions in his behavior. When Achilles' gang strikes him down in V.viii, we feel more disgust at Achilles than sorrow for Hector. Shakespeare often makes his military heroes look silly near the end—it's one of his ways of facing the truth about human nature. But with Hector anything that might redeem him is way back in Act II. We may contrast Coriolanus: when his resolution collapses in V.iii, it collapses not to pursue, against his reason, a war he knows to be foolish, wasteful, and wrong, but to bring peace to Italy and to save the lives of those he loves. And where Hector (ironically) sees his collapse as leading to a life of honor, Coriolanus knows that his collapse entails his death. Coriolanus's decision redeems the immaturity of much of his behavior and makes his end terrible as Hector's is not.

Nevertheless, the energy displayed by Troilus, Hector, and the rest of the pack, Greek and Trojan, is tragic in that it is destructive ("Lechery, lechery; still wars and lechery; nothing else holds fashion" [V.ii.190–91]), and it is this energy that gives the play its open-ended form, as if Shakespeare wondered what would happen in a world where tragic energy could not be consummated because no sense of community could oppose it, a world where there was no tension of this sort to create value. If there is "harmony" at the end of *Troilus and Cressida,* it lies in the universal acceptance of wars and lechery, a harmony based on eternal discord. Or, to use the method of my previous section, we may compare the final order with the nonexistent tragic deaths and conclude that in *Troilus and Cressida* the "new order" is so ironic as to be nonexistent. It mocks the "order" speech of Ulysses in I.iii and the "reason" of Hector in II.ii. Not that this matters much, since both Ulysses and Hector show by their subsequent words and actions that they don't have any great emotional stake in the substance of their arguments. But the final order manages to mock even what the characters do believe in—Hector's honor, Achilles' valor, Ulysses' policy, Troilus's romantic love, Cressida's faith, Menelaus-and-Paris's woman, Pandarus's sexual playpen, everybody's war—everything except Thersites' universal disgust, which isn't worth believing in.

I see *Troilus and Cressida,* then, as an exploration of tragic form, a flirting with its limits: a "tragic" story unfolds in a world where nothing can confer tragic values on the story's heroes. The play is a tragic structure which its characters, as Lepidus the role of triumvir, cannot fill: "To be called into a huge sphere and not to be seen to move in't, are the holes where eyes should be, which pitifully disaster the cheeks" (*AC* II.vii.14–16). So we see, short of absolute burlesque, the reductio ad absurdum of tragic roles—the military tragic hero, the political tragic hero, the romantic tragic hero, the philosophical tragic hero—all these are deflated in *Troilus and Cressida,* and we are left at the end with Troilus invoking destruction, and Pandarus, in his "tragic" fall from power, holding up the mirror to an unheroic sort of magistrate:

> O world, world! thus is the poor agent despised. O traders and
> bawds, how earnestly are you set a-work, and how ill requited!
> Why should our endeavor be so loved, and the performance so
> loathed? What verse for it? What instance for it? Let me see.
>> Full merrily the humble-bee doth sing,
>> Till he hath lost his honey and his sting;
>> And being once subdued in armed tail,
>> Sweet honey and sweet notes together fail.
> Good traders in the flesh, set this in your painted cloths:
> "As many as be here of Pandar's hall,
> Your eyes, half out, weep out at Pandar's fall;
> Or if you cannot weep, yet give some groans,
> Though not for me, yet for your aching bones.
> Brethren and sisters of the hold-door trade,
> Some two months hence my will shall here be made.
> It should be now, but that my fear is this,
> Some galled goose of Winchester would hiss.
> Till then I'll sweat and seek about for eases,
> And at that time bequeath you my diseases."
>
> (V.x.35–55)

In a world where destruction is permanent, a slaughter-minded idealist and a syphilitic pimp are fitting heroes.

Richard III and *Macbeth*, the other obvious exceptions to some of the things I was saying about the new order at the end of a tragedy, are quite different from *Troilus and Cressida* in their sense of the new community. The "new order" in *Troilus and Cressida* is simply an intensification and purification of the old disorder. In *Richard III* and *Macbeth* the new order takes on some of the aura of health, fertility, and superhuman harmony that surrounds the new order at the end of the comedies.

In writing *Macbeth* a dozen or so years after *Richard III*, Shakespeare comes as close as he ever does to repeating a tragic structure. In both, the tragic hero is a villain. Both Richard and Macbeth are military heroes who have been the main support of their kings in a civil war. (For Richard, see *3 Henry VI*, especially

I.i and IV.v.) Both betray their kings, turn regicide, and usurp the crown. The deeds of both are increasingly bloody, and both are increasingly isolated in their tyranny while there is a massing of forces opposed to them. Both are troubled by ghosts, and both die bravely in single combat against an opponent whom prophesy had designated as their bane. The successful new rulers bring order to the kingdoms, order associated with a return to health, fertility, and renewed generation. Both new political orders, Richmond's and Malcolm's, are also seen as part of a larger historical pattern and a divine order. It is the nature of the new orders in *Richard III* and *Macbeth*—the sense of promised generation and divine sanction—that makes these two plays exceptions to some of the statements I made above about Act V orders in the tragedies.[9]

There are of course important differences between the two plays, differences which reflect the maturing of Shakespeare's art in the dozen or so years separating their composition. There are differences in methods of characterization and consequently in the implications of the tragic deaths. Richard in soliloquy speaks to us; Macbeth speaks to himself. Richard's problems are mostly practical until the final scenes, but Macbeth feels his guilt early, and we move with him from fearful apprehension of guilt into metaphysical considerations that Richard never dreams of. When Richard realizes that "there is no creature loves me; / And if I die, no soul will pity me" (V.iii.201–2), I pity him though he says I won't. But I don't feel the existential terror I feel for Macbeth, whose death comes at the end of a long inward agony and has such cosmic reverberations. Macbeth can (and does) say what Richard says; no one loves *him* now, either. But he can say more:

> Life's but a walking shadow, a poor player
> That struts and frets his hour upon the stage
> And then is heard no more. It is a tale
> Told by an idiot, full of sound and fury,
> Signifying nothing.
>
> (V.v. 24–28)

Another important difference between the plays, a difference clearly related to the differences in characterization and metaphysical scope, is the far greater poetic richness of *Macbeth,* the greater mythic suggestiveness of its imagery; and this poetic richness has an important effect in shaping our sense of what is involved in the final scenes. The generative powers of England are restored by the return of Richmond in the last act of *Richard III.* But the problem of generation, or fertility, or organic growth, though certainly present and important in *Richard III,* is not as integral and extensive a part of the poetic texture as it is in *Macbeth.* Richard kills children too, but neither the play's language nor the various characters' preoccupations suggest in so intense a way as in *Macbeth* that the villain hero is a threat to the possibility of life as well as to individual lives. Richmond brings less than Malcolm.

Richmond *is* less than Malcolm, and this is the last difference between the two plays I wish to explore, a difference that is important in determining the different effects of the two endings, the different relations of the new order to the destructive tragic energy of the protagonists.

Only in *Macbeth* does the order established at the end of a Shakespearean tragedy give us any substantial compensation for the greatness we have lost. *Richard III* and *Macbeth* have, as we have seen, formally the same sort of ending: the good guys defeat the villain, to put it bluntly. But Richmond's strength is merely a matter of theory and of plot—of form, not of real substance. He wins, he says the right things, and so forth, but he lacks real vitality, or what I would call a concrete integrity. The group that defeats Macbeth—for Malcolm has allies who are not dramatically anonymous as Richmond's pretty much are—is different. Malcolm and Macduff (and Banquo, who is on that side and whose role they carry on) do have this concrete integrity, integrity one gets from a more vital contact with evil than we sense in Richmond. Macduff feels guilt for the death of his family. Malcolm imagines himself worse than Macbeth (thus managing to be both innocent and guilty). Banquo meets the witches and bids them speak to him; he understands Macbeth; and he has guilty dreams that show evil working in him as in Macbeth: "Merciful powers, / Restrain in me the cursed thoughts that nature / Gives way to in repose" (II.i.7–9). But as the sequel makes clear, he resists the evil that works in his unconscious, resists the temptation that Macbeth cannot. A simple enmity to evil, a refusal to have anything really to do with it except destroy it, is not enough—one must recognize one's own capacity for evil. Thus Richard's enemies are bland and Macbeth's are not. In *Macbeth* but not in *Richard III* the promise of generation is combined with a concrete integrity on the part of those who will fulfill the promise. Not only had Shakespeare's technique matured since the early 1590s, but also his sense of the world's moral structure had grown more complex. In fact, these two developments are complementary.

The new order in *Richard III* or *Macbeth* is richer in mythic implications than the new order in any of the other tragedies. Nevertheless the center of energy is still Richard or Macbeth. After all is said about the more magical promise of generation at the end of these plays and about the concrete integrity of the new leaders and the poetic richness of the generation theme in *Macbeth,* the new order in each case is still duller, more mundane, and dramatically less vital than the destructive energy of the tragic figures who die.

6

One of the structural devices by which Shakespeare forces us to see the death of the tragic hero in the context of the new, nontragic order is the isolation of the central figure, a stripping from him of power, wealth, friends, family, allies, people who understand him, a common understanding of the world, human contact generally, sanity, and finally life.[10] In his isolation we see more clearly what the tragic hero embodies, and we see what is left over when he dies.

It is not hard to find examples of tragic isolation: Titus in his unhinged hate; Richard III without even a horse; Richard II reduced to peopling his prison with thoughts; Brutus reduced to his sleepy sword-holder; Hamlet in his readiness; Hector among Achilles' thugs, Troilus in a world where no one can appreciate a sense of value, and Pandarus in a world where no one needs his services; Othello, having given up belief in his wife for belief in his friend, finding that in the end he has neither; Lear, alone in his ability to suffer, barely aware of an outside world, and then in an apparently trivial way ("Pray you undo this button"); Macbeth, once beloved and admired of all, now isolated even from his wife by madness and death, ending hated and despised by all; Timon actively seeking isolation from all that is human and all that is alive; Coriolanus, first going into exile like "a lonely dragon" to his fen, then going again to an alien land, to what he knows will be his death. Though some of the characters don't seem so very isolated *physically* (Titus, Hamlet, and Lear, for instance), all are terribly isolated in their imaginations and their apprehension of the world. Even Brutus must be, though, stoic that he is, he doesn't like to show it. It isn't necessary to go into more detail about this common structure. The similarities are clear enough. (So are the many differences. Even Richard III and Macbeth are different: Macbeth sees hardly any point in winning the last battle.) It is in those plays which during the nineteenth century came to be considered the "great" tragedies—*Hamlet, Othello, King Lear,* and *Macbeth*—that the mental isolation of the hero is most intense. Even if we no longer accept this traditional classification, it remains a good indication of the importance, in Shakespeare's tragic method, of the isolation of the central figure.

7

A special case, and a particularly interesting one given our concern in this chapter with the separation between the tragic figures and a surviving community, is the isolation of tragic characters in pairs; for an isolation of a pair of characters from the rest of society offers the possibility of an alternative kind of union to that of the surviving community, a kind of union embodying different, probably more exciting, values than those found among the survivors. The isolation of characters in pairs usually occurs in the plays where sexual love is an important shaping motive—*Romeo and Juliet, Troilus and Cressida, Othello, Macbeth,* and *Antony and Cleopatra.* In each of these plays, different as they are, the form of the final scenes depends in a significant way on the nature of the love relationship we have seen.

Sexual love, as a force that brings people together, provides the energy that moves Shakespearean comedy toward an end in marriage and in a community based on marriage, a community that, as we noted above, includes the best human possibilities found in the world of the drama and, at least implicitly, promises to reproduce them. But in tragedy the movement is not toward marriage but toward death, so that the best the characters can hope for is a metaphoric consummation, a *Liebestod,* in which the marriage bed is a tomb. Often they don't even get that, but instead find separate deaths after love has failed, perhaps after marriage has failed. Sometimes the enemy to love is society, sometimes the dangerous forms of passion that arise within the love itself. In any case, the outside community will survive and the "community" of love will not.

The community that survives after the lovers' deaths is held together by a duller bond than love. In not one of the tragedies does Shakespeare suggest that sexual love is a possibility in the surviving community. (He doesn't literally say that it is not a possibility, but the closest he comes to actually implying such a relationship is in Richmond's proposed marriage to Elizabeth. But, aside from the fact that we never see Elizabeth—indeed, has Richmond ever seen her?—any "love" in that pair is dynastic and emblematic, not romantic and sexual.) In fact, in all the tragedies only one named woman (I ignore crowds, as in *Coriolanus*) is both onstage and alive at the end of the play—Lady Capulet, who, though her age may be computed at under thirty, gives the impression (V.iii.207) of being old and ready to think of dying, unmetaphorically, as her Montague counterpart already has. The presence and absence of death aside, there is no difference between the tragedies and the comedies more striking than this—the comedies *must* have women present and alive at the end, the tragedies virtually can not. The absence of sexual love (in fact, the absence, really, of any kind of love whatsoever) is one of the most disturbing characteristics of these surviving communities. It is, as I say, one of the things that make these worlds tragic. The comedies will isolate the absence or the failure of love in a Shylock, a Jaques, a Malvolio, in order to celebrate love in the continuing community. But the continuing community in the tragedies loses the often disruptive energy of love without gaining any kind of bond beyond the civic or political, and thus fails to embody either tragic or comic values.

Within the group of plays in which the tragic characters are isolated in pairs, we may distinguish those plays where the pair is finally isolated in union from those plays where the pair is both isolated from society and divided within itself. In *Romeo and Juliet* and *Antony and Cleopatra* the sexual partners are felt to be united at the end—in death. The final scenes in both plays are achievements of that union, and in both there are two tragic figures. In *Troilus and Cressida, Othello,* and *Macbeth* the isolation of the pair of lovers involves separation, not union in death. In each case the male partner is the center of tragic interest. Troilus is more important than Cressida (I suppose because he is actively involved in the wars as well as in the lechery), even though the title gives her equal billing. Desdemona and Lady Macbeth obviously make less intense claims on our attention than their husbands. Nevertheless the love relationships in these plays are structurally crucial in ways that, say, the Brutus-Portia relationship, or even the Hamlet-Ophelia relationship, is not.

The plays that end in separation focus on the way love goes wrong in itself, not just in relation to an outside world. Therefore, in examining the effect of love as a shaping motive in the final scenes, we must clearly diversify our sense of love to include some of its varieties and perversions: sexual love, romantic love, idealistic love, lust, jealousy, need to be loved, possession, domination by means of love, and politic love. Most of these are likely to show up somehow in any given relationship, even in those plays which end in union, though I am mainly concerned here with kinds of love that have major structural influence on the plays. Moreover, these varieties are rarely separate from one another. Thus the love of Romeo and Juliet is probably the "purest" among these plays, by which I mean that there is comparatively little in it of jealousy, domination, or the more unredeemed forms of lust. Certainly it is not very politic (though see II.iii.91–92). Nevertheless, despite the fact that its interruptions are largely external, we can see in it disturbing (and as it turns out, fatal) traces of overromanticizing (principally in Romeo), idealism, and a hasty sexual desire which by some moralists might be called lust. But in general, their love is simply too uncompromising for the world they live in, and it drives them in the final scene to the only world where it seems they can be united, the world of death. They lack that balance of absolute love and common sense, of sexual desire and wise restraint, that we see, for example, in a Rosalind. But then happy, successful love is a comic mode.

In Othello a too unbalanced love turns into jealousy and a too unbalanced hate. Yet the love is never entirely lost, and the pressure of two absolutes tears Othello apart. Moreover, the transformation of love into hate also turns it into perverted lust, as Othello is driven by Iago to see Desdemona as "a cistern for foul toads / To knot and gender in" (IV.ii.61–62). The Othello who enters Desdemona's bedroom with murder on his mind has very mixed and compromised motives.

At the beginning of this final scene Othello's isolation is complete; he is isolated from the whole world by his monstrous notion of the truth. Desdemona too has become isolated, even from Emilia, since her husband's love has changed so mysteriously. Her own love does not fail, however, even after Othello has strangled her and she is dying. When Othello, having realized his error, kills himself, he creates a brief symbolic union:

> I kissed thee ere I killed thee. No way but this,
> Killing myself, to die upon a kiss.
>
> (V.ii.359–60)

This kiss creates here that ancient metaphorical association of sexual consummation and death that Shakespeare uses so extensively to celebrate the "eternal" unions of Romeo and Juliet and of Antony and Cleopatra. But the love union here, which follows such violent separation, separation much more violent than that in *Troilus and Cressida* or *Macbeth,* is as ironic as it is moving; for Othello kills both of them, they do not die mutually, and Othello places himself in hell as securely as he sees Desdemona in heaven. The kiss is ultimately an image not of sexual consummation but of sexual frustration.

Macbeth is really on the perimeter of this group, since love itself is not an important theme in the final scenes. But the structure of these scenes is very much the product of the love relationship between Macbeth and Lady Macbeth as Shakespeare has developed it in the early acts, where we see a perversion of sexual roles and the use of love as a means of domination.

In I.vii the sexual bond between herself and Macbeth is the means Lady Macbeth uses to force him against his better judgment into the murder of Duncan. To do this, however, she must destroy their sexual roles. She has already ritually unsexed herself (I.v.38–48), and here in I.vii she is herself identified with maleness (54–59, 72–74) and makes Macbeth's reluctance a sign of his unmanliness and a measure of the quality of his love (35–41, 47–54). When Macbeth declares that he "dare[s] do all that may become a man; / Who dares do more is none" (46–47), he is right, and his subsequent action is, despite Lady Macbeth's statements, an abandonment of his manhood. This confused love relationship between Macbeth and his lady becomes part of the play's pervasive fertility theme. Metaphorically speaking, because of what is essentially a kind of sexual perversion, Macbeth's marriage is not fertile, nor is Scotland under his reign fertile. (In both ways he is unlike the king he kills.) Macbeth's turning for support from Lady Macbeth to the weird sisters is part of the same metaphoric structure, since they do look like women who are men (I.iii.45–47), and the result of their persuasion is the cowing of his better part of man. Macbeth's great crimes after his murder of Duncan are either murders of those who, like Duncan, are fruitful (Banquo, who is manly in the way Macbeth has abdicated [II.iii.122–28], and Lady Macduff, who is so poignantly womanly and motherly in contrast to Lady Macbeth) or murders of all their children he can get his hands on. (The implied fruitfulness of Fleance, who escapes, is the ultimate horror in Macbeth's witch-induced vision in IV.i.) Macbeth's failure of manhood is further shown by the fact that the active and valiant warrior described in Act I performs none of these crimes with his own hands.

After the murder of Duncan, Lady Macbeth is progressively isolated from the partner of her crime, first by his failure to consult her before acting, then by her madness, finally by her death. One feels that their love relationship, like the relationship of Macbeth to Duncan, was once proper (and to that extent potentially fruitful—see I.iv.28–33), but that, again like Macbeth's loyalty to Duncan, their marriage was destroyed by ambition. There's not the least hint of union in the final scenes of this play. Macbeth has gone far beyond his wife in his willful destruction of his own proper nature. Yet it is the loss of this woman he loved that drives Macbeth to his bleakest meditation, his vision of life as "a tale / Told by an idiot, full of sound and fury, / Signifying nothing." He is now left completely alone to play out his meaningless role.

And he continues to play it out in the final scenes under the influence of the role perversion set up in Act I.[11] Macbeth's death is related to the sexual theme, because in giving up his manliness he has become the enemy of natural generation, of all who are "born of woman." So it is ironic justice that Macduff, the man not born of woman, the man whose birth implied a violent perversion of natural generation, should be the one to cow Macbeth's "better part of man" (V.viii.18) and then to kill him.

When we come to the warring lechers, whores, and idealists of *Troilus and Cressida,* all the varieties of love-motive I've somewhat arbitrarily listed above appear in one place or another, and by the end of the play the war has made the worst of them dominant. Romantic love is destroyed by the defection of Cressida and the scurvy opinion almost everyone has of Helen (a just opinion, to judge by the effect she makes in her one appearance). Here a classic "love-pair" story, a story of a "secret" love like that of Romeo and Juliet, becomes a story of separation, not of union in death. Cressida's love is more mortal than she. Not love, but a need to be loved is her primary motive. Troilus has Romeo's too-intense romantic idealism without the luck to find a Juliet and so is cheated of his love-death, or indeed of any death at all (but see Rosalind's comment, *As You Like It* IV.i.85–90). Troilus is jealous even before he and Cressida part (see IV.iv.57–107); in effect he is instructing her to be unfaithful, as if she needs to betray him to justify his expectations of her. Moreover, his sensuality seems to be in his imagination rather than his body:

> I am giddy; expectation whirls me round.
> Th' imaginary relish is so sweet
> That it enchants my sense. What will it be
> When that the wat'ry palates taste indeed
> Love's thrice-repured nectar? Death, I fear me,

> Sounding destruction, or some joy too fine,
> Too subtle, potent, tuned too sharp in sweetness
> For the capacity of my ruder powers.
>
> (III.ii.16–23)

> This is the monstruosity in love, lady, that the will is
> infinite and the execution confined; that the desire is
> boundless and the act a slave to limit.
>
> (III.ii.74–77)

It is appropriate that Troilus's suffering be mental too. Pandarus, who puts more stake in the act, gets the Neapolitan boneache. Achilles and Patroclus add homosexuality to the varieties of love, Thersites has a filthy mind, and with all the animal imagery in the play one suspects bestiality too. I've even seen a production (Oregon Shakespearean Festival, 1972) where, so we don't miss the point, Helen's ladies-in-waiting go at it on the forestage as Pandarus sings of "Love, love, nothing but love, still love still more!" and the talk turns to love's being apparently "a generation of vipers" (III.i.107, 122–23). And what shape do all these love-motives give to the final scene? A dying pimp, rejected by his best customer, spreads venereal disease among the members of the audience.

The love of Antony and Cleopatra also operates in many modes, if not in the more exotic types found in *Troilus and Cressida*. There is, for instance, the jealousy of Cleopatra over Octavia and of Antony over Thidias and Octavius; there are the repeated attempts by Cleopatra to use Antony's love to control his actions; there is the sense of lust and hedonistic self-indulgence surrounding the whole affair; there is the change of sexual roles when Cleopatra puts her clothes on Antony and wears his sword; there is the grand romantic stance, assumed by Antony in Act I and taken up by Cleopatra in Act V, which asserts that their love is a greater thing than the Roman Empire. (This is also the only one of the plays we've been considering where the love union is fruitful, an aspect of love in which Macbeth was so painfully frustrated. And yet this fruitfulness is incidental: Antony and Cleopatra simply produce children as a matter of course.)

The comprehensiveness of love here, however, is much different from the kind of comprehensiveness we found in *Troilus and Cressida,* because here it is concentrated in Antony and Cleopatra. It is unified, not diverse. Because it is unified, the "catalog" treatment I have just given their love is more obviously inadequate than a similar treatment of love in *Troilus and Cressida.* Shakespeare has designed *Antony and Cleopatra,* from Philo's categorizing speech on (that is, from the opening lines of the play), to make us finally abandon the attempt to categorize. He makes the love of Antony and Cleopatra something we can't describe neatly, as Philo thinks he can do. Moreover, though the final scene of *Antony and Cleopatra* is like the final scene of *Romeo and Juliet* in that what is finally achieved is a love union in death (complete with side-by-side graves and eternal fame), the final scene of *Antony and Cleopatra* is much more complicated because "love" is not the only important motive that gives the scene its structure and because Antony is already dead and Cleopatra is still very much alive and maneuvering.

Shakespeare won't allow Antony and Cleopatra to be easily romanticized as tragic lovers. In the first place, Antony commits suicide as "a bridegroom" and does a messy job of it. Then he is awkwardly heaved aloft to a Cleopatra who refuses to open her monument to him. In all this, of course, Shakespeare is dressing up what he found in North's Plutarch, adding the sexual suggestiveness and underlining rather than removing the absurdity of the situation. The gap between the deaths of Antony and Cleopatra is also from Plutarch, but instead of telescoping time in order to make his play more "dramatically effective," as he often did in reworking historical material, Shakespeare here exploits the "undramatic" gap in order to give his play an unusual double ending, so that we have "the Tragedy of Antony" ending in IV.xv and "the Tragedy of Cleopatra" ending in V.ii, with Antony no longer on stage. No simple *Liebestod* here.

8

In the world of Shakespearean tragedy, then, love fails as an associative alternative to the mere organization achieved by the survivors. In the final scenes we see those who can love, or those

27

who could love, die, while those who can merely associate, live. We are left with the separation between tragic figures who die and survivors who continue to live a life that is safer but less rich in possibilities for experience. At the end of *King Lear*, Edgar says that the life of a survivor, at least in the world of that play, will be neither so long nor so full as that of Lear and Gloucester, who have died: [12]

> The oldest hath borne most; we that are young
> Shall never see so much, nor live so long.
>   (V.iii.326–27)

In general, of course, *long* life is not required of a tragic hero, but all the tragic figures have seen more, seen more because they tried more, confronted more, than those, of whatever age, who survive.

Having looked, then, in this chapter, at the way the tragic process separates the tragic characters from the characters who survive to form a new order, we shall now turn to the experience of the tragic figures themselves, the characters who "see so much," however long they live. We will look at what they see, and at what they do in response to what they see. In the next chapter we will be involved not, as in the present chapter, with the way the structure of the play separates the "tragic" and the "normal" in the final scenes, but with the nature and shape of that experience in regions of pain or insight or triumph or failure beyond the reach of survivors. We will observe the tragic figures at the point where they see their death upon them, where they recognize the end of their power to shape the world around them and turn to assert their sense of the shape of their lives as those lives come to an end. The process of "shaping" which we see these characters involved in leads us to consider analogies between dramatic life and dramatic art, and between art and "real" life. In dramatic art, drama itself—the play—is the ultimate image of life, as the stage is the ultimate image of the world. Thus, almost inevitably, the final scenes of Shakespeare's tragedies are about the ending of plays as well as about the ending of lives.

2

❖ an art of Dying

I will be a bridegroom in my death.

DEATH, that first and most obvious characteristic of a Shakespearean tragedy, so often becomes for the tragic figures a thing to be desired. At least from Richard II on, a death wish is either acted on or deeply and extensively felt by nearly all of them. Actually there seems to be an almost absolute distinction between these alternatives: Timon excepted, those central characters who most profoundly wish for death, those characters for whom the death wish becomes a way of life, do not kill themselves. For the tragic figures who do kill themselves, death is desirable as an alternative to shame, to a life that must henceforth be lived on someone else's terms, or to continued existence in a world that no longer has in it a unique person whose death has made it, for the tragic hero, empty of value. This kind of death wish arises fairly suddenly and is fairly soon acted on, for it is a response to specific events, to "accidents." But the more deeply felt and extensive death wishes are responses to conditions, to the *general* possibilities of earthly life. This kind of death wish arises not simply from a specific, local grief—though there is that, too—but from an existential grief. It is a desire to escape the pain of life itself and its inherent, nonaccidental conditions. It is a desire for oblivion.

Among the first group, the suicides, there are those who kill themselves when a unique love has become impossible because of the death of the beloved. Romeo and Juliet are comparatively straightforward examples. With Othello, Antony, and Cleopatra,

considerations of honor and integrity are also important. We will
return to these love-suicides in chapter 5.

The sense of weariness, which is so marked a characteristic
of the members of the second group, appears in the suicides, too,
but only towards the very end. In them it has no metaphysical
resonance. The "Roman fools" Brutus and Cassius are weary.
"My bones would rest, / That have but labored to attain this
hour" (V.v.41–42), says Brutus, as he prepares to die. But Brutus
and Cassius kill themselves in order to remain, in Cassius's earlier
words, "masters of their fates." Their motives in dying are versions of their motives in killing Caesar. Had they defeated Antony
and Octavius, they would not be so weary, and at their deaths
there is little of the profound relief we feel, with Hamlet, amidst
our sorrow, when at last "the rest is silence."

Coriolanus and Timon, among the heroes of the mature plays,
fit least easily into these rough divisions. Coriolanus neither kills
himself nor expresses a wish for oblivion. He is so little inclined
to introspection that it is difficult to be sure what, if anything, he
is thinking as he approaches and meets his death. But when,
having realized that he is a man like other men and subject to
some of their infirmities, he gives up at his mother's plea his
unstoppable campaign against Rome, he sees this act as virtually
his death warrant:

> O my mother, mother! O!
> You have won a happy victory to Rome;
> But for your son—believe it, O believe it!—
> Most dangerously you have with him prevailed,
> If not most mortal to him. But let it come.
>   (V.iii.185–89)

He apparently returns to Corioles accepting his death, though not
welcoming it, for once in Corioles he proclaims himself still an
agent of the Volscians. Yet when he is goaded by Aufidius, what
might have seemed to be Coriolanus's new maturity disappears.
And yet again, when he is attacked, the man who had once
beaten the whole city single-handed now takes not so much
action as Julius Caesar or Hector to avoid death at the hands of
a gang. Does he trust in the influence of the temperate Volscian

lords (see V.vi.122–26), or does he finally welcome an end to
strife? The point may be that the confusion of role we see here (is
he the man or the boy?) is the appropriate conclusion to a life
unbalanced from the beginning by a confusion of roles—forced
to be a man while still a boy, still a boy once he is a man. Now
at the end he accepts like a man the implications of his mercy, but
denies like a boy that like a boy he granted the mercy.

If Coriolanus falls outside the main groups because he neither
kills himself nor expresses a desire for oblivion, Timon is an
exception because he does both. He commits suicide (at least in
effect) and holds a permanent grudge against life itself, not just
a specific event. For someone like Romeo, life would be good
again if Juliet were by some miracle still alive. But for Timon no
such redeeming event is even imaginable.

The second group, those who see death as a benefit yet re-
frain from suicide, includes Richard II, Hamlet, Troilus, and
Macbeth. Troilus we have already discussed in chapter 1; he
leaves the battlefield asking that destruction come quickly. The
other three are more meditative in their weariness with life. Beginning with his return to England and powerlessness in Act III,
Richard looks forward a number of times to the relief of not
having to face the pain of losing his crown, which for him means
losing his identity (see III.ii.144–70, III.iii.143–70, IV.i.255–62).
His wishing for oblivion culminates when he is in prison, where
he generalizes his case to include all men:

> . . . whate'er I be,
> Nor I, nor any man that but man is,
> With nothing shall be pleased till he be eased
> With being nothing.
>
> (V.v.38–41)

Though working of course from their own experience, Hamlet
and Macbeth go far beyond Richard in the philosophical reach
of their disillusionment with the world and their wish that all
experience would cease. Hamlet's long affair with death—the
most intense in Shakespeare—is part of the subject of chapter 3,
where I will consider it in detail.

Much is promised to Macbeth, but what he gets is not what

he thought it would be and not worth the suffering he has invested in it. In fact, it is not worth anything. But Macbeth is more than simply disappointed about the bad turn his life has taken; he comes to doubt that life can be otherwise than worthless. Early in Act V, when power is slipping away from him, Scotland is a chaos, and his wife is mad, Macbeth still feels that one might get from life that which he, because of his acts, will not; and because he has no longer any hope of getting it, he wishes to die:

> I have lived long enough. My way of life
> Is fall'n into the sear, the yellow leaf,
> And that which should accompany old age,
> As honor, love, obedience, troops of friends,
> I must not look to have; but, in their stead,
> Curses not loud but deep, mouth-honour, breath,
> Which the poor heart would fain deny, and dare not.
> (V.iii.22–28)

Two scenes later, when the invading army has grown larger and advanced further, when a siege is imminent, and when, finally, Lady Macbeth dies, Macbeth has come to feel that life can be no other way. Whether the Queen dies now or "hereafter" makes no difference. Life is a meaningless succession of days, leading only to death, which he wishes would come: "Out, out, brief candle!" (V.v.23). For Macbeth the world has not even so much meaning as an unweeded garden, and he makes his ultimate uncreative gesture, wishing that chaos were come again:

> I 'gin to be aweary of the sun,
> And wish th' estate o' th' world were now undone.
> (49–50)

In *King Lear* two characters carry on over several scenes what is in effect a debate about the merits of suicide, and a third character feels the pain of existence as strongly as Hamlet or Macbeth. In Act IV, Gloucester begins like the suicides we have examined. Blinded and alone, betrayed by the son he trusted and having cast off the son who loved him, Gloucester wants to take the quickest way to Dover and die by falling off the cliff. He commissions a mad beggar to guide him there, but though he doesn't know it, the beggar is his loyal son, Edgar, in disguise. I said a moment ago that if by some miracle Juliet had turned out to be alive (or, in practical terms, if Friar Lawrence's message had got through), Romeo would no longer have wished to kill himself. Gloucester tells us right away what the miracle would be in his case: "O dear son Edgar, / . . . Might I but live to see thee in my touch / I'ld say I had eyes again!" (IV.i.21–24). Since he has no hope of that, he wishes to die. Edgar, who has this miracle in his power, refuses to grant it because he disapproves of his father's attitude. Instead, he keeps Gloucester alive but ignorant, and as a result Gloucester becomes more and more like the characters we have been discussing who wish to die, who wish for oblivion, yet continue to exist in a world without hope. (I will examine the relationship between Gloucester and Edgar in more detail in chapter 4.)

Lear himself, like Hamlet and Macbeth, tries to come to terms with the meaning of existence, and like them he suffers terribly while doing so, like them suffers beyond the capacity of the other characters in these plays. But unlike them, he never cherishes death. It's not that he rejects the idea of suicide, as Edgar does. For Lear, the question of to be or not to be simply never comes up.

Hamlet, Macbeth, Lear—these are the characters with whom the pain of existence goes further beyond the pain of their own existence to the pain of human existence. The spheres in which Antony and, even more, Othello suffer, however powerfully, are more limited. Timon, it is true, extends his indictment of man and of life as far as anyone, but his rage seems too mechanical, too much a stance, finally too simple, to be comparable in effect to that of Hamlet, Macbeth, and Lear. The other figures we have been examining are less comprehensive in their suffering than these three. And not one of the three commits suicide. They either get over their death wish (Hamlet and Macbeth, though in very different ways) or they never experience it (Lear). Do these three men learn something or achieve a maturity that the others don't? Do they reach a "perception"?

33

2

Perception, sudden illumination, a moment of knowledge or recognition, a new clarity of vision, *anagnorisis*—these are various ways of describing what a central figure *may* arrive at late in a tragedy, and thus a character's movement toward perception may shape the final scenes in important ways. But we must be careful. The end of any play is likely to involve illumination or recognition as the dramatic knot is untied and the play's problem is solved. Is there anything we can call "tragic perception" or "tragic recognition" and is it a common characteristic of the final scenes of Shakespeare's tragedies? In general terms, yes. Tragic perception is the version of dramatic perception found in a tragedy—the tragic hero realizes how parts of his experience fit together, the tragic hero realizes something about the way the world works, the tragic hero realizes where he went wrong, the tragic hero realizes he can no longer live life on his own terms and so must make a decisive action, and so forth. But he may equally well *not* realize these things and the play may still be a tragedy.[1]

The primary question is not "What does the tragic hero learn?" but "What does the tragic hero experience?" If *King Lear* is more profound than *Othello,* it's not because Lear learns more than Othello or because what he learns is of higher quality. It's rather because in his pilgrimage through five acts of pain he engages a wider range of human experience than Othello, or, to recall the terms used earlier, he stirs up and encounters disorder on more levels. This may make his experience more profound, but I don't think it makes it more tragic. In other words, I wouldn't use quality of perception as a defining characteristic of the genre "Shakespearean tragedy." To insist that a character in a tragedy must learn the truth about something profound is Rymerism. It's moralist criticism. It implies that the *point* of tragedy is to learn something, that dramatic meaning is the same as didactic meaning. And after all, I suppose good wives *should* take good care of their linen. But lessons of this sort are trivial, no matter how important the subject. I don't suppose one should murder one's wife either. These are lessons any moralist can supply, and Shakespeare, like life, is full of them. They are not the point.

This doesn't mean, on the other hand, that Shakespeare's tragedies are not about moral problems, nor does it mean that we can't learn anything from them. Johnson, who understood Shakespeare so well even when he objected most strenuously, saw lack of serious moral concern as Shakespeare's gravest fault:

> His first defect is that to which may be imputed most of the evil in books or in men. He sacrifices virtue to convenience and is so much more careful to please than to instruct that he seems to write without any moral purpose. From his writings indeed a system of social duty may be selected, for he that thinks reasonably must think morally; but his precepts and axioms drop casually from him; he makes no just distribution of good or evil, nor is always careful to show in the virtuous a disapprobation of the wicked; he carries his persons indifferently through right and wrong and at the close dismisses them without further care and leaves their examples to operate by chance.[2]

This description is pretty fair; it makes Shakespeare sound like life. The difference is that Shakespeare has more art than life does, so that he shows us moral problems without as many irrelevancies as we find in nature and thus shows them in a way that makes their complexities easier to see. This is his "moral purpose," at least to judge from the plays. The tragedies give us the experience of moral problems, but rarely any solutions that aren't trivial. (Even *Richard III*, accidentally perhaps, is complicated by the fact that Richard is so much more vital than Richmond.) The complex problems he does solve are dramatic, that is, artistic.

That neat moral lessons are not the point of the plays doesn't mean we shouldn't make moral judgments about the characters. Making such judgments is properly part of the experience of a morally complex world—whether life's or Shakespeare's. Abandoning moral distinctions is as bad as making distinctions that are too simple. Either course means stopping, giving up, while the thing to do is go on, and go back, and go on again, through the complex world. This is one of the things we should be doing when we write about Shakespeare and when we scribble sarcastic question marks in the margins of someone else's piece of Shakespeare criticism—*and* when we come back two years later, erase the question marks from the other fellow's stuff and scribble them beside our own (with more sympathy, of course). Perceptions come and go. The moral structures of the world and Shakespeare stay complex.

Perception is a *formal* element in the final scenes, like suicide, takeover by a new order, or death, and as with the others, Shakespeare uses it in a variety of ways. A tragic hero's perception *may* be profound; it may have been achieved before the final scenes; it may be contradicted by his actions; it may be ironic, trivial, or pointedly absent. It is to the various uses of perception as a structural device that I now turn.

In *Titus, Richard III,* and *Romeo and Juliet* the use of tragic perception in the hero is comparatively uninteresting. Titus is a single-minded revenger right to his death, Richard comes to a fairly predictable recognition of his guilt and its range, and Romeo and Juliet accept the implications of an absolute love. It is probably not coincidental that these are the earliest of the tragedies. As he moved into the second half of the 1590s, Shakespeare apparently began to make perception more than simply a necessary part of any dramatic structure. He began to exploit perception as a significant (not merely a customary) tragic device.

In *Richard II* Shakespeare makes virtually explicit use of tragic perception, for he gives Richard, early in his death scene, a long soliloquy in which the deposed king tries to put the pieces of his life together. In moralizing the break of rhythm in a piece of music, Richard shows that he now accepts what Gaunt and York were trying to make him understand back in Act II, before Bolingbroke's return:

> Ha—ha—keep time! How sour sweet music is
> When time is broke and no proportion kept!
> So is it in the music of men's lives.
> And here have I the daintiness of ear
> To check time broke in a disordered string;
> But, for the concord of my state and time,
> Had not an ear to hear my true time broke.
> I wasted time, and now doth time waste me.
>   (V.v.42–49)

But Richard, as self-indulgent in grief as he was in power, cannot stop there. He must elaborate the moral anatomically ("For now hath time made me his numb'ring clock" [50]), and he goes on to tell us in great detail how the analogy works. Then, having done this, he returns to a clear recognition that he is doing now what he has always done:

> But my time
> Runs posting on in Bolingbroke's proud joy,
> While I stand fooling here, his Jack of the clock.
> (58–60)

He ends in contradiction, both infuriated by the enforcer of the moral and grateful for the love that tried, if ineptly, to bring him harmony.

What finally ennobles Richard is not his perception, not his self-recognition, not what he learns. What ennobles him is his isolation and the fact that though he does learn through his suffering, he cannot ever use what he has learned. I don't mean that he has no opportunity to escape and try again. I mean that he cannot make what he learns more than an intellectual part of himself. He cannot change, but must always "stand fooling" there. It may be this useless clarity, finally, which is the most tragic thing about Richard. He does not lose his crown because he is naïve, even about the power of his crown. Richard's intellectual clarity appears throughout the play in his assessment of Bolingbroke (I.i, II.i, III.iii, IV.i), but it does him no good because it has no effect on his own irresponsible action and because it actually forces Bolingbroke to move more quickly in taking power and putting Richard where we see him in V.v, in prison.[3] And in prison, with no one but himself to contend with, his clarity of vision only drives him back into the self-indulgent exercise of language which since Bolingbroke's takeover has necessarily replaced his self-indulgent exercise of power.

Brutus and Coriolanus are, except for Cleopatra, the most silent of Shakespeare's tragic heroes in the sense that they almost never let us hear their deepest thoughts, if they have any. In Brutus this is an effect partly of his Stoicism, partly of his absolute belief in his honesty. In him, tragic perception is notable by its absence. Once he has gulled himself with an analogy (II.i.10–34), or, to put it more kindly, decided that Caesar is a threat to

Roman freedom because of what he might do in the future, we
see no more of those moments when he is "vexed . . . with
passions of some difference" and "with himself at war" (I.ii.39–40,
46). Brutus refuses, so far as we can tell, to perceive even the
need to reexamine his deeds. He never questions the rightness of
the course he has taken. He never questions his ideals, even when
they have led to civil war, his own defeat, and the victory of the
very tyranny he had originally acted to prevent, a tyranny we
never see under Julius Caesar, a tyranny which is now present,
not future.

Coriolanus's silence is not so complete. In lines that are apparently spoken "aside," he threatens perception but then retreats
into the absolute:

> My wife comes foremost; then the honored mould
> Wherein this trunk was framed, and in her hand
> The grandchild to her blood. But out, affection!
> All bond and privilege of nature, break!
> Let it be virtuous to be obstinate.
> What is that curt'sy worth? or those doves' eyes,
> Which can make gods forsworn? I melt, and am not
> Of stronger earth than others. . . .
>   Let the Volsces
> Plough Rome and harrow Italy! I'll never
> Be such a gosling to obey instinct, but stand
> As if a man were author of himself
> And knew no other kin.
>
> (V.iii.22–29, 33–37)

Coriolanus, at least, is "with himself at war." When finally he does
melt, in lines we have already considered, he sees this relenting
as likely to be fatal to him. A tragic perception seems to lie behind
this; but we never learn what it is, and when he returns to Corioles he apparently expects fair treatment, even praise, not death.
With its inarticulateness, its suggested alternation of mature
recognition and adolescent stubbornness, its swings between
shrewdness and naïveté, Coriolanus's mode of perception seems
appropriate to the tragic hero in whom the struggle between boy-
hood and manhood was never resolved.

Troilus and Timon provide us with clear examples of ironic

perception. In V.ii Troilus sees that Cressida is false and thus
arrives at the perception that all women are false. In V.x he has
seen that Hector is slain and thus arrives at the perception that
the war should become more bloody and violent than ever. In the
middle of Act III Timon thinks he learns, and he changes. But he
changes only superficially. Fundamentally he learns nothing. He
is as absolute as ever and is incapable of perceiving the unique
nature of his three principal visitors in the woods, Alcibiades,
Apemantus, and Flavius, three men who are foils to his notion of
"man." Timon regards even Flavius not as a man but as an
absolute, in this case the exception that proves the rule.

In marked contrast to Timon, Antony accepts uniqueness, the
uniqueness of Cleopatra, and that acceptance is his perception or
recognition. It is all the more noble and tragic and wonderful for
being instinctive. He has passed beyond "learning," the most
trivial form of perception, to immediate apprehension of the
truth.

Antony's perception, and his tragedy, depend a great deal on
the nature of Cleopatra. Cleopatra is an even more "silent" tragic
figure than Brutus or Coriolanus. Shakespeare never directly
presents what goes on below her "public" surface. She has no
soliloquies at all, no asides. We see and hear what the world—
including Antony—sees and hears. At several points in Acts III
and IV Antony seems to be wrong about Cleopatra, but given
Cleopatra's character one can't be sure. She *could* have betrayed
him, even if in fact she hasn't. It is apparently one of her traits
to consider seriously every possibility offered her, to ask somewhere in her mind what a given action might bring her. (This
trait does much to shape V.ii.) What we can see in Acts III and
IV is a repeated pattern of rejection and acceptance. No matter
how mad Antony becomes, he always comes back:

> Fall not a tear, I say: one of them rates
> All that is won and lost. Give me a kiss;
> Even this repays me.
>
> (III.xi.69–71)

The simple diction of his returns is always a moving contrast to
the purple splendor of his rages.

39

For Antony the final scenes of the tragedy come in Act IV. In IV.xiv he receives the false news of Cleopatra's death. Knowing that she is dead, having less than ever to live for, he asks Eros to kill him, but Eros kills himself. Antony then sees himself as a learner and stabs himself:

> Thou teachest me, O valiant Eros, what
> I should, and thou couldst not. My queen and Eros
> Have by their brave instruction got upon me
> A nobleness in record.
>   . . . Eros,
> Thy master dies thy scholar. To do thus
> I learned of thee.
>
> (96–99, 101–3)

Laboring under a false "recognition" (Cleopatra's true love of him, from which she died), Antony is even now a poor pupil; he does his work ill in comparison to the efficient Eros. But it is when Diomedes brings the true report that Antony shows his real stature, his mastery. The recognition in itself is nothing, trivial, but his mode of recognition is impressive. When Diomedes gives his news and says he fears he has come too late, Antony replies very simply:

> Too late, good Diomed.
> (128)

He shows no rage, no reproach towards Cleopatra, and no regret, either here or in the next scene, when he is taken to her monument. His acceptance is a recognition of her uniqueness, a uniqueness that includes the kind of petty thing she has just done. He loves her for that, too, and his acceptance is a final assertion that their love *is* on a higher level of value than the Roman lands. This assertion here lacks the touch of bombast it had in Act I (i.33–40). Here it is tragic.

When I began my discussion of "tragic" perception, I had been examining Hamlet, Macbeth, and Lear, those men who range furthest in questioning the order of things and who seem to us the most comprehensive in their suffering, and yet who either reject suicide or never consider it. I ended by asking whether these three men learn something or achieve a maturity that the other tragic heroes do not. And I might ask further whether they reach what we could call "superior" perception. I think not, not as a group anyway. Antony, for instance, achieves as much maturity as any of them. In *Hamlet, King Lear,* and *Macbeth* perception is important as a formal element, but that may be as far as we can generalize, because the actual relation of perception to form is so different in each play.

Of all Shakespeare's tragic heroes Hamlet and Lear seem to be most consciously in search of perception, of illumination. In their final scenes (and here I mean specifically *Hamlet* V.ii and *King Lear* V.iii) we see that they have consolidated their experience into an acceptance of what the world has offered them. They each offer what amounts to a statement of their acceptance, their recognition. (See *Hamlet* V.ii.208–13 and *King Lear* V.iii.8–26.) But that is as far as the similarity goes. Hamlet's actions right up to the end are consistent with his new stability of soul. Lear, on the other hand, when he returns to the stage with Cordelia dead in his arms, is once again torn apart, showing no trace of his "perception." He ignores anything he might have learned as completely as he ignores the possibility of suicide. He is out of touch again, ignoring the people around him. He has become again the proud, tormented, self-absorbed, questioning, testy, pitiful old man of the first four acts. Lear may have learned something along the way, but it isn't reflected in the scene of his death (V.iii.258ff.).

Macbeth concludes in V.v that life is meaningless. Nothing happens to him afterwards to change his mind or to redeem the world in his eyes. This clear vision of life is the general form of Macbeth's perception; it is the result of a long series of specific perceptions, those repeated disillusionments about the oracular promises which have been made to him. The series continues into the final confrontation with Macduff, confirming his general belief.

But is Macbeth right? Or is he at least not demonstrably wrong? Maybe. I suspect that such a vision would not be clearly wrong in the other mature tragedies, but once more the special nature of the new order in *Macbeth* is important. The fact that Malcolm, Macduff, and the rest achieve a political and moral unity associated with life-giving forces suggests that Macbeth's view of life is simply tainted, sick, like Scotland under his rule. It suggests that instead of being more perceptive than his enemies he is simply self-abused (cf. III.iv.142), that he is ironically deceived in his vision of life just as he is in the conclusions to be drawn from the witches' predictions, that he has turned life inside out: "Fair is foul and foul is fair." By the standards of the play he is in, Macbeth seems to be wrong, perverse. The good life was possible under Duncan, exists in England under Edward the Confessor, and will be possible again in Scotland under Malcolm. We see here the importance of the new order in which the tragic disaster is set: it is Macbeth, not the nature of things, that has robbed his life of meaning—*his* life, not life in general.

And yet Macbeth finally does not act as if life were meaningless and he wished the candle would go out. His instincts, apparently, rebel against the logical conclusion of his perception. He rejects suicide in favor of continued destruction of life:

> Why should I play the Roman fool and die
> On mine own sword? Whiles I see lives, the gashes
> Do better upon them.
>
> (V.viii.1–3)

His motive here does not seem to be humanitarian; that is, he is not rescuing men from meaninglessness. Rather, he may envy these men; he cannot bear to see lives that *have* purpose, as these lives so clearly do. When he meets Macduff, and perceives the last equivocation of the "juggling fiends," he still does not seek death, nor will he yield his life into the power of another. He seeks victory:

> . . . I will try the last. Before my body
> I throw my warlike shield. Lay on, Macduff,
> And damned be him that first cries "Hold, enough!"
>
> (V.viii.32–34)

Macbeth dies in opposition not only to Macduff and Malcolm and men of women born, not only to all order, but also to what he has learned about life, to his perception. He goes on as if life, his life, means something, as if it were worth too much to give it to a Malcolm. After concluding that life is meaningless, Macbeth gives his own life meaning by continuing in it as long as he can.

I have saved the problem of Othello's "tragic perception" for last because, as far as Shakespearean criticism is concerned, this may be the most celebrated case. In his well-known, provocative, and perceptive essay on "Senecan" attitudes in Elizabethan drama, T. S. Eliot uses Othello's final long speech as his primary example of a self-deceiving self-dramatization which he identifies as an Elizabethan adaptation of the original Senecan "tragic" stance: [4]

> Soft you! a word or two before you go.
> I have done the state some service, and they know't.
> No more of that. I pray you, in your letters,
> When you shall these unlucky deeds relate,
> Speak of me as I am. Nothing extenuate,
> Nor set down aught in malice. Then must you speak
> Of one that loved not wisely, but too well;
> Of one not easily jealous, but, being wrought,
> Perplexed in the extreme; of one whose hand,
> Like the base Indian, threw a pearl away
> Richer than all his tribe; of one whose subdued eyes,
> Albeit unused to the melting mood,
> Drop tears as fast as the Arabian trees
> Their med'cinable gum. Set you down this.
> And say besides that in Aleppo once,
> Where a malignant and a turbaned Turk
> Beat a Venetian and traduced the state,
> I took by th' throat the circumcised dog
> And smote him—thus.
> *He stabs himself.*
>
> (V.ii.339–57)

In Eliot's view, Othello's real, though unconscious, purpose in this speech is not to set down the truth about his life but to make himself feel better about how it has turned out:

> I have always felt that I have never read a more terrible exposure of human weakness—of universal human weakness—than the last great speech of Othello. . . . It is usually taken on its

43

face value, as expressing the greatness in defeat of a noble but erring nature. [At this point Eliot quotes the speech.] What Othello seems to me to be doing in making this speech is *cheering himself up.* He is endeavouring to escape reality, he has ceased to think about Desdemona, and is thinking about himself. Humility is the most difficult of all virtues to achieve; nothing dies harder than the desire to think well of oneself. Othello succeeds in turning himself into a pathetic figure, by adopting an *aesthetic* rather than a moral attitude, dramatizing himself against his environment. He takes in the spectator, but the human motive is primarily to take in himself. I do not believe that any writer has ever exposed this *bovarysme,* the human will to see things as they are not, more clearly than Shakespeare.[5]

I accept the last sentence here (though I don't believe it is illustrated by this speech of Othello's). And I agree with Eliot that the point of the speech is not to express "the greatness in defeat of a noble but erring nature." (The speech may or may not express such greatness but to see that as the point would be to trivialize it.) But, in saying that Othello at this point is "adopting an aesthetic rather than a moral attitude," Eliot seems to be claiming that what is *required* of Othello at this moment is the adoption of a moral attitude, and in doing this Eliot would seem to be making the same kind of assumption that we saw Johnson make about Shakespeare in general, that Shakespeare "seems to write without any moral purpose." Both Johnson and Eliot apparently assume that aesthetic stances and moral stances must be distinct, that an aesthetic stance can not in fact be a moral stance in the most profound sense. On the contrary, aesthetic stances do have moral value, and later in this chapter I will return to the nature of Othello's aesthetic attitude here and its moral implications. For the moment, let us simply note that Eliot would, after all, appear to be drawing moral conclusions from Othello's aesthetic stance. In other words Eliot treats the speech as if it expressed, unconsciously, a moral attitude. But even taken as purely a moral assertion, Othello's speech does seem to me to be a just assessment of Othello's career—a balanced statement of reality, not an attempt "to escape reality," as Eliot claims. The speech is indeed not a moment of "perception," but I think it is the result of a sound perception and thus ultimately an expression of one.

Othello sums up his case as that "Of one that loved not wisely, but too well; / Of one not easily jealous, but, being wrought, / Perplexed in the extreme." The problem is that Othello has behaved rather oddly for one who loved well and who was not easily jealous. But Othello is saying what he feels, and I think it is an accurate statement about the conflict of passions in the play we have just seen. Because of her powerful appeal to Othello's senses, Desdemona had gotten under the armor of self-confidence and self-sufficiency which had always protected him in times of crisis. Othello's jealousy is lack of confidence in himself. His cry of "Cuckold me" (IV.i.196) shows habitual self-esteem confronted with evidence that he is not esteemed. Iago works by undermining Othello's self-confidence and by arousing his strong sensual imagination, as in that cruelest of lines, "With her, on her; what you will" (IV.i.34), which sends Othello into his trance. The important thing to observe is the rare power needed to reach the nearly inaccessible (heretofore invulnerable) core of Othello's being, from whence his great passions break. This power is Desdemona's, not Iago's. Iago merely exploits it. The whole play testifies to Othello's previous self-containment at all times. Even now, he says, "But that I love the gentle Desdemona, / I would not my unhoused free condition / Put into circumscription and confine / For the sea's worth" (I.ii.25–28). The best account of the strong appeal of Desdemona's "parts and graces" and their impact on Othello's self is his own:

> Had it pleased heaven
> To try me with affliction, had they rained
> All kinds of sores and shames on my bare head,
> Steeped me in poverty to the very lips,
> Given to captivity me and my utmost hopes,
> I should have found in some place of my soul
> A drop of patience. But, alas, to make me
> A fixed figure for the time of scorn
> To point his slow unmoving finger at!
> Yet could I bear that too; well, very well.
> But there where I have garnered up my heart,

> Where either I must live or bear no life,
> The fountain from the which my current runs
> Or else dries up—to be discarded thence,
> Or keep it as a cistern for foul toads
> To knot and gender in—turn thy complexion there,
> Patience, thou young and rose-lipped cherubin!
> Ay, there look grim as hell!
>
> (IV.ii.47–64)

Othello "loved not wisely but too well" because when he did finally engage his passions, he lost all control of them, and he was "not easily jealous" because the object was not easily found which could so engage his passions. (No one has ever doubted that he was "perplexed in the extreme.") It is not necessary to pay such attention to these lines when Othello delivers them because they are no flash of insight. They indicate neither presence nor absence of "tragic" perception. They express Othello's character as the rest of the play has presented it.

Othello's important perception, his actual recognition of truth, comes earlier and is very simple: he was gulled. This is a trivial perception, but it is sufficient. It is an important shaping element in the final scene. Again, Othello best expresses the perception: "O fool, fool, fool!" (324).

Helen Gardner, in a footnote to her remarks on the use of historical criticism in looking at *Hamlet*, comments on Eliot's view of self-dramatizing death-speeches and relates Othello's speech to a "historical" genre:

> Mr. Eliot's general complaint about the death-scenes of Elizabethan tragic heroes, whose *apologias* he ascribes to the influence of Seneca, ignores the historical fact that this was an age of public executions in which men were judged by the courage and dignity with which they met public death, and when it was thought proper that at this supreme moment of their lives they should submit their case to the judgement of their fellow-men.[6]

Othello's speech, then, is a putting of his case before the Venetian public (though it is more than that), and, as Eliot observes, he is not the only tragic hero to make this sort of presentation. Since speeches like this naturally fall in the final scenes, we come to another important element in the structure of these scenes—the tragic hero's assertion of self.

3

Assertion of self, or (what lies behind it) a strong sense of self, does much more to give a play a feeling of tragedy than perception does. The assertion of separateness which it involves is never a major structural influence in comedy, or at least not in Shakespearean comedy, where the final scenes assert union centrally. (*Love's Labor's Lost* is the exception.) In the tragedies the separateness dominates, in our response, the new order (union) against which it is set. Only in *Romeo and Juliet*, among the tragedies, does a union seem to be at the center of the structure of the final scene. Romeo and Juliet assert their identity, their integrity, by a merging of selves in a sexual union, a consummation in death. As in comedy, love conquers all.[7] This doesn't happen in *Troilus and Cressida*. It is one of the things that happens in *Antony and Cleopatra*, but because Antony is absent from the final scene, it happens by means of a far more complicated process, in which Cleopatra, not the union, is central.

One form tragic self-assertion takes, one that, in a sense, we have already looked at, is self-justification, a desire by the tragic hero that his story be judged correctly, that it be accurate to the facts, that it not be biased in favor of the most recent developments. (Of course, this attitude takes it for granted that the tragic hero's career is worth remembering in the first place. This assumption too is part of the tragic sense of self.) We have already examined the case of Othello. Hamlet, Coriolanus, and Antony offer us versions of the same device. Hamlet hasn't the time to tell his own story, as Othello does, so he entrusts the job to Horatio:

> Horatio, I am dead;
> Thou livest; report me and my cause aright
> To the unsatisfied. . . .
> O God, Horatio, what a wounded name,
> Things standing thus unknown, shall live behind me!
> If thou didst ever hold me in thy heart,
> Absent thee from felicity awhile,

> And in this harsh world draw thy breath in pain,
> To tell my story.
>
> (V.ii.327–29, 333–38)

Coriolanus is rushed too, but it is his self-assertion that helps to bring on his death. He lacks the balance of Othello, Hamlet, and Antony. Goaded by Aufidius, Coriolanus utters *in* Corioles those parts of his story that will make it easier for the conspirators to get away with killing him:

> Your judgments, my grave lords,
> Must give this cur [Aufidius] the lie; and his own notion—
> Who wears my stripes impressed upon him, that
> Must bear my beating to his grave—shall join
> To thrust the lie unto him. . . .
> Cut me to pieces, Volsces. Men and lads,
> Stain all your edges on me. Boy? False hound!
> If you have writ your annals true, 'tis there
> That, like an eagle in a dovecote, I
> Fluttered your Volscians in Corioles.
> Alone I did it. Boy?
>
> (V.vi.104–8, 110–15)

With Antony, we find a fourth kind of self-justification, for he makes his plea for a just assessment of his life neither to the public nor to someone he directs to make it to the public. He speaks only to Cleopatra:

> The miserable change now at my end
> Lament nor sorrow at; but please your thoughts
> In feeding them with those my former fortunes,
> Wherein I lived the greatest prince o' th' world,
> The noblest: and do now not basely die,
> Not cowardly put off my helmet to
> My countryman. A Roman, by a Roman
> Valiantly vanquished.
>
> (IV.xv.51–58)

The self-justifying speech naturally implies a strong self-image, but the absence of such a speech hardly means that the tragic hero lacks a strong self-image. The self-image may be conscious or unconscious. It is conscious in the case of Cleopatra, who stages the elaborate ritual of V.ii in order to assert her integrity as woman, as wife, as queen, as tragic heroine. The best example of the unconscious assertion of heroic self-image is Macbeth, who by his final act instinctively claims his worth in spite of his declared belief in the valuelessness of all life. Gardner observes that Shakespeare has made this Thane of Cawdor a contrast to his predecessor, who, it is reported (I.iv.3–11), made the "just" death-speech expected of a nobleman.[8]

One kind of dying stance found often in the tragic literature of the sixteenth century and earlier seems to have been regarded by Shakespeare as something of a joke—the mirror, the warning, the tragic figure pointing to himself in his fall as a moral lesson.[9] At least, none of Shakespeare's greatest tragic heroes sees himself as a mirror. When Shakespeare does use the mirror notion, its effect is almost always local, not structural, and it is likely to appear in ironic contexts. Cleopatra, for instance, apparently mocks Caesar with it during their exchange of diplomacy: [10]

> See, Caesar: O, behold,
> How pomp is followed! Mine will now be yours,
> And should we shift estates, yours would be mine. . . .
> Be it known that we, the greatest, are misthought
> For things that others do; and, when we fall,
> We answer others' merits in our name,
> Are therefore to be pitied.
>
> > (V.ii.150–52, 176–79)

I think there are only two examples of characters adopting the "warning" stance in an important, structural way. The clearest example is the extremely ironic one of Pandarus, who, in what is essentially a dying speech at the end of the play (quoted above, p. 16), holds himself up in his fall as a mirror for all his "Brethren and sisters of the hold-door trade" (V.x.50). The other is Timon:

> . . . let my gravestone be your oracle.
> Lips, let sour words go by and language end.
> What is amiss, plague and infection mend!

> Graves only be men's works, and death their gain.
> Sun, hide thy beams; Timon hath done his reign.
>
> (V.i.217–21)

Timon sees himself here as a king who wants his dying declaration, the epitaph on his gravestone, to teach men a moral lesson. But what a lesson—shut up and die off as fast as possible, following his example! The contradictory statements in the epitaph read in V.iv ("Seek not my name . . . Here lie I, Timon") combine the moral lesson that all things human should be obliterated with the self-assertion of the dying tragic hero who, like Hamlet, Othello, and Antony, is concerned that his name be remembered and his story viewed with balanced eye.[11] We are to remember that "Timon . . . alive all living men did hate," that for him there was no balance. Ironically for Timon, Alcibiades seems well on the way to giving him the just and truly balanced assessment that an Othello, a Hamlet, or an Antony would have desired.

4

Alcibiades' explanation of Timon's gravesite on the sea is that "rich conceit / Taught [him] to make vast Neptune weep for aye / On [his] low grave, on faults forgiven" (V.iv.77–79). Yet Timon seems to have had in mind a kind of eternal daily laceration and a situation that catches symbolically the restlessness of his soul and his desire for an ambiguous oblivion:

> Lie where the light foam of the sea may beat
> Thy gravestone daily.
>
> (IV.iii.375–76)

> Come not to me again; but say to Athens,
> Timon hath made his everlasting mansion
> Upon the beached verge of the salt flood,
> Who once a day with his embossed froth
> The turbulent surge shall cover.
>
> (V.i.212–16)

In any case, it is clear that Timon has chosen a place of death that is symbolically rich—the point where sea and land crash together, a point of ceaseless opposition appropriate to Timon's "latter spirits" (V.iv.74), his hatred for humanity, his constant contradiction even of himself. Timon's death itself must be considered a suicide: death by simple refusal to live. The simplicity of this opposition, too, suits his character well, as does the fact that the death occurs offstage, for Timon now wishes to avoid entirely the sight of men, the public show, and Shakespeare makes the suicide of Timon so private that not even the theater audience can witness it. Timon goes away from all men, all life.

The choice, as by Timon, of a symbolically appropriate death is a form of tragic self-assertion that we find in all those plays where the tragic figures commit suicide. "Rich conceit," to use Alcibiades' phrase, teaches these characters to give their deaths a shape that expresses their sense of the quality of their lives. Sometimes this rich conceit is a conscious exercise of imaginative power; sometimes it is apparently instinctive. Sometimes the shape the character wants to give his life is suggested by metaphors alone, sometimes by metaphors elaborated into parable or personal ritual. Romeo, for instance, as he prepares to drink the poison, is perhaps not aware that he uses again the images he used as he went to the Capulet feast where he first met Juliet (compare I.iv.106–13 and V.iii.109–18); but he does observe a brief ritual in drinking the poison as a toast to Juliet:

> Here's to my love! O true apothecary!
> Thy drugs are quick. Thus with a kiss I die.
> (119–20)

Again, Juliet is not conscious of repeating either Romeo's life-sex-death metaphors or (with "poison" replacing "sin") the exchange of kisses from their first meeting (I.v.103–10): [12]

> O churl! drunk all, and left no friendly drop
> To help me after? I will kiss thy lips.
> Haply some poison yet doth hang on them
> To make me die with a restorative.
> (163–66)

Nor is she aware of the symbolic significance of the language she uses at the very moment of suicide (a moment when dramatic word and deed are united), but her intuition of the forces within Romeo and herself that have led them to this tomb now leads her to the happy metaphor that makes her marriage to Romeo complete and final:

> O happy dagger!
> This is thy sheath; there rust, and let me die.
> (169–70)

In all these lines the two characters' imaginations are bringing forth images and romantic gestures appropriate to the story of a couple that prefers sexual union to life and thus finally can find consummation only in death.

In rushing, as Cleopatra says, "into the secret house of death / Ere death dare come to us" (IV.xv.81–82), the tragic figures who kill themselves are not only choosing their own death rather than letting others choose it for them (or what would, in their opinion, be worse, letting others choose for them an unacceptable life), but also they are choosing the *manner* of their death, the style.[13] They are declaring that their death shall be an extension of their life, rather than its negation, that death is not an uncharacteristic accident but a final assertion of the power to give personal shape to life.

In contrast to the kind of self-justifying speech we examined earlier, in which the man about to die tries to set the record straight with those who will go on living, the self-assertive suicide appeals not to the reason but to the imagination, and correspondingly the language that gives the suicides their style usually depends not on balance ("Nothing extenuate, / Nor set down aught in malice") but on metaphor ("I will be / A bridegroom in my death"). The language of suicide is witness not to the facts of life but to its poetry. The characters who use this language are not so much concerned that their true story be remembered by their survivors as that in dying they be true to themselves.

With both Antony and Othello we can see a character use one of these modes of self-assertion and then the other. Antony, in IV.xiv, where he actually gives himself his mortal wound, makes his suicide a wedding night: "I will be / A bridegroom in my death, and run into't / As to a lover's bed" (99–101). Here he is not the valiant Roman who would rather die than be shamed in capture but rather the man who would give "all for love," the man who would be shamed not to give all as Cleopatra (he thinks) and Eros have done.[14] Later, in IV.xv, where he finally dies, he brings together the two spheres of his accomplishments —the lover in the reunion with Cleopatra, the movement aloft into her monument, and the final kiss; and the great Roman conqueror in his declaration as he is brought in that "Not Caesar's valor hath o'erthrown Antony, / But Antony's hath triumphed on itself" (14–15), and in the balanced, soberly worded speech (51–58) we examined earlier in which he asks Cleopatra to remember his life in proper proportion. (The one metaphor in this speech—"feed"—is not central to what he is saying and does not refer to Antony's view of himself or his actions.) At least in this play Shakespeare sees the speech justifying one's life, setting one's life in order, as a peculiarly Roman genre. The Romans are making them constantly, Cleopatra virtually never. The use of visual spectacle, of image and symbol, on the other hand, seems to be Egyptian. (Consider Cleopatra on her barge, for instance.) Thus as Antony dies in Cleopatra's arms, in her monument, speaking of being "a Roman, by a Roman / Valiantly vanquished," he is verbally a Roman, visually an Egyptian. Cleopatra, when she dies, will be concerned mostly with image in both spectacle and word.

Othello, in the middle of his final long speech (V.ii.339–57), changes significantly from one mode of self-assertion to another, from the plea for a balanced assessment of his whole life to the metaphorically powerful suicide itself. The former appears in the balanced phrasing of the speech up to "Set you down this" (352), the latter in the anecdote, with its "bloody period," about the incident in Aleppo. It is clear in the context of the whole last scene that Othello's suicide is part of an elaborate ritual. In fact, Othello creates two rituals in the final scene, the second (the suicide) reversing the moral structure of the first (the murder of Desdemona). I will examine these rituals in detail in chapter 5. For the moment, it is important to see what Othello is doing with his anecdote about the Turk in Aleppo. Most immediately he seems to be reporting a minor incident as if it were to be remembered as a major accomplishment of the Moorish general who has "done the state some service"; this would tend to suggest that Othello is ironically undercutting the greatness of the general. But Othello's real purpose in telling the story becomes apparent when he stabs himself at the end of it. Now we realize that the anecdote is an extended metaphor, a parable in which both the Turk and "I" are Othello. The parable first makes a distinction between the Christian servant of the Venetian state, who loved Desdemona, and the presumptuous infidel who killed her; but the parable also shows, in the image of self-killing that ends it, Othello's recognition that these two are one, that he cannot, like Hamlet to Laertes, speak of another self who was Othello's enemy too. No, even more than with Antony, the death of Othello shows a tragic figure accepting his wholeness—in this case the capacity for love being inseparable from the capacity for hate.

Othello's final speech shows particularly well another important quality of the language of suicide and demonstrates the way its kind of self-assertion—its revelation of the character's sense of self—differs from the speech of self-justification. The speech of self-justification refers away from the dramatic moment in which it is uttered, away to other times and other places, either to the past in which the speaker performed his deeds or to the future in which they are to be remembered and reported. The language of suicide, on the contrary, usually brings everything down to the moment it is uttered.[15] Everything in the person's life is brought to bear on the deed we see and hear at that moment—the taking of the life. This is nowhere more evident than in Othello's use of the Aleppo incident. Having requested his hearers to "Speak of me as I am," he has been talking about his career, especially about the recent past, so full of "unlucky deeds." With his offhand "And say besides that in Aleppo once" Othello lulls his audience into thinking that he is continuing to talk about the past, an even more distant past. But by stabbing himself Othello suddenly makes us realize that he is now using the past as a metaphor, or a parable, for what is taking place in the present. Two people, a distant place, a far-off time, a punishing blow—"Turk" (or "dog"), "I," "Aleppo," "once," "smote"—are poetic tools for describing one man acting here and now. Like Juliet's "dagger" and "sheath," Antony's "lover's bed," or Timon's seaside grave, the Aleppo incident is a character's way of expressing his sense of the essential truth about the life that has brought him to this present, this moment of death.[16]

And when we consider the end of this speech as it occurs on a stage, a unity of word and deed, we recognize that the language of suicide is a language of act as well as of word, of visual image as well as of verbal image. The words alone may seem to allow a separation of the "dog" and the general, the bad and the good. But the words are not alone. Othello utters them in a visual context that insists on their unity—the Othello who kills is the Othello who dies, the Othello we see and hear, the only Othello there is.

If Antony and Othello are interesting for using both the speech of self-justification and the ritual suicide, Brutus is remarkable for using neither, remarkable because earlier he had insisted so strongly on performing the murder of Caesar as a ritual and had delivered an elaborate speech of self-justification to the Roman mob.[17] To be sure, Brutus, in killing himself, does see his suicide in relation to the murder of Caesar, as does his "brother" Cassius. But there is an ironic difference between the ways these two men make the connection. Brutus had said earlier (in his speech of self-justification) that he would turn the dagger that stabbed Caesar on himself if Rome ever needed his death (III.ii.44–46).[18] But when he does kill himself, he does not explicitly use the same dagger; he merely compares the two slayings: "Caesar now be still. / I killed not thee with half so good a will" (V.v.50–51). Cassius, on the other hand, who was less interested in making the assassination a ritual, makes his own death a ritual of symbolic retribution:

> Now be a freeman, and with this good sword,
> That ran through Caesar's bowels, search this bosom.
> . . . Caesar, thou are revenged
> Even with the sword that killed thee.
> (V.iii.41–42, 45–46)

Brutus needed ritual to hide, from himself more than from others, the true nature of the assassination, but now, dying, he neither doubts his moral superiority nor imagines anyone else can doubt it; that superiority itself justifies the acts of his life and the manner of his death. Cassius, on the other hand, saw the nature of the assassination more clearly; it was an act that might call for revenge.[19] And now, consonant with his new belief in "things that do presage" (V.i.78), his new belief that events are morally as well as physically connected, he wants to make his death symbolically appropriate to his life.

The most elaborate, prudently prepared for, gracefully executed suicide in Shakespeare displays magnificently (and appropriately) the most elaborate, carefully cultivated, consciously maintained, and yet at the same time most elusive sense of self— Cleopatra's. For all her "infinite variety," her idle moods and ambiguous motives, her mixing of oblique and direct, her lapses from decorum and her insistence on due rank, her wild passions and her cool reserves, her openness and her opacity—all this, and more, apparent even in the final scene—still she seems *whole*. She is inconstant (always changing) without being essentially inconsistent, perhaps because what she embodies centrally is the power of continual change. And yet in the scene of her death, the main subject of chapter 5, below, she even manages to assert and make everyone accept her constancy. She is crowning forever not only her image but also a royal self of her own creation, albeit in the end a simpler one than she has shown us earlier.

5

The magic of Cleopatra in the last scene not only asserts the wholeness of her own life but also, like the magic of Isis tending to Osiris, patches up the fragments of Antony's. And we have seen how, in the case of Othello, a character asserts the wholeness of his life by recognizing a split in himself. Following these lines perhaps we can ask, without becoming inappropriately psychoanalytical, whether we find characters whose sense of self is in some way fragmented during the play and who then achieve a more integrated sense of identity in the final scenes, or, to put it another way, we can ask whether achievement of a whole sense of self is, like tragic self-assertion, a frequent formal element of last scenes.

Antony himself, for instance, when he has lost both the final battle and, apparently, the love of Cleopatra—when he has lost, that is, the centers of both his "Roman" and his "Egyptian" powers—says that his identity has become as shifting and indeterminate as a cloud:

> That which is now a horse, even with a thought
> The rack dislimns, and makes it indistinct
> As water is in water. . . .
> My good knave Eros, now thy captain is
> Even such a body: here I am Antony,
> Yet cannot hold this visible shape, my knave.
>
> (IV.xiv.9–14)

We can see him, through the "suicide" of Cleopatra, his own suicide, and his last reunion with Cleopatra, trying to rebuild and reassert his "shape" as Antony. To a certain extent he succeeds, as we noted above, for he dies in Cleopatra's arms and manages to see himself as having been conquered by himself rather than by Caesar. And certainly his final acceptance of his life as it was, including the "miserable change now at [his] end" (IV.xv.51) and of Cleopatra as she is, including her last trick, does much to redeem the shabbiness of his suicide. Still, the suicide *was* shabby, and his contention that his valor, not Caesar's, has triumphed seems as good an example as any of what Eliot describes as cheering oneself up. And his "ascension" into Cleopatra's monument blends pathos and comedy in a way that stresses the variety of Antony's personality more than its unity. The scene of his death makes him a richer, more complex figure than the valiant Roman he claims to be in his final speech. It is left to Cleopatra's speeches about him after his death, both in IV.xv (especially "The crown o' th' earth doth melt," etc. [63–68]) and in V.ii (especially her "dream" [76–100]), to produce a conventionally unified great man. Thus the process of Antony's reintegration can be said to continue somewhat ironically after his death, as a man of great (if not infinite) variety becomes, in the surviving imagination of Cleopatra and thus in the world's memory, a simple superhuman Emperor Antony.

Richard II is perhaps the clearest example of the fragmentation of identity in a tragic hero. Originally man and king were one. But as Richard began to neglect the legal and traditional responsibilities of the king (in effect allowing the man to use the king), he opened a split in this original identity which eventually allowed Bolingbroke to break the two completely apart. This split is the origin of Richard's obsession with the *role* of king; it's not that he is an actor at heart but that for the first time he must see "king" as a separate thing from man, and because they were originally one, he fears that ceasing to be king may mean ceasing to be anything at all. Yet being nothing might be preferable to this intermediate state of being in doubt. He finds oblivion attractive, as we noted earlier. Richard's obsession with the breakdown of his identity continues right through the final soliloquy and the dialogue with the groom. Only at the moment of his death, like the dying lion thrusting forth his paw (cf. V.i.29), does he clearly assert once more the unity of man and king:

> Exton, thy fierce hand
> Hath with the king's blood stained the king's own land.
> (V.v.109–10)

Exton, says Richard, is killing more than a man. And though this assertion, like his physical resistance, may strike us as simply a matter of last-minute histrionics, the future proves him right.

Fragmentations of identity are not so simple in later tragic figures as they are in Richard. Lear, for instance, not only has the roles of man and king to reconcile, but also the role of father, in some ways his most difficult. Moreover, his sense of what it means to be a *man* is much more complex than Richard's. "Who is it that can tell me who I am?" (I.iv.220), he asks early in the play, and his long search for an answer is not successful until IV.vii, when—reconciled with Cordelia—man, father, and king again become one.[20] But when Cordelia is killed, his identity is once more shattered and he ends still searching—not for an identity now, but for her life or a reason she is dead. By the end he has become the least ego-conscious of these dying heroes and makes no explicit assertion of self.

Hamlet's sense of identity is threatened in many ways. In the first half of the play he is progressively broken down by the world he experiences, and in Act III his behavior is so frantic that if it is not madness it might as well be. But also in Act III he seems to begin putting himself back together again. Each new experience from III.ii through V.i he brings into a new unity, a new sense of self. The process is painful; perhaps it involves learning to live with pain. But I think there is a great sense of relief, for us and for Hamlet, when he breaks into the funeral party with the cry, "This is I, / Hamlet the Dane" (V.i.244–45). The violence of this assertion is followed in V.ii by a calmer acceptance of himself and his role. His apology to Laertes (V.ii.215–33) seems sincere in its distinction between a former madness and the Hamlet who stands there now. Hamlet's selfishness is largely gone. He is "open and free"—to his own cost, in practical terms. He has no regrets, so long as his story is told. Hamlet maintains to the end a wholeness we can believe in. Of all the tragic figures, Hamlet probably achieves the most remarkable reestablishment of the sense of self, the most remarkable because he comes back by himself from a chaos of soul nearly as complete as Lear's, and unlike Lear he maintains his self-possession to the very end. He who had rejected so much in his world is now ready for anything, including death. Among the tragic figures who find their identities threatened, only Antony rivals Hamlet in his final acceptance of his life, and death; and Antony had not had to come so far to reach that acceptance.

Coriolanus's problem, because of the importance of his relation to his mother, is in some ways related to Hamlet's, but it is really much more limited. One might even state it as simply as this: is he man, superman, or boy? Unlike Richard, Hamlet, Antony, and Lear, Coriolanus seems barely conscious of his problem. Others are at fault; he almost never considers the possibility that he might be. There are some glimmers of recognition in V.iii, but they seem to have gone out by the final scene of all. He remains fragmented, the boy-man. In the absence of a really solid sense of self, his final self-assertion, quoted above, lacks the expressive balance of a Hamlet or an Othello or an Antony and lacks also the magical assurance of a Cleopatra. He lacks as well the persistent questing of a Lear, lacks even the single clear (if futile) assertion—physical and verbal—of a Richard, and, strangest of all, lacks even the plain physical defiance of a Macbeth. Yet perhaps this is not so strange after all.

59

Art of Dying

His last assertion *is* merely verbal, its force ironically undermined by his fragmented identity. Claiming to be a man, he is acting like a boy. Man to man Aufidius was no match for Coriolanus, and knew it, but he finally found a way to reach that point where Coriolanus was not solid, where Coriolanus could not effectively oppose him, where Coriolanus was not a man. The last irony is that Aufidius's victory is itself so unmanly and that his cue was Coriolanus's most manly act—giving in to his mother.

There is, I suppose, a kind of triumph in those characters whose deaths either explicitly or implicitly maintain their sense of self (whether solid or fragmented) in the face of opposition. This triumph is present in most of the tragic characters we have been discussing. But also in most the triumph is so like defeat that calling it a triumph is the same thing as saying that the tragic figures are simply creatures of greater possibilities than those who survive them, potentially finer human types, if you will, and that the tragic process, by exploring their possibilities, has revealed their superiority. But in at least three cases—Brutus, Antony, and Cleopatra—the characters themselves explicitly transform defeat into a triumph. All three are from the Roman world, and this attitude towards death is specifically identified by one of them—Cleopatra, the foreigner—as Roman: [21]

> We'll bury [Antony]; and then, what's brave, what's noble,
> Let's do't after the high Roman fashion,
> And make death proud to take us.
>
> (IV.xv.86–88)

The triumph is partly a matter of dying "like oneself":

> I dare assure thee that no enemy
> Shall ever take alive the noble Brutus.
> The gods defend him from so great a shame!
> When you do find him, or alive or dead,
> He will be found like Brutus, like himself.
>
> (*JC* V.iv.21–25)

Brutus, says the captured Lucilius here, will assert his sense of self triumphantly in life or death, and since capture would prevent such assertion, Brutus will die when capture is inevitable.[22]

In the event, Brutus sees his triumph as greater than his adversaries':

> I shall have glory by this losing day
> More than Octavius and Mark Antony
> By this vile conquest shall attain unto.
> (V.v.36–38)

Their triumph is vile, his is glorious, the difference presumably being that he is Brutus, "the noblest Roman of them all," and as Strato points out, "Brutus only overcame himself, / And no man else hath honor by his death" (V.v.56–57). It is, so to speak, a "moral victory," one whose ironies we have already discussed. In the later play, the later Antony, whose sense of self is wilder and more flamboyant than Brutus's, and who, after losing the final battle against Octavius, says that his identity has become as insubstantial as a cloud, nevertheless sees himself in death in the terms Brutus and Strato used for Brutus:

> Not Caesar's valor hath o'erthrown Antony,
> But Antony's hath triumphed on itself. . . .
>   [I] do now not basely die,
> Not cowardly put off my helmet to
> My countryman. A Roman, by a Roman
> Valiantly vanquished.
> (*AC* IV.xv.14–15, 55–58)

As we noted above, since Antony killed himself on the basis of a lie, and didn't do it very neatly, his assertion here may seem a little forced, his death a little shabby; but Cleopatra turns his tragedy and her own into a grand triumph over Caesar, one we can almost accept without ironic reflections. She does this by making her death a work of art. She stages her suicide not only with grace of execution (so different from Antony's!) but also with a sense of dramatic control: Shakespeare shows Cleopatra achieving her triumph by an art analogous to his own.

6

Shakespeare's presentation of Cleopatra as a stage-conscious artist creating her own life and manipulating the characters around her is the principal subject of chapter 5. For the moment, it is enough to note that he has made the action of V.ii essentially a comic intrigue in which Cleopatra attempts to circumvent the wishes of the antisexual Caesar in order to accomplish the union of herself and her lover, Antony. This scene has the kind of structure we find in so many comedies in which we see the young lovers outmaneuver the father figure who wishes to keep them apart. Enthroning herself in a regal tableau, Cleopatra succeeds in ritualizing a reunion and marriage with Antony. She even manages to make the marriage fruitful by turning the asp into a baby. She escapes into a bright new life free of the bonds of Caesar and the kind of life he represents. It is true that this comic victory is ironic, for Antony and Cleopatra are not only old, but also dead, and the world, the normal sphere of comic activity, is left for the young Caesar to bustle in. But at the same time the victory over Caesar, achieved by dying in rituals of their own creation, is what makes Antony and Cleopatra tragic figures. It was a greater thing to be Antony and Cleopatra than to be "the universal landlord," and thus they triumph over Caesar in the tragic structure as well as the "comic" structure of the final scene.

The characters, Cleopatra above all, who assert their triumph in the face of the continuing society, the supposed winners, the new order, are claiming that they are really in control of events and are masters of their own fates. (Cleopatra may go so far toward remaking the world, the dramatic show, that perhaps only the fact that she does indeed die makes her story a tragedy.) But the claim of control is essentially made also by the tragic figures who without an explicit sense of triumph commit a suicide that is symbolically appropriate to their life, for they insist that they themselves are giving their life its final shape. And those too who ask that their story be told correctly are exercising a kind of control, for they are imposing a specified structure on the consciousness of posterity. All these figures, most of whom were accustomed to shaping in an important way the life of their times, are making in whatever way they can a last assertion of their will to control, their desire to give the world a shape that answers to their sense of themselves and the life they think they have lived. Sometimes the attempt to control is literally directed toward the surviving world, sometimes solely to themselves, sometimes to both at once. Of course the world can be put into various kinds of structure—political, moral, psychological, metaphysical, poetical, historical, even (as with Antony and Cleopatra) mythical—and the various tragic figures seek to impose a variety of shapes on life.

And yet, is it really an illusion, this sense of control? Is it the last illusion, rather than the last exercise of power over reality? Are any of them really better off than Macbeth, who refuses to compromise his instinctive sense of his own value by submitting either to Macduff or to Malcolm or to his own nihilism, who at the end continues to fight in opposition to the structure of his life as announced by the witches and as accepted for so long by himself, and who yet, for all his defiance, is obviously not in control? All the tragic figures, after all, end up dead, and they are defeated to the extent that the world didn't turn out the way they wanted it to, defeated by human enemies, or fate, or the nature of the world, or in fact by the very sense of self which seems to triumph. Are they all ironically more deluded than Lear, who has clearly lost all power to shape, and now, unconcerned with death as his own certain future, is left trying, and failing, to deal with Cordelia's, unable to accept her death or deny it, since to him it is an event that makes no sense?

And this leads to a further question: who or what is ultimately in control of the worlds of these plays? [23] Who shapes the tragic process the characters get involved in? Is it the individual human will, or is it a society which will not tolerate a certain kind of human greatness (and so destroys and survives that greatness), or is it something altogether beyond human control or comprehension—time, fate, chance, providence, the gods, God? Or is it the artist himself with his own incomprehensible mystery? (And to what extent are we stepping outside the work of art to ask the question in this last form?) These questions involve not only the relation of the tragic figures to the final order, but, perhaps more important, the characters' sense of their own powers to shape the events of the final scenes, which are, after all, the final scenes of their own lives. To speak this way of an analogy between the "scenes" of art and the "scenes" of life raises the question of the artist's participation in the final scenes and thus involves Shakespeare both as a shaper of his final scenes and as a possible analogue to his own characters. And the problems of art and the problems of life are explored together, for we find that in the greatest plays an extension of tragic form leads to an extension of human experience into more intense relation to something "outside."

Again, Shakespeare gives us variety. Though the sense of something beyond man is rarely, if ever, completely absent, there are some plays which seem almost completely secular. There are others that have a structurally important religious dimension, a sense of control by something beyond. These are usually the plays where a good deal of metaphysical disorder occurs. One could arrange the plays on a rough secular-to-religious scale, beginning with *Titus* and *Coriolanus,* proceeding through *Othello* and *Romeo and Juliet,* and ending with *Hamlet* and *King Lear.*

With *Hamlet* and *King Lear,* we come to Shakespeare's most complex uses of superhuman controls—providence in *Hamlet,* "the gods" in *King Lear.* The new calmness and acceptance of life and death we see in Hamlet in Act V is associated with a belief in providence. In *King Lear* the gods are powerful, they are mysterious. Their relation to the human events they presumably preside over is obscure. They are not associated with the new order. The reestablishment of a human order at the end of this play is the most tentative in Shakespeare. Even in *Troilus and Cressida* the ironic new order—chaos—is firmly established. In *King Lear,* though we do return as usual from the tragic depths to the business of daily human existence, there seems to be nothing for that daily existence to do.

The new order usually brings us back to the secular, if we have been away. In any case, it brings us back to the ordinary. The tragic heroes have gone up against the ultimate. The greatest of them have gone up against the mystery, up to the barrier that separates human life and human understanding from whatever it may be that lies beyond. The new order stays, safely, well back from that barrier. In the comedies there is normally no such sense of retreat, but instead a promised advance into the future where life will go on not away from the mystery but in harmony with it, accepting it, whatever it is.

The tragedies do not *decide* what the relation is between human control and whatever lies beyond it. They present the problem as it presents itself in life: the question of the ultimate nature of what is beyond man's control is left open, as it must be if one is serious in asking it, as Shakespeare was. Any answer would be reductive. It would not do justice to the gods or to God. It would imply a comprehensive human intellect. It would deny the power of the irrational. And this is what the greatest of the tragedies are about—man's confrontation with things that don't make sense.

Cleopatra's form of this confrontation with things that don't make sense is to embrace them as a source of creative possibility, for in that lack of sense lies the chance of wonder. She "dreams," for instance, of an Antony who never was and never could be except in the vision of a poet (see V.ii.76–92), an Antony, certainly, whom we never saw; and yet she boldly proves that her dream Antony could only be real:

> But if there be nor ever were one such,
> It's past the size of dreaming: nature wants stuff
> To vie strange forms with fancy, yet t' imagine
> An Antony were nature's piece 'gainst fancy,
> Condemning shadows quite.
>
> (V.ii.96–100)

Through Cleopatra's art the most wonderful becomes the most natural, the most real. But Cleopatra's art is really the art of her creator, and the process she performs with Antony is the basis of the dramatist's art, a process Shakespeare performs in each play, making his dreams seem real.

Since it's the nature of great art to be about, among other things, itself, the final scenes of the tragedies are about the ending of plays as well as about the ending of lives. We can most clearly see the poles of Shakespeare's exploration of this situation in the contrast between the endings of *Antony and Cleopatra* and *Timon of Athens*, two plays which, besides being written near each other in Shakespeare's career, have, curiously enough, a common source in Plutarch's *Life of Antony,* where Antony, in one phase of his career, is compared to the man-shunning Timon.

Timon, we noted above, leaves the stage to die, in marked contrast to Cleopatra, who occupies the center of it triumphantly. In fact, Timon dies in marked contrast to all Shakespeare's other tragic figures, for he is the only one who dies offstage, the only one, that is, who leaves the world of the drama in order to die.[24] We may even see it the other way around: *he dies by leaving the world of drama.* In the absence of more specific information on his death, we may render the verdict of "self-inflicted death by rejection of the medium of his existence."

Clearly Shakespeare uses this offstage death as one important way of characterizing Timon. He makes Timon uniquely anti-dramatic. Timon gives an appropriate shape to his death by refusing to let us see it, by refusing to be a character in a drama, by refusing, as it were, to go along with Shakespeare's art.[25] That art depends on an analogy (though not a simple one) between the world of man and the world of drama; but then if all the world's a stage and the stage is all the world, Timon, by dying offstage, expresses in an absolute way his hatred for the world by ceasing to be part of it, by leaving the stage where the human drama is played out. His rejection of drama is a way of expressing his rejection of life. "My long sickness / Of health and living now begins to mend," says Timon, "And nothing brings me all things" (V.i.184–86). Other Shakespearean characters flirt in various ways with "nothingness," but only Timon actually becomes nothing because only he so completely leaves the place which in drama contains everything and is every where—the stage.

In Timon's offstage death Shakespeare has, in a sense, violated the principles of his art, an art which involves placing dreams *on the stage* as if they were real. One might almost say that Timon's death doesn't happen, because what happens in the world of drama is what is done and said onstage, and the death of Timon is not even narrated to us by "offstage" witnesses. His grave and epitaph are found, and that is all.

The fact that Shakespeare built a play around a character who denies drama may suggest that Shakespeare himself was experiencing a kind of despair in the value of dramatic art. Or it may mean that he was simply experimenting with the extremes of tragic form. Certainly the play is an extreme of tragic form, and certainly Timon, if not the play, is an image of despair as he rejects the very power which created him.

Speculating on Shakespeare's motives is a risky, irresponsible, and amusing activity, and it is always a mistake to identify him with any of his characters. The characters and their attitudes must always be considered in the context of the play's structure as a whole. Thus in the case of *Timon* we see that Shakespeare carefully shows the limitations of Timon's "absolute" world view by confronting him in Act IV with Alcibiades, Apemantus, and Flavius, who do not fit his notion of "man," and by setting his uncompromising rejection of Athens and man and life against the balanced, responsible, and conciliatory behavior of Alcibiades in Act V. Thus it may be that Timon's rejection of drama, in his offstage death, is simply another way, perhaps the ultimate way, of showing Timon's limitations. Just as Timon wishes for the perversion of nature's creative powers and for the self-destruction of human sexuality, both male and female, so he rejects the creative powers of the dramatic imagination. The structure of the play does not suggest that Shakespeare finally endorsed his creature's desires.

Nevertheless, the question of the value of his art must have been somewhere in Shakespeare's mind as he wrote *Timon,* for he puts into the play, in fact begins the play with, a direct image of himself—a poet who is writing about Timon.[26] And the "Fortune's wheel" poem this poet describes has the same simple view of life and of human nature, the same reductive two-part structure, that we find in the history of Timon's own world view. Moreover, the Poet's aim in writing is clearly to get money, and his reappearance at the beginning of Act V does less than nothing to reveal any limitations in Timon's view of man. It is tempting to see the Poet as Shakespeare's self-parody—a pompous man with no imagination and no sense of life's variety, a glib, flattering hypocrite, a man whose motive in writing is not artistic and creative but economic, a man, in short, for whom Timon's latter opinion might be adequate—Wm. Shaxper, the facile upstart crow with a finger in the Globe's every financial pie, borrowing feathers, never blotting a word, pleasing both royalty and rabble so he can get a coat of arms and buy that big house back in his hometown. The inaccuracy of the self-parody, like the inaccuracy of Timon's world view, is apparent in both the poetry and the structure of the play; still, *Timon* seems to consider the possibility that drama is a fraud.

Drama would be a fraud if the process on which it depends—the creation of lifelike illusions—turned out to be false to life. But this primal fact that drama is illusion needn't make it false to life. It would be essentially false to life only if life made absolute sense, as Timon wants it to do, and thinks it does, one way or the other. Ironically, Timon rejects the world partly because he has found that things (human nature, for instance) are not what they seem. He might have concluded from this, as Shakespeare seems generally to have done, that drama, with its traffic in illusions, is a highly appropriate way of dealing with life lived in a mysterious, various, constantly changing world. But Timon doesn't so conclude because he doesn't finally see that kind of world. Instead he would regard himself as "disillusioned." Now he knows what the truth is, and drama must be rejected. Drama is essentially a fraud, rather than an illusion, only if one can be as positive about life as Timon is.

In contrast to Timon, Cleopatra dies by entirely embracing the world of drama. Instead of despising human creative powers, she celebrates them, in a sense creating her life as she lives it. Thus if Timon is an image of despair in dramatic art, Cleopatra is an image of faith, faith that for any moment, including death, the dramatic imagination can make a better life.[27] Cleopatra's primary concern in her final scene is neither to justify her behavior nor to ask anyone else to do so nor to offer a philosophical or moral summary of her opinions about the world. Instead, what she most wants to do as she dies is to put on a good show, for herself and for us. And the show does all the rest.

We come to the paradox that death can be a creative art for the tragic characters, and in this they imitate the tragic art of their creator, who in his own way is making death a creative art. We began this chapter by noting how often the tragic characters experience a desire for death. It is apparent now that this desire for death can take on some aspects of being an aesthetic impulse, that the ending of a life becomes the ending of a play.

This parallel of life and play, death and final scenes, appears even when the character himself is unconscious of his dramatic significance. If Cleopatra and Timon are opposite poles with respect to *acceptance* of the dramatic event, Cleopatra and Lear are poles with respect to *consciousness* of it. Where Shakespeare has made Cleopatra so very conscious of putting on a show, he has made Lear supremely unconscious. In contrast to Albany, who tries to make a neat conclusion to a play that isn't neat (especially with "All friends shall taste / The wages of their virtue, and all foes / The cup of their deservings" [V.iii.303–5]), Lear persists as a dramatic character, occupying the center of the stage with his own interests and obsessions, continuing in his role, refusing to give up the play. For Albany as for Timon, everything was answered; for Lear, nothing. Albany's impulse to see moral balance in the world, whether it's there or not, has the "aesthetic" result of leading him to conclude the play prematurely. The impulse that keeps Lear going is the impulse to continue the process by which he has been attempting to come to terms with life, the process of dramatic confrontation with the elements of his world. In Act I Lear had attempted a more conscious kind of play in an attempt to assert his control over the emotional life of his daughters and subjects, but his play failed because one of his actresses wouldn't keep to her assigned role. In the acts that follow, drama becomes an unrehearsed dialogue with all that couldn't be contained in the terms of the Act I play, a dialogue through which he explores human nature, his own nature, the nature of family, of society, of the gods, of the macrocosmic forces of the storm, of death, trying to discover whether there is any moral purpose, any moral order to it all. As there has been no conclusion to his search (in contrast to Albany's), so there is no conclusion to his life, no conclusion to the play, but only a death, an end. Lear doesn't consciously give his death a shape, but since it becomes clear after his death that the survivors can't give a shape to the new world they inherit, the "shapelessness" of Lear's death is the only ending appropriate to the story. Lear's dramatic confrontation with a world that doesn't make sense is reflected in the lack of final order—of political "sense"—in the ending of the play.

We noted earlier that Shakespeare's tragic figures generally, in shaping their ends, their final scenes, are responding to a world they can no longer control. Whether they are conscious or unconscious of their shaping acts, whether their shaping takes the form of measured speeches about their lives or of symbolically appropriate suicides or of expressive rituals or simply of *self-*assertive acts, the characters are insisting, in a sense, on an artistic right, at times almost a creative right, over their own lives. This artistic control is particularly appropriate at those moments when the characters are confronting things in the world which don't make sense, because artistic control is control of illusion and, as I suggested above in talking about Timon, that very lack of strict sense that illusion implies can be the dramatist's means of doing justice to a world that doesn't make sense, to things that are finally beyond human control, like the inevitability of death. Art, the control of illusion, is a compensation for loss of control over "reality," and not only compensation, of course, but also confrontation, exploration, and, ultimately, exploitation of the mysterious "real" world, exploitation because the sense of mystery is engaged on the side of the artist. Certainly, artistic control does nothing to make the world more sensible, whether we consider the elaborate form used by Cleopatra or the brief form used by Antony. It certainly makes no sense to say that one "will be / A bridegroom in [one's] death, and run into't / As to a lover's bed." It seems absurd to say that a movement toward creation is in fact a movement toward death. Yet out of that absurdity is born the paradox that the act of death becomes a creative act, and in that paradox lies the secret of the tragic hero's value as an exemplary human figure facing part of the mystery.

And what can be true of the tragic hero is more constantly true of the tragic dramatist, Shakespeare himself. All his control of dramatic form and style serves finally not to make a world whose primary quality is to make sense, but to make dramatic worlds that exploit the paradoxical power of illusion to preserve, explore, and confront the complexities we experience in life. If the power of the dramatist is in some ways divine, if in some ways he is the one who controls the (dramatic) world absolutely, in other ways the power of the dramatist is a great image of human power extending itself fully in the face of a world that is mysterious and senseless or perhaps mysterious and wonderful but in any case beyond our control. In our experience of this world the moment of death is particularly crucial, since it's a moment when the mystery can no longer be put off, and for this reason the final scenes of the tragedies are of particular importance. "More are men's ends marked than their lives before," and so too we have been "marking" the plays' ends. As the tragic figures assert themselves most fully in the scenes of their death, so Shakespeare's art is most fully extended in *his* final scenes, where he puts the power of human creation against what seems most destructive in the world.

And, as the world is not only mysterious but also various, mysterious partly because various, no single dramatic form can be definitive. Thus Shakespeare's variations and extensions of tragic form become a way of experiencing a strange, shape-changing world. Among these dramatic experiments, three plays seem to me to have dramatic shapes and, correspondingly, dramatic worlds that are more complex and strange than the rest—*Hamlet, King Lear,* and *Antony and Cleopatra.* They even more than the rest are unique and daring explorations of what can be accomplished by tragic art. I now turn, in the chapters that follow, to detailed examinations of the final scenes of these plays, attempting to respond to the particular music of each close, to the way Shakespeare has shaped each of his worlds.

3

✻ hamlet

Sir, in my heart there was a kind of fighting
That would not let me sleep.

HAMLET, more than any of the other tragedies, is structured by a mutual, personal, increasingly recognized antagonism
between two characters. The antagonism is apparent from Hamlet's first words, in I.ii; and with the disclosure of the King's
crime and with Hamlet's vow of revenge in I.v, we know how
the antagonism will end—we know that a final showdown between these two men will end the play. The dramatic tension
builds to this point and builds through a series of displacements
or versions or avoidances of the principal conflict. Hamlet sees
this conflict between himself and the King as a long duel and the
King's substitutes as interferers in the duel:

> 'Tis dangerous when the baser nature comes
> Between the pass and fell incensed points
> Of mighty opposites.
> > (V.ii.60–62)

Claudius does the best he can to avoid fencing with Hamlet
directly; their personal exchanges are rare and brief, right to the
end. Instead, Claudius sends a series of substitutes to uphold his
part of the duel. Much of the action of the play, then, is a series
of local duels which become more dangerous as the nature of
the contest becomes increasingly clear to Claudius. We have
Hamlet against Polonius, Hamlet against Rosencrantz and Guildenstern, Hamlet against Ophelia, and Hamlet against Gertrude.
We even have Hamlet against himself. Hamlet must fight his

way through all these preliminary matches before he can get to the King; this makes the play a web of attack and defense. Indeed, one could say that Hamlet's real problem is the constant danger he's in, not least from himself.

From the beginning Claudius finds Hamlet's behavior unreasonable. He becomes more and more interested both in finding out a reason for it and, when he does find one out, in getting rid of Hamlet. After his sensible fatherly advice (I.ii.87–117) fails to have any effect, Claudius resorts to indirect means of accomplishing his goal. He spies on Hamlet and sends others to spy on him, to sift him, to play upon him, and "by [their] companies / To draw him on to pleasures, and to gather / So much as from occasion [they] may glean" (II.ii.14–16), all to "pluck out the heart of [his] mystery" (III.ii.351–52). Decoys are laid for him— Ophelia and Gertrude. The King's method here—indirection— is described by a more shallow practitioner, Polonius:

> Your bait of falsehood takes this carp of truth,
> And thus do we of wisdom and of reach,
> With windlasses and with assays of bias,
> By indirections find directions out.
> (II.i.63–66)

Of course Hamlet has his own plots and indirections to answer theirs. The antic disposition is a defensive indirection which allows him to avoid their traps, though it also encourages the setting of them. And if Claudius and Polonius use Ophelia as a mousetrap to catch Hamlet's mystery, Hamlet springs his own Mousetrap to catch the conscience of the King, and springs it with rather more success, though of course with ironic success since by succeeding thus he virtually tells Claudius what all the spying couldn't bring to light. The Mousetrap, like the antic disposition, works both ways. This is a world of plotters where the plots always fall on the inventors' heads, where enginers are always hoist with their own petars.[1]

Hamlet's aim is to kill the King, the King's is to defend himself by killing Hamlet. The local duels are displacements of this basic antagonism, and the process of *Hamlet* is the decreasing of the displacement to the point where the deaths occur.

2

In its first stage, the fencing is verbal. One of the characters on Claudius's side will make some sort of advance toward plucking out the heart of Hamlet's mystery, an advance typically in the form of a question, and Hamlet will defend himself verbally by turning his opponent's words in an unexpected direction. This sort of wordplay is more important in *Hamlet* than in any of the other tragedies; indeed, I think it is integral to the play's structure.[2] The wordplay one finds in *Hamlet* is akin to the wordplay of the professional fools, the word experts who use their employers as straight men. It is Feste who observes that "a sentence is but a chev'ril glove to a good wit. How quickly the wrong side may be turned outward!" (*TN* III.i.11–13, 34–35). But it is the "corrupter of words" who is in the end the restorer of words, for by calling attention to the words, he calls attention to the truths which they do or do not express.

Hamlet's first four lines are attempts (which may at this point seem churlish) to break through the language to the truth, to find the full relevance of the words to which he is responding (I.ii.65, 67, 74, 76). Hamlet's technique in these lines is one we will see him use over and over. In response to an inquiry he will pick up his questioner's words and pun on them; he will seem to interpret literally what was intended metaphorically (or sometimes the other way around), but his own "literal" statement will have a different metaphorical thrust. A pun is an equivocation, a dealing in ambiguities, and it is the key to Hamlet's verbal fencing. He uses it to ward off an inquirer's thrust at the heart of his mystery and to make his own thrust in return. In the language of fencing, the pun is his parry and riposte.

The pun, the equivocation, the ambiguous word, is particularly suited for anatomizing a country like this Denmark where the king is hedged by the Divinity he has violated, where his queen is also his sister and his nephew his son, where the very image of innocence sings bawdy songs, where the dead seem to walk abroad dealing in the affairs of the living, where Death itself is an uncertain end, and where the prince who worries so much about these ambiguities is himself a mass of ambiguities, as reams of criticism will testify. The master of the pun is the fool, the corrupter of words, who is also the antic—a retailer of the grotesque and the mad who is at the same time the most clear-sighted man of all. In holding up his side of the duel with Claudius, Hamlet assumes an "antic disposition," and the corruption of words is the method of his madness. It is a common-place in "antic" lore that the apparent fool is really wise while the apparent wise man is foolish. In this Denmark which though apparently sane is fundamentally mad, the apparently mad man is the sanest of the lot, though he takes enough of the general taint to fall with the rest. That is why he is a tragic hero instead of only a fool.

When the attack on Hamlet becomes particularly threatening, his fencing becomes even more skillful, as he mixes his parries and ripostes with feints (that is, with set-up lines, like "Will you play upon this pipe?" [III.ii.336–37]). But even a simple question like the King's "How fares our cousin Hamlet?"—hardly a threatening inquiry—will receive an answer like "Excellent, i' faith, of the chameleon's dish. I eat the air, promise-crammed. You cannot feed capons so" (III.ii.89–91), which not only makes the King's bland, long-dead metaphor suddenly concrete, in a "mad" sense, but also makes a self-revelation, an indictment, and a threat. This is Hamlet's language of defense—an upsetting of his opponents by refusing to accept the socially accepted meanings of words. Related to this is the upsetting of his opponents by refusing to accept the socially accepted relation of ideas (see, for example, II.ii.173–85 and IV.iii.16–36).

The complement of language as defense is language as attack, or what Hamlet calls "speaking daggers." At the end of his first soliloquy, having faced his life's grief in the frailty of his mother, Hamlet says that his heart will have to break in silence, "for I must hold my tongue." But by giving him the facts that answer to his soul's prophecy, the Ghost frees his tongue, frees it first to explode into the "wild and whirling words" which (after the Ghost's revelation and after Hamlet's proof of that revelation in the Mousetrap) are the direction his suddenly released flood of energy takes when no true object of that energy is present; frees it later, when an object is present and yet no physical expression of the energy is possible, to explode into verbal attacks.

This is the offensive side of Hamlet's verbal fencing. His most notable verbal attacks are those on Ophelia (III.i) and Gertrude (III.iv), and in these attacks, especially the latter, Hamlet works himself into a frenzy. He loses control, and when a fencer loses control he becomes vulnerable; he gives too much away. In the closet scene this happens in the stabbing of Polonius, which puts Hamlet more surely in the King's power, and in Hamlet's reaction to the Ghost, which convinces the Queen irrevocably that her son is mad. Hamlet's frenzied verbal attack led both to Gertrude's physical fear, which led to the stabbing, and to the appearance of the Ghost, who must come to sharpen Hamlet's "almost blunted purpose" (112), "blunted" because he has been dulling his passion by using it in verbal combat instead of in a physical attack on the King. Verbal attack is a displacement of Hamlet's real purpose—when he can't act, he must resort to words.

Hamlet's soliloquies have often been taken as showing his preference of words (or thoughts) to deeds. While I wouldn't call it a preference, I do think we can see Hamlet using some of the verbal fencing techniques against himself, and therein lies much of Hamlet's danger to himself that I spoke of earlier. The verbal attack appears as the self-laceration which reaches its peak in "O what a rogue and peasant slave am I" (II.ii.534–74), where Hamlet "unpacks his heart with words" and then accuses himself of doing so. The verbal defense appears in his attempts to curb or direct his passionate frenzy by reason, as in the soliloquies of II.ii, III.ii, or (ironically) III.iii, and in reason's own arguments with itself, as in the soliloquies of III.i and IV.iv. The parallel with his dialogue method is perhaps not so clear here as with the attacks, but we do see him involved in trying to discover the true meanings of words like "revenge," "man," "death," and "reason" itself. He wishes to find the reality beneath the word, the truth beneath the socially accepted corruption, the truth about Claudius, Gertrude, himself, the world, death. Ultimately, of course, his fencing with himself comes to the same impasse as his verbal dueling—the proof lies only in the physical event.

In general, Hamlet's verbal fencing, when it is observed, is interpreted by those around him as his madness. His language is normally and necessarily oblique—he suppresses the "real" point of his antagonisms. He cannot attack directly the forces that oppose him, so he must displace the attack into more socially acceptable forms. That the more socially acceptable form is madness is a measure of the forces being suppressed, for madness is not entirely acceptable; but it is safer than direct action, or direct statement. (His verbal attacks on Ophelia and Gertrude would have been even less safe if he hadn't already a reputation for insanity.) It is the displacement of his antagonism which makes Hamlet in one aspect a satirist, for it builds up pressure which must issue somehow and so issues in grotesque verbal attack—satire—one aim of which is to put man in his place (which is always lower in the scale of things than he would expect).

The verbal attacks appear irrational because his victims generally don't understand the cause for his antagonism. Claudius, however, realizes more and more where Hamlet's oblique language is really aimed, so that in III.i, after the nunnery scene, the King finds Hamlet reasonably sane:

> . . . what he spake, though it lacked form a little,
> Was not like madness. There's something in his soul
> O'er which his melancholy sits on brood,
> And I do doubt the hatch and the disclose
> Will be some danger.
>
> (163–67)

Thus the King's verbal fencing, as in IV.iii, has an ironic dimension missing in the other responses to Hamlet's thrusts—he is now no more anxious than Hamlet to have the cause of the mad behavior discovered.

Hamlet's problem is to get to the point where he no longer has to verbalize his antagonism, indirectly or directly. He must somehow get to the point where he can take physical action against Claudius with certainty that he will succeed in his revenge. "Succeeding" of course involves more than simply killing the King: he must be sure that his soul and the Ghost have not been false prophets and that the killing will be true revenge, and he must have the answers to a complex set of questions which are themselves not clear but which still seem vital to his enterprise. Hamlet's problem, then, is to resolve the duel with Claudius into its simplest form.

3

One of Shakespeare's favorite tropes is the theatrical metaphor, the comparison of the world to the stage, of life to play. The
ultimate effect of this metaphor may be to make life less "real,"
to make life, play, and dream one, as in the "Our revels now are
ended" passage:

> We are such stuff
> As dreams are made on, and our little life
> Is rounded with a sleep.
> (*Tem* IV.i.156–58)

But drama itself depends on the opposite implication of the
theatrical metaphor, on the irony that play, or make-believe, or
the player in "a fiction" or "a dream of passion," can become as
real as "real" life.

With the theatrical metaphor as it usually works, the
boundaries between worlds remain distinct until they become
nonexistent. But one way in which drama can operate is to exploit this metaphorical equivalence, which is, after all, a total
equivalence, by making an apparent fiction within the world of
the play, such as a play-within-the-play or a masque, partially
real within that world. Mere play suddenly becomes real in a
literal way. In *The Spanish Tragedy*, for instance, with a group
of actors which includes Bel-Imperia, Lorenzo, Balthasar, and
himself, Hieronimo is supposed to be putting on a "mere" entertainment for the King of Spain, the Viceroy of Portugal, the
Duke of Castile, and the rest of the court. But, with the help
of Bel-Imperia, Hieronimo breaks the supposed fiction, drawing
it into the real world of *The Spanish Tragedy* by having Balthasar
and Lorenzo factually instead of fictionally stabbed. (Bel-Imperia
carries the device even beyond Hieronimo's fiction by making
her suicide real.) The relation between characters in the broken
fiction is not always a direct equivalent of their relation in the
outer play. Soliman's desire for Perseda, her revenge on him, and
her suicide are direct metaphorical equivalents for the relation of
Bel-Imperia and Balthasar; but Lorenzo's role as Erasto has an
ironic relation to his role in the real world of *The Spanish*

Tragedy, for as Erasto he is more or less in the position of Andrea and Horatio, and Hieronimo as the Bashaw is in Lorenzo's. In this play the supposed fictional world becomes more than just a metaphorical equivalent of the real world, as a normal fictional world would be, yet less than a total equivalent.

The boundaries which are simply evaporated by the theatrical metaphor are rudely violated—broken—by this partial realization of an internal fiction. Because of its inherent theatricality (in both senses), this device seems particularly forceful at the end of a play, and as an ending it seems particularly appropriate to revenge tragedies, since it allows not only the simple irony of a straightforward revenge at a moment when the guilty victim least expects it ("This isn't the real world, where my crime was committed, so I'm safe here"), but also the more complicated irony of a transposed world where the original deeds and the original roles can be reversed and replayed, the wheel brought full circle. The revenge can be an ironic image of the original crime: the original murderer becomes a victim, and the revenger (who represents the original victim) becomes a murderer.

A different but related way of ending a play is to make a situation which at the beginning exists only in words—an oracle (or prophecy, or riddle), a promise or a lie, a relationship between characters—come true in fact at the end. The broken fiction and the words-come-true ending are two ways in which "fiction" becomes fact. When they are combined in a single play, the broken fiction begins to have a literal as well as metaphorical equivalence to the real world of the play. The fiction becomes an image of the play as well as a part of it. *Hamlet* is such a play.

In *Hamlet* there is both a play-within-the-play and a fencing match. The inner play comes after the real event that it mirrors, and for most of the spectators (and for the actors) it remains fiction—it is simply "the image of a murther done in Vienna," a murder which doesn't concern them or affect their response to the performance. The fiction of the inner play is not "broken" (though it is halted abruptly!). But for Hamlet and Claudius the inner play mirrors a real murder done in Elsinore, a murder that has a real place in their lives. Personal associations force them to make an allegorical interpretation of the play. For

Claudius and for Hamlet, "The Mousetrap" is real murder speaking with most miraculous organ.

A fencing match has the same relation to "real" fighting that theater has to "real" life. In fact, a fencing match is a kind of theater, a particularly stark kind, with its actors and its audience, its props and its rituals, its questions and answers, its dialogue and resolution. It is a theater in which the conventions are especially evident.

In V.ii the fencing in *Hamlet* finally turns from verbal to physical. It becomes more literal. But as far as Hamlet knows, it is still going to be one remove from full reality, for fencing is a socially acceptable, "safe" form of a fight for blood, a fight to the death. (Often it is also a form of revenge, a satisfaction of one's sense of honor, as in various ways it is here, though again Hamlet does not know this at first.) But as we have already learned in IV.vii, Claudius and Laertes will carry the fencing to its literal, physical extreme: the fictional duel will suddenly become real.

The inner play, "The Mousetrap," is preceded by a dumb show, which was preceded by the original crime. So in temporal order the crime moves from real action to play action to words. That is, it moves "backwards," from literal poison to verbal. The revenge reverses this order; it moves forward from words to play (the "brothers' wager") to real action: the poison is literally returned to its source.[3] The gap between the last two steps is very short in the case of the crime—they are consecutive. And it is virtually nonexistent in the revenge—they overlap in the broken fiction of the duel. The center of this movement from "fact" to "fact," at the climax of the play scene, is Hamlet's shrewd verbal thrust, first by the player's tongue, then driven home by his own:

> *Lucianus.* Thoughts black, hands apt, drugs fit, and
>   time agreeing,
>   Confederate season, else no creature seeing,
>   Thou mixture rank, of midnight weeds collected,
>   With Hecate's ban thrice blasted, thrice infected,
>   Thy natural magic and dire property
>   On wholesome life usurps immediately.
>   [*Pours the poison in his ears.*]

> *Hamlet.* 'A poisons him i' th' garden for his estate. His name's
> Gonzago. The story is extant, and written in very choice Italian.
> You shall see anon how the murtherer gets the love of Gon-
> zago's wife.   (III.ii.245–54)

By making the King "blench," these words prove to Hamlet that
the crime was indeed committed; they tell the King that revenge
for that crime may lie ahead. Hamlet's fiction recreates the fact
of the crime. It also prefigures the revenge: it is what Hamlet
calls "false fire" on the King's position (256), but the thrust is
that in the future Hamlet will load his gun with shot as well as
powder.

In the inner play, then, a real murder in the past becomes a
fictional murder in the present. At the end, as I suggested earlier,
the fencing match, an elementary kind of theater, becomes real
murder. Fiction no longer follows fact, nor prefigures it, nor substitutes for it. The fiction itself is "broken" into fact. When Hamlet
realizes this, that it has happened whether he will or no, he finally
accomplishes with poisoned sword and poisoned cup what he
had been doing with poisoned words since his first line—he
puts down the King.

4

The duel with the King is what we may call the "outer"
structure of *Hamlet,* and the broken fiction ending is the solution
to Hamlet's external problem. At the same time the play has an
"inner" structure and Hamlet an internal problem—that mass of
concerns which do not directly involve *practical* aspects of his
relation to the King. There is his sense of duty, of purpose, which
troubles him because it conflicts with his belief that the world
has nothing in it of sufficient value to justify a purpose. There is
his sense of his mother's sexual guilt, and it is this sense of her
guilt that leads him to see all women as "frail," to see mankind
generally as bestial or worse, and to see the world as empty of
value, as "an unweeded garden / That grows to seed" (I.ii.135–
36). And there is his desire for death, for escape from this kind
of world, a desire which conflicts not only with his sense of duty
but also with a fear of death, a fear which itself conflicts with

his sense of duty. It is these concerns that make Hamlet a character of frenzied activity and thoughtful pauses, a character of constantly shifting moods, a character of brilliant dialogue and of soliloquies, a character so fascinating and finally so important. In what follows I use "demon" as a convenient term for this combination of conflicting concerns, a term that suggests the way they drive and torment him in the first four acts.

I realize well enough how clumsy and tactless it is to separate "external" and "internal" as I have just done, and I don't intend to insist on the division. The two actions proceed simultaneously, with the same cast of characters; this is not a matter of plot and subplot. Indeed, in discussing the "external" problem I have already, inevitably, spoken of things which are part of the "internal" problem, things such as Hamlet's self-dueling and the "complex set of questions" which seem to stand between Hamlet and his revenge. But I hope that the distinction between Hamlet's external and internal problems will be useful in helping us see what is odd about the final scenes of this play. The scenes are odd because the first two hundred lines of V.i are a kind of pause in which the revenge plot is not advanced but in which, I will argue, Hamlet, without realizing it, finally becomes "ready" for the ultimate duel, which will come in the next scene. And the scenes are also odd because Shakespeare doesn't really show us until about two hundred lines into V.ii what the significance of the "pause" in V.i probably was—how it resolved Hamlet's internal problem and made him "ready."

Similarly, I realize that the collective term *demon* disposes too neatly of much that is most fascinating about Hamlet. And yet the complexities the term hides are mainly apparent in the first four acts, which are not my subject here. When Hamlet returns from his sea voyage, the demon is all but gone. Indeed this is the reason I feel that the last two scenes are the concluding phase of the play. I have described the demon briefly only to have some sense of what is missing when we come to V.i.

5

When Hamlet returns from the sea in V.i, he returns to a graveyard, where his search for death reaches a new plane. The graveyard is a world of death, a land inhabited by those who have died and are now in various stages of decay on the way to dust. Hamlet's imagination brings the bones and the dust back to life and populates the opened grave he finds there with lawyer, courtier, and politician, with my Lord Such-a-one and my Lady Worm, with original murderer, world-conqueror, and emperor, with the king's jester, the antic, until the grave, crowded enough as it is, seems indeed "not tomb enough and continent / To hide the slain" (IV.iv.64–65).

The presiding figure in this world is a grave-maker, and Hamlet converses with him in the fencing style which has been characteristic of his conversation in the earlier parts of the play. Now, however, it is Hamlet who, in his search for the meaning of death, seeks to pluck out the heart of the Grave-maker's trade, his mystery. It is Hamlet who asks the questions and is put off by equivocating replies, by refusals to take the socially accepted meanings of words. In this fencing match it is Hamlet who loses:

> *Hamlet.* I will speak to this fellow. Whose grave's this, sirrah?
> *Clown.* Mine, sir.
>   [*Sings*] O, a pit of clay for to be made
>   For such a guest is meet.

(109–13)

The Grave-maker goes on with his business, as Hamlet went on with his reading when Polonius was questioning him. And Hamlet, like Polonius, persists:

> *Hamlet.* I think it be thine indeed, for thou liest in't.
> *Clown.* You lie out on't, sir, and therefore 'tis not yours.
>   For my part, I do not lie in't, yet it is mine.
> *Hamlet.* Thou dost lie in't, to be in't and say it is thine.
>   'Tis for the dead, not for the quick; therefore thou liest.
> *Clown.* 'Tis a quick lie, sir; 'twill away again from me to you.
> *Hamlet.* What man dost thou dig it for?
> *Clown.* For no man, sir.
> *Hamlet.* What woman then?
> *Clown.* For none neither.
> *Hamlet.* Who is to be buried in't?
> *Clown.* One that was a woman, sir; but, rest her soul, she's dead.

Hamlet. How absolute the knave is! We must speak by the
card, or equivocation will undo us.

(114–29)

Thus the Grave-maker's equivocation prevents Hamlet from finding out (what we know) that the grave is to be Ophelia's, that
she will soon join the danse macabre which his imagination ani-
mates. And the Grave-maker is "absolute"—positive, perfectly certain, decided [4]—but more than that—cocksure, obstinate, perverse. Hamlet gets a taste of what it must have been like for
Polonius, Rosencrantz and Guildenstern, and Claudius to question him.

In his next series of questions Hamlet does get, towards the
end, a couple of real answers—some information on the natural
history of corpses and the identity of a certain skull. But he also
gets some more empty information:

Clown. . . . young Hamlet . . .—he that is mad, and sent into
England.
Hamlet. Ay, marry, why was he sent into England?
[The correct answer—to be killed—is of course beyond the
Grave-maker's knowledge. But the answer he does give an-
swers nothing at all:]
Clown. Why, because 'a was mad. . . .
Hamlet. How came he mad?
Clown. Very strangely, they say.
Hamlet. How strangely?
Clown. Faith, e'en with losing his wits.
Hamlet. Upon what ground?
Clown. Why, here in Denmark.

(138–41, 146–51)

We have already heard this kind of logic applied to the cause of
Hamlet's lunacy. Polonius likes to think he's an adept with words,
as Hamlet indeed is, but when Polonius is delivering matter at
the top of his bent, his words tend to take a long time to get
almost nowhere:

I will be brief. Your noble son is mad.
Mad call I it, for, to define true madness,
What is't but to be nothing else but mad?
(II.ii.92–94)

(This if anything tells us less than that he went mad with losing his wits.) Polonius then proceeds to an elaborate logical explication of his diagnosis, which amounts to little more than his concise first reaction to Ophelia's report ("Mad for thy love?" [II.i.85]). As Polonius using words is in some ways a tedious, inept, and therefore pompous Hamlet, so the Grave-maker is a kind of extreme Polonius. He is, apparently, like Polonius, impatient of interruption and absolutely confident of his own knowledge of human affairs. We can see this earlier in V.i, before Hamlet arrives:

> *Clown.* Is she to be buried in Christian burial when she willfully seeks her own salvation?
> *Other.* I tell thee she is. Therefore make her grave straight. The crowner hath sate on her, and finds it Christian burial.
> *Clown.* How can that be, unless she drowned herself in her own defense?
> *Other.* Why, 'tis found so.
> *Clown.* It must be *se offendendo;* it cannot be else. For here lies the point: if I drown myself wittingly, it argues an act, and an act hath three branches—it is to act, to do, and to perform. Argal, she drowned herself wittingly.
> *Other.* Nay, but hear you, Goodman Delver.
> *Clown.* Give me leave. Here lies the water—good. Here stands the man—good. If the man go to this water and drown himself, it is, will he nill he, he goes, mark you that. But if the water come to him and drown him, he drowns not himself. Argal, he that is not guilty of his own death shortens not his own life.

(1–18)

As Polonius's argument after II.ii.86 is a tedious way of coming to a comparatively simple point, so the Grave-maker's argument proves no point at all. It is simply an indication that he disagrees with the coroner's decision. Even more than Polonius's speech, the Grave-maker's words form their own pattern with scant reference to reality. In fact, he goes so far beyond Polonius that I think we do not feel that he is inept, or foolish, or wrong. The standards by which one makes those judgments (reality, experience, social custom) seem not to apply. He reduces the Polonian method to the most basic level—his is the tautological mind itself. In his logic, distinctions disappear altogether. In Polonius's analysis of Hamlet's "declension" into madness (II.ii.146–51), the distinctions between the stages seem to be minute, largely verbal, and of little importance. In the Grave-maker's analysis of "an act," the distinctions between the stages are nonexistent, wholly verbal, and of no importance whatsoever. He seems to feel that anything in his system proves anything else—thus his confident "argal." Polonius wishes to demonstrate his own powers of intelligence by expanding his point verbally to make it seem more massive. The Grave-maker bluntly assumes his superior powers—thus his patronizing attitude towards his associate, towards the coroner, and towards Hamlet.

But if the Grave-maker is a reduction of Polonius to the level of tautology, there is also a sense in which he is a reduction of Hamlet himself. I have already mentioned his refusal to take the socially accepted uses of words and the way this practice is ironically turned against Hamlet, though in the Grave-maker it seems less a conscious defense than simply the way of the world. And as with Hamlet this refusal can be used in the kind of logical progression that violates socially accepted relations of terms. Hamlet addressed Claudius as "mother" because "father and mother is man and wife, man and wife is one flesh, and so, my mother" (IV.iii.50–51). By a logic of the same sort the Grave-maker argues that since "the Scripture says Adam digged," and since digging implies arms, and since arms are the sign of a gentleman, Adam and those who dig, as he did, namely "gard'ners, ditchers, and grave-makers," are all gentlemen, and moreover gentlemen of the oldest lineage.

In fact, I think the similarity goes beyond this. It seems to me that the Grave-maker's "reasoning" about manner of death is a grotesque reduction of Hamlet's reasoning earlier in the play, in particular of "To be, or not to be—that is the question":

> For here lies the point: if I drown myself wittingly, it argues an act, and an act hath three branches—it is to act, to do, and to perform.
>
> (8–11)

The connection I make here may be a distortion caused by the prominence the "To be or not to be" soliloquy has come to assume in one's thinking about *Hamlet,* and I'm not sure that the Clown's logic is a deliberate parody (on Shakespeare's part) of Hamlet's now-famous speech. But I think Hamlet's reasoning has ultimately led him no farther than the Grave-maker's leads him. The difference is that the Grave-maker isn't interested in going anywhere; he's already there. In I.ii Hamlet knows where he wants to go but doesn't know how to get there. By III.i he is dividing possible actions into logically distinct groups, with the result that he no longer knows where he wants to go. The country he was interested in is still "undiscovered." Any reasoning within a closed system leads ultimately to a set of tautologies. If the truth one needs isn't in the system already, one can't get it by further reasoning. One needs some new givens—a new incursion of reality, new experience. The Grave-maker's logic requires no new experience. Its tautologies are entirely sufficient for his purposes. He is secure in his function and will handle what the future brings as he has handled reality since Hamlet was born. He is, as Hamlet says, "absolute."

Hamlet is not. Possibly what changed Hamlet's view of death between I.ii and III.i was his experience of the Ghost, and if he has advanced at all from III.i it may have been as a result of lugging an actual corpse around, one that he himself had made, and of discussing, in IV.iii, the activity of worms and the "progress" of kings "through the guts of a beggar" (30–31). Hamlet's experience here in V.i confirms him in the new direction suggested by IV.iii, with its strong sense of physical decay, and apparently leads to the end of all reasoning. His experience here is an imaginative trip to that undiscovered country.

This is to begin to take the scene symbolically, and when one takes the scene symbolically, the Grave-maker comes to represent Death. He has a good deal of Death's impersonality, his easiness with corpses, an easiness born of long experience, and his peculiar logic—senseless but irrefutable. In his own way he is precise, but his own way is not the ordinary human way. A man who reasons as he does would be "foolish," or "wrong," but he is not—that is, in the dramatic experience of the scene, I think we feel that he is "right." His view of life is tautological—"an act hath three branches—it is to act, to do, and to perform," "he that is not guilty of his own death shortens not his own life," madness is losing one's wits. Seen from Death's point of view, life is itself a tautology—birth implies death, as death implies birth, and what happens in between doesn't much matter. This may be why Shakespeare is so particular, on a realistic level, about the Grave-maker's service beginning on the day of Hamlet's birth, for from that day Hamlet's encounter with the Grave-maker was symbolically inevitable.

For Death, man is born of dust and will return to dust. Man is the quintessence of dust and what he may seem to have in common with the angels and the gods is of little importance, in Alexander or in anyone else. The Grave-maker neither knows nor cares that Hamlet is in the process of becoming a tragic hero, that he is a Great Image of Western Man. To the Grave-maker Hamlet is just another fool, a dull ass. The Grave-maker is outside the action, the "life of the play." Hamlet's duel with him is Hamlet's first with someone who is neither involved nor interested. For the Grave-maker all men are more or less alike, mere prospective tenants for his sturdy houses. The only important distinction between men is in the length of time they will hold out water. The Grave-maker, like Death, is a thorough democrat:

> . . . the more pity that great folk should have count'nance in this world to drown or hang themselves more than their even-Christen.
>
> (24–26)

And being put down by the "absolute" Grave-maker's equivocation, Hamlet notes the knave's refusal to observe degree: [5]

> By the Lord, Horatio, this three years I have taken note of it, the age is grown so picked that the toe of the peasant comes so near the heel of the courtier he galls his kibe.
>
> (129–32)

This lack of respect for place is natural for someone whose daily life has shown him a procession in which "Golden lads and girls all must, / As chimney-sweepers, come to dust." So too "The sceptre, learning, physic" (*Cym* IV.ii.262–63, 268). What is at the realistic level the Grave-maker's "democracy" is symbolically the commonplace of Death's.

Having said thus much about the Grave-maker's symbolic role as "Death," one must note that he also represents the comic spirit in the play. He shows us the life that goes on despite the presence of death and tragic careers, the life that ignores mortality and goes on singing and drinking. It is interesting that Shakespeare often brings the comic spirit and an uncommon awareness of mortality together in a single character, often in a context of "madness" and folly, drinking and singing. In a number of the comedies, and in *King Lear,* it is the professional fool who has the clearest perception of the death that must put an end to song—Feste, Lavatche, Lear's Fool, even Touchstone. This is an important source of the thread of sadness in a play like *Twelfth Night.* And Shakespeare's greatest comic character, Falstaff, who is so intent on thriving, on staying alive, on bouncing back up whatever the tragic Hotspurs and Sir Walters do, is at the same time intensely and painfully aware of his own approaching end. By the end of *2 Henry IV* he has come to represent both England's healthy comic spirit and her anarchic mortal disease. (Prince Hal's major difficulty is that he cannot get rid of one without the other.) And as these jesters—even Falstaff is in some ways a "professional"—are haunted by death, so in *Hamlet* the Grave-maker is professionally accustomed to death to the degree that he can go merrily on with life in death's constant presence. Death will live merrily till Doomsday, and until then the Grave-maker will go on building his houses, singing about mortality, and sending out for stoups of liquor.

The Grave-maker, like the professional fools and Falstaff, and like Hamlet himself, is an antic, a grotesque, one who demonstrates to men how foolish and grotesque they are by showing them the reality behind the appearance, the reality behind the socially accepted words and behavior. In doing this the antic is naturally "mad." He is not a "good citizen." The antic's basic tool is equivocation, that double-edged sword which can hide or reveal the truth. Death too is an antic, the Great Antic, the Great Equivocator, who is also king in his own court (as, for example, in *Richard II* at III.iii.155–70). The grinning death's head shows man what a grotesque fool he has been to trust in such superficial qualities as those of birth and rank, power and beauty. Man is himself an equivocation. He seems to be "the beauty of the world, the paragon of animals"; and yet he is but a "quintessence of dust," and it is Death which makes this clear. Death reduces man's pretention—he gets to the material truth beneath the mere verbal titles, so that the question is not one of "great folk" or lesser but of how long a man will lie in the earth ere he rot back to his original dust.

The first part of V.i, then, is symbolically Hamlet's duel with death. And of course he loses. He loses because, in what is still a verbal duel, the Grave-maker is more literal than Hamlet is prepared for. The Grave-maker has one principal metaphor which is the basis of his occupation—namely, that he is a builder of houses that will last till Doomsday. Other than that (I ignore the incidental references to oxes and asses) he refuses to accept the metaphors society has come to associate with certain words. Thus "arms" are certain bodily parts, "ground" is land, possession implies a living possessor, a corpse is neither a man nor a woman but an object which might once have been one or the other. This method is a "mad" method since it denies certain social norms. As I said, Hamlet had used this equivocating method earlier against other opponents. Fencing itself, whether with words or swords, is a kind of equivocation as long as it seems to be doing less than aiming to kill. It is a putting off of the real question. It is both hostile and not hostile, fact and fiction, deadly combat and play. The difficulty in *Hamlet* is in being sure which side of the ambiguity your opponent *means,* which side of the pun has the burden. It is dangerous to assume he will mean the obvious. The play, for instance, means more than the King thought it would. In the graveyard scene Hamlet loses verbally to the Grave-maker because he depends on socially accepted metaphor and gets something more literal in return. This is a symbolic death and prefigures his actual defeat by Death in the final scene, where again the weapons are more literal than he expected.

Hamlet also dies in V.i in the sense that he makes an imaginative progress through the world of death, a world of graves, skulls, and physical decay. Here he seems to find answers to some of the questions which had troubled him earlier. There recurs in this scene, up to the entrance of the court party, that

sense of Hamlet's being cut loose from the action of the play,
a sense which in particular was characteristic of "I have of late"
(II.ii.292–305) and "To be or not to be" (III.i.56–88). And the
questions that have troubled him in these passages are to some
extent answered here in V.i, questions about death and the
nature of man.

The first thing Hamlet notices upon entering the graveyard is
what seems to him the incongruity of a singing grave-maker. Then
he notices the incongruity between the hollow skull the Grave-
maker throws up and the head which once had a tongue and
could sing as the Grave-maker sings. And there is the further
incongruity between what the skull's position might once have
been and what it is now:

> This might be the pate of a politician, which this ass now
> o'erreaches; one that would circumvent God, might it not? . . .
> Or of a courtier, which could say "Good morrow, sweet lord!
> How dost thou, sweet lord?" This might be my Lord Such-a-one,
> that praised my Lord Such-a-one's horse when 'a meant to beg
> it, might it not? . . . Why e'en so, and now my Lady Worm's,
> chapless, and knocked about the mazzard with a sexton's spade.
> Here's fine revolution, an' we had the trick to see't.
>
> (73–75, 77–80, 82–84)

Hamlet's satire, which has been operating on the living to find
the reality beneath the appearance, now operates on the dead
to find the skull beneath the living face. The skull is the ultimate
reality about a man, and satire which leads to the skull leads to
death. The incongruity between the living occupation and the
mere skull suggests the vanity of life, the ultimate uselessness of
one's frantic activities. This appears especially in the long *ubi
sunt* portrait of the lawyer, all of whose intricate legal con-
trivances cannot now protect him against a simple action of battery—he must "suffer this mad knave now to knock him about
the sconce with a dirty shovel" (93–95), no doubt one of the
slings and arrows of outrageous fortune.

Hamlet's imagination raises a modest danse macabre. This
becomes clearest when he meets the skull of Yorick. Here the
imagined flesh touches his own:

Alas, poor Yorick! I knew him, Horatio, a fellow of infinite jest, of most excellent fancy. He hath borne me on his back a thousand times. And now how abhorred in my imagination it is! My gorge rises at it. Here hung those lips that I have kissed I know not how oft.

(172–77)

Both living and dead, Yorick was an antic. For the living Yorick he remembers, Hamlet gives an *ubi sunt* elegy; the dead Yorick, the skull, he uses as a *memento mori*—the grinning skull of the danse macabre, the face that reminded the living they must die:

Where be your gibes now? Your gambols, your songs, your flashes of merriment that were wont to set the table on a roar? Not one now to mock your own grinning? Quite chapfall'n? Now get you to my lady's chamber, and tell her, let her paint an inch thick, to this favor she must come. Make her laugh at that.

(177–83)

As the living antic (like Hamlet at III.i.142–44) strips the paint off the flesh, so the antic Death strips the flesh off the bone. In this scene Hamlet fleshes the dead in order to unflesh the living. The false covering is stripped off the truth.

"To this favor she must come." Death is inevitable. Hamlet didn't have to come to a graveyard to find that out. Everyone knows that from a more or less early age. But in this scene Hamlet comes to an uncommon physical apprehension of death's inevitability. He now knows it in his bones, not merely in his mind. Death becomes a material reality instead of a vague future state. Partly this new apprehension is unpleasant, even painful:

Did these bones cost no more the breeding but to play at loggets with 'em? Mine ache to think on't.

(85–86)

He hath borne me on his back a thousand times. And now how abhorred in my imagination it is! My gorge rises at it. Here hung those lips that I have kissed I know not how oft.

(174–77)

And smelt so? Pah!
(188)

93

Hamlet has ridden on the back of death, kissed its grotesquely grinning mouth, felt his bones ache along with the dead bones. Yet in the end it seems to me that the danse macabre is for Hamlet a comforting spectacle too, for if death is inevitable and material, it must be a release, a total disintegration of the human form back into dust. The "noble dust of Alexander" may end up being used to "stop a beer barrel" (191, 199). Hamlet to be sure sees this as a return to "base uses" (190). But I think the sudden breaking out of prose into rhymed verse at the end of this part of the scene suggests a kind of joy:

> Imperious Caesar, dead and turned to clay,
> Might stop a hole to keep the wind away.
> O, that that earth which kept the world in awe
> Should patch a wall t' expel the winter's flaw!
> (200–203)

Hamlet's experience in this scene has been largely a matter of digesting incongruities. Though all the incongruities involve death and are therefore not entirely free from sadness, some have tended to be humorous ("Why does he suffer this mad knave now to knock him about the sconce with a dirty shovel, and will not tell him of his action of battery"), some wistful, elegiac ("That skull had a tongue in it, and could sing once"), some fearful (those in the Yorick passage). The incongruities involving Alexander and Caesar, the declensions of these world conquerors to bungstopper and chinkfiller, are funny, whimsical, like the progress of a king through the guts of a beggar (IV.iii). They are also the most hyperbolical. The closeness of Yorick leads directly to the distance of Alexander, not as an evasion but as a conclusion:

> Dost thou think Alexander looked o' this fashion i' th' earth?
> (185–86)

Hamlet's experience in this scene resolves the paradox of "What a piece of work is a man." Man is ultimately a quintessence of dust, whatever role he has played in the dance of life. At this point the fact seems almost more a curiosity than a source of anguish. The experience of this scene also resolves for Hamlet the problem of "the undiscovered country." In the world of the graveyard, death has become simply this material thing, this return to base uses, to dust. This conclusion is perhaps not the most reassuring or flattering that one could reach, but it has the virtue of being both inevitable and thorough, so that one needn't worry much about it. I say that Hamlet learned this in the first part of V.i, that his "search" for death led him into a symbolic and imaginative death where he acquired that which satisfied his demon. But that his demon was satisfied in this way by his "death" in V.i is not obvious from the scene itself. I think it only becomes clear in V.ii that something like this happened and I will return to the point shortly.

6

After all this talk about corpses and what happens to them, a funeral procession brings into the graveyard for burial a new corpse, the one the Grave-maker has been exercising his logic on, the one whose identity he has kept Hamlet from learning. Now of course Hamlet himself is not literally dead, and after his imaginative death his vital energy is ready to surge up at the first opportunity in order to proclaim its continuing, if temporary, superiority to death. The realization that death is inevitable and that the flesh will rot into dust is not the only possible effect of a *memento mori*. The skull also says *carpe diem,* that one should seize the day one has.[6] The principal sphere of *carpe diem* activity is sexual love. And who does Hamlet (at least the untroubled Hamlet) love but Ophelia? So when he learns that it is Ophelia who has died and hears Laertes' unrestrained passion, all Hamlet's vital force finds the only outlet available and bursts forth in a violent verbal attack on Laertes. Denied its true object by the very death it seeks to keep away, the vital force can express only grief, jealousy (for Hamlet now has less right in Ophelia than Laertes), and frustration generally. (Perhaps guilt, too, though this is not by any means clear; Hamlet never acknowledges any responsibility for Ophelia's death.)

But Hamlet's verbal attack on Laertes is in a different style from his earlier verbal attacks. The imagery is different. There is nothing in his speeches here which suggests the operation of his demon, no reference to those topics which had obsessed him earlier, to the diseased world, to woman's frailty, to man's sinful, bestial nature. Instead we have his clearly "artificial" parodies of Laertes' hyperbole, his sarcastic taunting of Laertes toward more such hyperbolic gestures; and at the same time such direct, achingly literal statements as "I loved Ophelia" (256), "What is the reason that you use me thus? / I loved you ever" (276–77), and "This is I, / Hamlet the Dane" (244–45).

Nothing Hamlet says here is "mad," by craft or otherwise, though the others may interpret his speeches that way because by now he has a reputation for madness and because they cannot know the experience he has just been through. However, Hamlet seems to have rather strangely forgotten some of his earlier actions, such as murdering Laertes' father. Is he simply a hypocrite? That seems out of tune with the rest of his character. An explanation may lie in the meaning of Hamlet's assertion, "This is I, Hamlet the Dane." Partly this is an expression of that surge of *carpe diem* energy built up by his contact with death. Identity, like love, must be claimed while one is alive, before one returns to dust which is indistinguishable from Alexander's or any other's. To say "This is I, Hamlet the Dane" is to say "I am alive." But it is also to say "I know who I am." (It is probably also to suggest, "I am the true king here.") Hamlet's assertion of identity suggests that he now sees himself as in some way a different person from the one who did all those wild things earlier, and that this new person is the real Hamlet. From his present point of view those earlier things are irrelevancies, easily forgotten, or at least not chargeable to the new man.

The same problem comes up in V.ii where Hamlet, while admitting his deeds, excuses himself to Laertes:

> Give me your pardon, sir. I have done you wrong,
> But pardon't, as you are a gentleman.
> This presence knows, and you must needs have heard,
> How I am punished with a sore distraction.
> What I have done
> That might your nature, honor, and exception
> Roughly awake, I here proclaim was madness.
> Was't Hamlet wronged Laertes? Never Hamlet.

If Hamlet from himself be ta'en away,
And when he's not himself does wrong Laertes,
Then Hamlet does it not, Hamlet denies it.
Who does it then? His madness. If't be so,
Hamlet is of the faction that is wronged;
His madness is poor Hamlet's enemy.
Sir, in this audience,
Let my disclaiming from a purposed evil
Free me so far in your most generous thoughts
That I have shot my arrow o'er the house
And hurt my brother.

(215–33)

I think one's first reaction—and that is probably all one gets at
a performance—is that Hamlet's apology is manly, humble, and
candid. Yet if one is not swept away by the catechism, if one
pries into what he is saying, one may ask how ingenuous Hamlet
is being here? Earlier he had denied that he was really mad
(especially at III.iv.140–43, 188–89). Is he now using a crafty
madness as an excuse for murder? Hamlet tries to refuse responsibility for his actions even while acknowledging them. But I
think we can accept as honest Hamlet's belief in something outside himself which had used his body to commit certain deeds.
Hamlet calls it his "madness." I think this is what I have called
his demon. The point is that by the end of V.i Hamlet is no longer
"mad" (in his terms) or "demon-driven" (in mine). It is probably
impossible to be precise about when the change occurred. The
process may well have begun in the wild words and deeds themselves. But it seems to me that the experience of V.i before the
entrance of Laertes and the rest is likely to have been its culmination. The search for death came to the fullest conclusion
it could find short of death itself, and this very experience of
death, an imaginative experience, aroused the reintegrating impulse in Hamlet. The Hamlet we see resume the duel here in the
last forty-five lines of V.i is not the same nervous, divided, driven
man who fought the first part under the same name.

In the grappling between Hamlet and Laertes the dueling
action of the play becomes physical. This particular opposition
is one we have been waiting for, with increasing consciousness,
for some time. First there was the juxtaposition in I.ii of the

King's fulsome permission to Laertes to return to France and his "bending" of Hamlet *not* to return to Wittenberg. Then in I.iii there was Laertes' animosity towards Hamlet's interest in Ophelia. And of course there was Hamlet's murder of Polonius, Laertes' consequent return to Denmark for revenge, and the further inflaming of Laertes caused by the madness and death of Ophelia. Finally we know that to accomplish his revenge Laertes has conspired with the King, albeit ignorant of the King's ultimate motive. Both Hamlet and Laertes have fathers to revenge, and since Laertes is working with the King, since he is another of the King's substitutes, we know that their revenges must eventually cross. And we have some notion of where the revenges will cross since we know that Laertes and the King are planning to set up a literal fencing match and kill Hamlet in a "pass of practice" (IV.vii.137), the King's pun expressing both the superficial play of the match and the treachery at its heart. The struggle in V.i is a kind of preview of the match, and the fact that this struggle takes place in a grave is a kind of forecast of the result—death on both sides.

7

The last scene of *Hamlet* brings to an end the long fencing match between the Prince and the King. The revenge is accomplished. It is the King, however, not Hamlet, who is now the moving force, the man who shapes the action. Hamlet seems, to an even greater extent than the King had imagined, "free from all contriving" (IV.vii.134). Why is Hamlet so passive? Has he adopted a conscious policy of counterplotting, of letting his enemies choose the weapons and then turning them against the choosers? Or has he put his trust in providence, and if so is this trust a confident acceptance of a bright new truth to which his experience has led him, or is it a stoic resignation to what can't be helped anyway? Or is Hamlet simply tired of fighting? In other words, at this point in the play what does Hamlet really want?

As the last scene opens, Hamlet is telling Horatio how the King plotted to have him conveyed to England by Rosencrantz and Guildenstern and killed there, how he discovered this plot, and how he proceeded to set up a counterplot. As he had intended, Hamlet has contrived "to have the enginer / Hoist with his own petar" (III.iv.207–8). The weapons in this phase of the fencing match are again words, this time written and this time with an ultimately physical effect, a deadly effect. The thrust is the King's command, and Hamlet's parry and riposte, satiric as usual, are a kind of parody of that command. Rosencrantz and Guildenstern are the King's substitutes in this action, and Hamlet deals with them as he would with the King himself, for he arranges that they be "put to sudden death, / Not shriving time allowed" (46–47), which is the kind of fate he has wished for the King himself in III.iii. As Claudius did to Hamlet's father, so Hamlet wishes to do to Claudius and to anyone he has enlisted to shield himself from Hamlet's revenge. As far as Hamlet is concerned, anyone who helps the King becomes an accessory to a capital crime. It doesn't seem to matter whether the accessories actually knew what they were doing or not. They got in the way, and that is enough:

> Why, man, they did make love to this employment.
> They are not near my conscience; their defeat
> Does by their own insinuation grow.
> 'Tis dangerous when the baser nature comes
> Between the pass and fell incensed points
> Of mighty opposites.
>
> (57–62)

But perhaps the most interesting thing about this description of plot and counterplot is the framework Hamlet puts it in. He attributes his counterplotting action to the prompting of providence:

> Sir, in my heart there was a kind of fighting
> That would not let me sleep. Methought I lay
> Worse than the mutines in the bilboes. Rashly,
> And praised be rashness for it—let us know,
> Our indiscretion sometime serves us well
> When our deep plots do pall, and that should learn us
> There's a divinity that shapes our ends,
> Rough-hew them how we will.
>
> (4–11)

99

An ominous disturbance in his heart sets him forth. Acting on impulse, not according to some careful plan, he goes to his escorts' cabin and takes their commission. Only in his specific response to the King's plot revealed in the commission does he reason out a plan, and even then it is a kind of parody of the King's, so that Rosencrantz and Guildenstern are ironically paid for following the King's will blindly. The episode seems to have left Hamlet with little faith in carefully thought-out plans—deep plots seem too likely to pall. Instead he expresses a belief which almost amounts to saying that if one just plunges ahead into action heaven will take care of everything, even minor details like a convenient signet (48–49). One might also expect that the episode would give him a belief in omens, or "augury," so that instead of simply being swept along in what others are planning he would jump in at the prompting of an ominous feeling and redirect the action to his own ends. But we will see in a few moments that if his experience on the ship did give him a belief in augury, he has since lost it.

In speaking of his revenge Hamlet now seems calmer, more temperate, more reasonable, more sure of himself than before his journey, and less convinced that the whole of creation is diseased:

> Does it not, think thee, stand me now upon—
> He that hath killed my king, and whored my mother,
> Popped in between th' election and my hopes,
> Thrown out his angle for my proper life,
> And with such coz'nage—is't not perfect conscience
> To quit him with this arm? And is't not to be damned
> To let this canker of our nature come
> In further evil?
>
> (63–70)

Claudius is now but an abnormality in what seems to be a normal world. He is diseased tissue from which infection might spread further than it has if not cut out, but now prompt surgery will save the patient. This summary of what's wrong with Claudius is very straightforward and untortured. Gertrude now appears to be more victim than guilty party. Hamlet no longer expresses any animosity towards her. That he puts this summary in the form of a rhetorical question implies that there is no question, that he is ready to act. (Horatio apparently assumes that no answer is required to the question of "whether," for he gives none but goes on to the question of "how.") This is the culmination of a process of settling, of calming the demon, which probably began on the eventful night of the play. Hamlet is now relatively unperturbed, steady.

So if Hamlet is now clear-headed and steady, what is his plan? "It must be shortly known to [the King] from England / What is the issue of the business there" (71–72), so he hasn't got much time:

> It will be short; the interim is mine,
> And a man's life's no more than to say "one."
>   (73–74)

That the interim is his might imply that he intends to do something specific with it, that finally he will undertake a carefully planned revenge. The plan needn't be elaborate, since a man can be killed very quickly. But in fact it appears that Hamlet has no plan at all, except to be nice to Laertes. Hamlet never speaks of a plan, now or later. In fact, he seems to have dropped the subject to speak of Laertes (that is, Hamlet's "But" in line 75 appears to me to be a non sequitur). Even his statement of Claudius's guilt in the form of a rhetorical question begins to seem empty when nothing follows from it. Hamlet's experience with providence on the ship seems to have convinced him that deep plots have a tendency to pall and that he'd do better to take what the moment provides.

What the next moment happens to provide is Osric, and an invitation to fence. With Osric himself Hamlet returns to the purely verbal fencing of the earlier acts. In fact the dialogue here is an exaggeration, almost a parody, of the earlier fencing. Earlier Hamlet had used combative language (sometimes excessively) to get at what he saw as the truth of a situation, to upset the socially accepted meanings of the words which obscured this truth, to upset those who wished to hide, or did not know, what they were really doing. But for Osric (one whom "the drossy age dotes on" [181] and, we may assume, an epitome of its virtues), words have come to have social value in themselves, not in their relation to the things or situations which are their supposed occasion, not, that is, in their meanings, whether true or false. The socially accepted words, clearly in excess of their content, are simply a matter of fashion. Osric uses words as he uses his hat, to make flashy, affected gestures. The precise relation of words and what they propose to describe is not even an occasion for deceit—it is not something one worries much about. Osric is not trying to *hide* anything with his words, and the message does leak through, but verbal communication seems to be on the verge of breaking down completely, with Osric unable "to understand in another tongue" (124) and Hamlet needing to be "edified by the margent" (150–51).

Hamlet does win this match, I suppose, though it matters little, since Osric is not really vulnerable. He is probably as sure as the others that Hamlet is difficult and perverse, but he hardly cares, because he is not really interested in Hamlet the way the earlier opponents were. Osric, like the Grave-maker, is not interested in the duel between Hamlet and Claudius, and he is involved only by accident, as a messenger. There is no intended threat behind his words, nor in the verbal combat.[7] He is interested in the upcoming match between Hamlet and Laertes, as he is interested in language, solely as a sporting affair, a game. Thus the verbal fencing between Osric and Hamlet is trivial—a comic interlude. The Osric scene is highly amusing—which is of course highly ironic, since Osric is ignorantly setting up the treacherous fencing match and we know it, though neither Osric nor Hamlet does. When Osric leaves to deliver the "effect" of Hamlet's words "after what flourish [his] nature will" (173–74), he leaves with Hamlet's commitment to a sporting event that will mean his death.

When Osric has left and Hamlet and Horatio have made some additional sarcastic remarks about him, remarks which in Hamlet's case are ironic because his sense of superiority to the frothy Osric is also ignorance of Osric's solid, unyeasty threat to him, a lord comes to confirm the arrangements for the fencing match made through Osric. Hamlet says he remains ready to play the match:

I am constant to my purposes; they follow the king's pleasure.
If his fitness speaks, mine is ready; now or whensoever, provided
I be so able as now.

(190–92)

Hamlet has said that the "interim" was his, but here he seems to
be giving the direction of that interim to the King. His words
might be deceitful flattery except that this is exactly what he
does. He seems only determined that he shall have his "fitness"
ready to take advantage of the King's pleasure.

Horatio thinks Hamlet "will lose this wager" with Laertes
(198), but Hamlet disagrees:

I do not think so. Since he went into France I have been in
continual practice. I shall win at the odds.

(199–200)

"I shall win at the odds" is both a noble, judicious self-assessment
and, at the same time, fatuous, self-satisfied ignorance. Hamlet
expresses confident "knowledge" of the future, because he thinks
his skill has power to shape it, and insofar as the fencing match
is what he thinks it is going to be he is perfectly right: he does
fence better than Laertes, so much better that the King's plans
are upset. But the irony of course is that Hamlet doesn't really
know what the odds are. We do, and we know that they are
against Hamlet.

Despite his confidence, however, Hamlet feels uneasy:

I shall win at the odds. But thou wouldst not think how ill
all's here about my heart. But it is no matter.

(200–202)

At this point we must be reminded of the fighting in Hamlet's
heart that would not let him sleep that night on the ship and of
what his troubled heart implied for him there about providence
and his course of action. One can see providence as a process in
which one participates or as a process in which one acquiesces.
Actually it is both, inevitably, if it exists at all—that is, if one
believes it does describe the way the world works. But the aspect
which predominates in one's sense of providence will determine

the nature of one's actions in facing the future. On the ship Hamlet's perturbed heart was a cue to rash suspicion and rash action, to an active participation in the working out of providence. Here, on the contrary, he dismisses his heart's trouble as unimportant, as "foolery," as "such a kind of gaingiving as would perhaps trouble a woman" (204–5). When Horatio suggests that what he ought to do is obey his qualm and let an excuse be made for him, Hamlet refuses his advice:

> Not a whit, we defy augury. There is special providence in the fall of a sparrow. If it be now, 'tis not to come; if it be not to come, it will be now; if it be not now, yet it will come. The readiness is all. Since no man of aught he leaves, knows what is't to leave betimes, let be.
>
> (208–13)

The virtual absence of imagery in these lines (there is only one image, and that one is biblical, with a traditional implication), the bareness of the diction, and the simplicity of the syntax suggest that Hamlet has come to some sort of conclusion, some final distillation of his experience of the world. The evidence of his senses has been reduced to this simple knowledge. This knowledge is a source of stability. He is "ready" for what will come, not in the sense that he has a plan of action or even that he is prepared to be suspicious of the actions of others, but in the sense that he is ready to die if death is what comes. In the space of a few lines Hamlet has turned, strangely turned, as if he didn't see the connection, from the belief that he can shape the future in some precise way to the belief that the future will shape him.

Hamlet's assertion that "the readiness is all" is clearly a recognition of human limitation, of the impotence of man in controlling events. This limitation appears in dramatic form in the backfiring plots of the play. But what is the mood of Hamlet's recognition? Is it a calm, energetic, even triumphant aligning of himself with providence, a willing, even joyful acceptance of a guiding force beyond his own? This is perhaps the implication of "There is special providence in the fall of a sparrow," taken by itself, if we consider the biblical context from which it is taken. But the line isn't "by itself" in the play. It has its own context in

Hamlet's speech, where, in contrast to Matthew 10:29, the emphasis is on human limitation, not divine care. In the context of *Hamlet* the sparrow suggests how thoroughly out of man's control the world is. This is not to deny that the biblical allusion has a point. Divine control and human impotence are complementary; the Bible stresses one, *Hamlet* the other. The literal meanings are the same, or at least compatible. The allusion calls attention to the difference.

It seems to me that the mood behind "the readiness is all" is one of profound weariness, a feeling, derived from his experience, that it's no use to plan—we are too ignorant—and thus no use to hearken after omens. Hamlet doesn't seem to say this with reluctance. He seems rather to say it with relief ("But it is no matter" [202]); there is the less for him to worry about now. Hamlet's lines *sound* weary. The brief, simple, unadorned clauses, and their measured, not excited, flow; the thrice-repeated rising and falling rhythm (recalling the sparrow?) of "If it be now . . ." with its closely patterned, incremental development; the interwoven repetitions of short words identical or similar in sound patterns ("now . . . not . . . not . . . now . . . not now . . . no . . . aught . . . knows," "come"[3], "be[4] . . . betimes . . . be," "leaves . . . leave . . . let"), as well as the pattern of [i] and [z] sounds in "Since . . . be"—all this, in contrast to Hamlet's normal energy and variety, works with the content of the lines to suggest that Hamlet is tired of his frenetic activity, of his agony, even of his talking, tired of plotting and even of active counterplotting.[8] The "demonic" fencing, in words and deeds, has worn him out. He is ready for it all to end. The moment will call forth his action, but he will not call forth the moment. He will participate passively in providence, not actively, as on board the ship. On the ship acceptance of augury had saved his life; now he defies augury. An uneasy heart is no longer a cue.

This difference between his attitude toward providence on the ship and his attitude here before the fencing match naturally makes one look to the time between for a cause for the change. (Both attitudes are present in this scene—one described, before Osric's entrance, the other expressed, after it—so that the change is readily apparent.) Hamlet tells us what he learned from his experience on the ship. He doesn't tell us what he has learned since that experience that has changed his mind. He may not even be aware that he has changed. Again we are faced with the indefinite relation of cause and effect in Hamlet's developing consciousness. But, as I have said earlier, what has intervened, and what I think we feel behind his new attitude, is the experience of the graveyard.

Hamlet's imaginative experience of death in general gave him a "carnal" proof that death is both inevitable and annihilating and thus makes our mundane purposes and distinctions seem to have little ultimate point. Death reveals the vanity of the lawyer's careful plottings and, by extension, of mortal plottings generally. In the graveyard Hamlet also learned of the death of Ophelia. Since it seems that before his familial troubles arose he really loved her, one can see how her death would make him weary and more frustrated. There was now even less worth living for. Reflecting on Ophelia's death one might say that she died earlier than she should have. But when one asks what "early" means, the answer is either arbitrary or vague. One dies when one's career, one's story, is finished, and the career is clearly defined by an unknown providence which doesn't observe human standards of "early" and "late." Thus it is finally meaningless to say that someone dies "early" ("Since no man of aught he leaves, knows what is't to leave betimes, let be"). One must be prepared at any time. Caesar finds it "most strange that men should fear, / Seeing that death, a necessary end, / Will come when it will come" (*JC* II.ii.35–37). Hamlet's "the readiness is all" is Caesar without the bravado. Providence in *Hamlet* seems to be simply the normal working of time, bringing careers to a close at what it for inscrutable reasons finds the appropriate moment. It does not appear to lead to a life after death. Laertes speaks of Ophelia as destined to become a minist'ring angel, but, so far as Hamlet is concerned, there is no sense in V.i or here in V.ii of any afterlife, any bad dream, or good dream, after death.[9] The end is an end. The sparrow falls when his career is done. So will Hamlet.

8

As Hamlet says "let be," the court enters for the fencing match toward which the whole drama has been leading. The

King, of course, is still using a substitute—this time Laertes. Hamlet, as he had promised, courts Laertes' favors. His apology is apparently noble, candid, and sensible. Indeed this is virtually the first time Hamlet has been civil at court. And he is more than civil—he is friendly, relaxed, gracious, eager for the match, and, as the King predicted, "remiss, / Most generous, and free from all contriving" (IV.vii.133–34). As far as we can tell, he suspects no danger and plans none. He is no longer weary, for the "brothers' wager" makes him forget the duel with Claudius.

Laertes, on the other hand, is clearly hypocritical:

> I do receive your offered love like love,
> And will not wrong it.
>
> (240–41)

We know that two plots have been laid against Hamlet, one with an unbated, poisoned foil, the other with a poisoned cup. As the foil plot and the cup plot unfold, simultaneously, quickly, and chaotically, Gertrude's maternal enthusiasm spoils the latter and Hamlet's skill the former to the extent that Laertes can't make the murder look like an accident. Again human plans have not been able to control the events; we see here what Horatio will call "purposes mistook / Fall'n on th' inventors' heads" (373–74). The poison is quickly spread around in a violent symbolic justice.

When Hamlet discovers that the fencing match is a more literal fight than he expected and that it is part of his duel with Claudius, he plunges into his revenge. Though he was weary of the revenge duel almost, it seemed, to the point of not caring, he rises here to a momentary burst of passion and makes the direct attack we have been waiting for so long:

> The point envenomed too?
> Then, venom, to thy work. . . .
> Here, thou incestuous, murd'rous, damned Dane,
> Drink off this potion. Is thy union here?
> Follow my mother. [*King dies.*]
>
> (310–11, 314–16)

In the graveyard the death of Ophelia had called Hamlet out of an imaginative death to a passionate assertion of his life—the attack on Laertes amounted to a cry of "I, Hamlet, still live, and care." Here, his mother's death and his own call forth a similar cry, though now the "still" sees a real, personal end, not an imagined general one. The attack on the King is a final assertion of life, in an act which completes it.

Hamlet's weariness in the augury speech and his fierce action when he has received his death wound is remarkably similar to a change in the King's mood. When Gertrude drinks the poison meant for Hamlet, the King seems to give up, to cease to care ("It is the poisoned cup; it is too late" [281]), so that when Laertes whispers that he'll "hit him now," the King replies "I do not think't" (284). "It is too late . . . I do not think't." The lines are so brief that one must be careful about reading too much into them. But first there may be a kind of reluctance that Laertes should succeed where he himself has just so miserably failed. Or there may be disgust that all of his substitutes and he himself should have been so incompetent. But, recalling the King's prayer in III.iii and his genuine, if guilty, love for Gertrude, I think there's a greater anguish in the lines than this. Like Hamlet's final weary distillation of his experience, the King's lines here are short and simple. In them I think Claudius is saying that she whom he loves is dead, his aims can no longer be accomplished, nothing matters any more. And yet when Hamlet wounds him, life instinctively cries out:

> O, yet defend me, friends. I am but hurt.
> (313)

Both Hamlet and Claudius awake out of careless weariness into an assertion of life. But where Hamlet's final assertion is an unequivocal attack, the King's is characteristically a final attempt to depend on others. Since pouring the poison in his brother's ear, he has been in his way as impotent and bedrid as old Norway. And in the end his devious, cowardly poison is publicly returned to its source.

If from the beginning Hamlet has been moving toward his attack on Claudius, he has also been looking toward death. In V.i he found that death is an annihilation, a material annihilation, a return to dust. Life seems vain, not because what we find after death is a truer life, but because our mortal strivings only bring us to the grave where they are worth nothing. Even Alexander and imperious Caesar become dust indistinguishable from the rest of us. And yet life is all that we have to build on, and among the living, Alexander *is* more than anonymous dust. His name and his story survive; *otherwise* he is dust. His name survives because the story of his life has been told. The career of a man may have some importance in the world even after he himself has ceased to be. Thus Hamlet so strongly desires to have the story of his career told, and told right, after his death:

> Horatio, I am dead;
> Thou livest; report me and my cause aright
> To the unsatisfied.
>
> (327–29)

When Horatio shows his strong feeling of the situation by trying to kill himself, Hamlet stops him and reproaches him:

> O God, Horatio, what a wounded name,
> Things standing thus unknown, shall live behind me!
> (333–34)

And Hamlet asks Horatio to stay alive long enough to tell the world the story we have seen and heard. Hamlet apparently wishes to die thinking that he will be immortal to the extent that he will be remembered by the living, that he will be justified among the living. If Hamlet's dying concerns were Christian, he would presumably be interested in the immortality of his soul, not of his good name, and would be concerned with God's judgment, not the judgment of the men he leaves behind. But it doesn't seem to trouble Hamlet that like his father he dies "Unhouseled, disappointed, unaneled" (I.v.77). His interest in having his story told is a very pagan interest. It is, for instance, one of the unchristianized elements in *Beowulf*, the story of another hero who dies of an envenomed wound, in victory over his foe, leaving his country open to foreign domination.

Hamlet's story is the thing that will survive; otherwise he sees no afterlife. Death is not therefore necessarily terrible, however, as the terms of his instructions to Horatio make clear:

> Absent thee from felicity awhile,
> And in this harsh world draw thy breath in pain,
> To tell my story.
>
> (336–38)

In dying, Hamlet makes it clear that for him death is something to be wished for, while life is painful and the world harsh. The ten slow monosyllables of that second line suggest the long, drawn-out pain they describe. "Felicity" does not mean "heaven" because Horatio couldn't get to "heaven" by killing himself. Hamlet means that death itself is felicity, an end to the pain. In some ways Hamlet has returned to the position of his first soliloquy, the weariness, the wish that his "too too sullied flesh would melt." But that soliloquy was sentimental in a way that the present scene isn't. In I.ii a particular had colored the universal: Hamlet had extended his own hurt through all creation, which became rotten in his own image. The world was rotten because he was miserable. But this anguished sense of a world thoroughly diseased drops off, or is worked off, and by opening himself up to experience beyond his purely personal problem, he reaches a sense of a more general human predicament in which his special griefs no longer have an all-absorbing place. We can see this process working at least as early as the "To be or not to be" soliloquy, though the ultimate form of his new sense of the world is much different, being, as I said, in some ways closer to the mood of I.ii, except that by V.ii the universal has come to color the particular. Hamlet learns to accommodate himself to a world governed by an inscrutable providence which leads to an annihilating death. And yet he has also learned to be heroic in the face of this world by being "ready," by suffering out his career, by waiting for the moment which made sense of his career and gave his story shape.

"The rest is silence," Hamlet says (347), and dies. And as the mundane drums of Fortinbras close in on the Danish court, Horatio sends Hamlet on his way:

> Now cracks a noble heart. Good night, sweet prince,
> And flights of angels sing thee to thy rest!
>
> (348–49)

But Hamlet doesn't speak of singing angels, or of howling devils. For him the "rest" is something different. It is, first, all he has left to say, and, beyond that, all he has left to do, and the rest is simply silence—finally. What he has left to say and do is nothing, and this nothing is his peace, his bliss, his undisturbed sleep. Silence is his rest, too. Long ago he had urged his heart to break in silence because he had to hold his tongue. But events freed him into a frenzy of saying and doing, an exhausting agony. Now his heart does break and at last he *may* be silent.

9

Just before he dies, Hamlet, like a responsible prince, takes care of a piece of practical business, the settling of the succession. He wishes to ensure renewed stability and order in a Denmark whose leaders have just been chaotically slaughtered, even if that renewed order requires foreign domination. And the restoration of order duly occurs. By survival and opportunism Fortinbras takes control of his father's lands and his father's enemy's lands— a neater, more thorough revenge than Hamlet or Laertes could manage. Fortinbras accepts the kingdom before it's offered him— he knows what the "tragic" deaths of Claudius and Hamlet really mean:

> For me, with sorrow I embrace my fortune.
> I have some rights of memory in this kingdom,
> Which now to claim my vantage doth invite me.
> (377–79)

Fortinbras, like Octavius Caesar and Tullus Aufidius, can afford to be sad, can afford to appreciate the tragic spectacle unfolded before him. There is nothing like dying an untimely death for getting the world to speak well of you. Your erstwhile political enemies will be especially gracious. They can show their good will, their high regard for admirable human qualities, and their generous pity, without having to pay the consequences. In fact, they will get the benefit of being associated with your virtues. So Fortinbras expresses his sorrow and (somewhat patronizingly) speaks of Hamlet's royal qualities, and begins to give orders.

When Hamlet's father died and his mother so quickly re-married, "the funeral baked meats / Did coldly furnish forth the marriage tables," a notable example of "thrift" (I.ii.180–81). Now, Hamlet, like Polonius, is "at supper," along with other company:

> O proud Death,
> What feast is toward in thine eternal cell
> That thou so many princes at a shot
> So bloodily hast struck?
>
> (353–56)

And Fortinbras is the thrifty one: this supper is his inaugural breakfast. And the entertainment at this breakfast will be "The Tragedy of Hamlet," as presented by Horatio. If *Hamlet* were about the restoration of health to a diseased land, it would be cynical indeed.

4

※ King Lear

Great thing of us forgot!

ONE can see why the last scenes of *Hamlet, Othello, Macbeth,* and even, in its own queer way, *Antony and Cleopatra* must be as they are. In these plays the end seems to be inevitable, given the action that leads up to it. In *Hamlet,* for instance, the plot moves through a series of displacements toward that inevitable confrontation between Hamlet and Claudius —one senses this from the beginning. Inevitability is sometimes considered necessary to the sense of tragedy, and when it is absent one is likely to feel that one has stumbled upon a melodrama. In *King Lear* one does not have this sense of a foregone conclusion to the action: *King Lear* is the least inevitable of Shakespeare's tragedies.

Towards the end of *Lear* it really begins to look as if things will turn out well after all, as they do in *King Leir* or, so far as this phase of the action is concerned, in the story as given by Spenser and Holinshed and Geoffrey of Monmouth. True, there is the blinding of Gloucester, and the permanence of that act might suggest that things can't be put right again. Nevertheless, after the blinding in III.vii, the good characters begin to rally and unite, and the evil characters begin to confound themselves in their own greed, lust, and cruelty. Edgar begins the difficult reconciliation with his father. Cornwall dies in a manner that Albany sees as poetically just; his death is evidence for the justice of the gods. Albany emerges from his vague ambiguity to fight actively for the good; he is the first person to declare opposition to Edmund. Regan and Goneril no longer "hit together" and begin to fight over Edmund. Cordelia returns to rescue her father. Edgar kills Oswald and obtains important evidence against Goneril and Edmund. And, most important, Lear and Cordelia are reunited. Indeed this reconciliation is the point towards which the plot seemed to be heading ever since I.i. It is also the point toward which the melodrama *King Leir* moves, and at which it arrives, inevitably, and stops.

Shakespeare's play, of course, goes on. The Restoration and eighteenth century saw its unusual lack of inevitability well enough and preferred the happy ending restored and augmented by Nahum Tate. Shakespeare was simply too perverse when, as Johnson says, he "suffered the virtue of Cordelia to perish in a just cause, contrary to the natural ideas of justice, to the hope of the reader, and, what is yet more strange, to the faith of the chronicles." [1] Johnson was so horrified by the end of Shakespeare's *King Lear* that he concurred in the public preference for the "poetical justice" of Tate's version:

> A play in which the wicked prosper and the virtuous miscarry may doubtless be good, because it is a just representation of the common events of human life; but since all reasonable beings naturally love justice, I cannot easily be persuaded that the observation of justice makes a play worse; or that, if other excellencies are equal, the audience will not always rise better pleased from the final triumph of persecuted virtue.

The point is not that situations like that in Shakespeare's *Lear* needn't be faced. But poetically just drama may help one face such situations. A "representation of the common events of human life" which does observe poetic justice is a comforting spectacle because it makes the universe a moral place, a place where one can easily see the point of virtue. And I suppose that if one believes that the universe is a moral place, one is better able to put up with such "common events of human life" as might seem unjust; one would know that the injustice was only superficial.

But Shakespeare seems to have been not so much interested in comforting his audience as in entertaining them, and the final defeat of persecuted virtue can be very entertaining. It can also be very instructive—morally. For if one is merely entertaining, there is no need to assume a connection between morality and success. One may ask, or have one's characters ask, whether the universe does operate according to principles we would call "just." Even leaving aside Cordelia, whose "guilt" or "innocence" may be disputed, and considering Lear, who clearly does do something slightly immoral in trying to destroy the bond morality has set up between himself and his daughter, should we see what happens to him as a punishment which his crime deserves, or is it cruel and excessive? And what about Gloucester? Is what happens to him a just retribution for his careless lust? Are the gods just, or malevolent, or capricious? This is a problem that discomforts some of the characters in *King Lear*.

The action of a play in which poetic justice is observed need not seem dramatically inevitable. In fact, one problem with "moral" plays is that they so often do not. (This is true of comedy as well as tragicomedy—for example, Vanbrugh's *The Relapse* makes this point about *Love's Last Shift*.) But *King Lear* is perverse dramatically as well as morally. It is not for the sake of dramatic inevitability that persecuted virtue is killed off. Our dramatic expectations are fairly well answered by the reconciliation of Lear and Cordelia in IV.vii. That reconciliation is the scene the play seems to have been trying to bring about.

A play whose plot seems to unfold inevitably is a comforting spectacle too, though often in a way quite different from that of a play whose plot implies a moral universe. For though an inevitable plot may crush the great man or the good man, it nevertheless suggests that the universe operates according to certain laws, however cruel they are, however inequitable, however immoral by human standards. And a world with unjust laws is more comfortable (at least psychologically) than one with no laws at all. The inevitable plot may suggest a Fate against which the man may struggle, or it may simply work out the logic of the situation in which he finds himself. In any case the ultimately crushed man can feel that his life has a shape and a meaning. Hamlet, Othello, Antony, and Cleopatra, for instance, take some trouble to be sure that the shape, and thus the meaning, of their lives is perceived.

In *King Lear*, so far as plot is concerned, Shakespeare was perverse, and the last act is a gratuitous continuation. But though plot be the soul of tragedy, it is not everything, and Shakespeare's perverse continuation from tragicomedy into tragedy takes the form suggested by the nature of the world of the play—specifically by the nature of human relationships evident throughout the play. In a "poetically just" play where the plot is not inevitable, the plot implies the nature of the world. In *King Lear* the nature of the world implies the plot. The action is finally inevitable not because of our dramatic sense but because of our sense of the possibilities of human association and human action in the world of this play.

And what are the possibilities of human association in *King Lear*? Very slight. All but nonexistent. *King Lear* is a spectacle of human insularity.

Characters in plays are often at odds with each other—such conflict is the essence of drama, so that almost any play can be said to be about "the failure of communication." But conflict in *King Lear* goes beyond this because it comes to seem inevitable, no matter who the characters are, no matter how much they would prefer some sort of peaceful, harmonious union. The characters in *King Lear* are consistently unable to establish, much less maintain, a free contact of souls. They are a set of separate egos who can collide but not combine. They can all too easily hurt one another, but they cannot help. Love is impotent, pity is impotent, and so, finally, are their opposites. For all the characters eventually need help, need association and fellowship, and since they cannot get it, they cannot even accomplish their insular aims. In this world there is only isolation and ineffectiveness, and conflict leading to death.

One sees this insularity throughout the play. Indeed it is the source of all the difficulties. Lear loves his daughter, and Cordelia loves her father. But this love between father and daughter must manifest itself in a way that forces them apart instead of bringing them together. In Lear's case it's not the "evil" characters who set things moving toward disaster. (We're not even aware at first that "evil" characters exist.) And the action of the play, from the first act on, is almost entirely a continual and progressive isolation of the characters from one another, even when they are onstage at the same time, even when they would seem to be on the same side. It should suffice to mention one example—the scenes in Act III with Lear, Kent, Edgar (as Tom), and the Fool, scenes which are so remarkable for the failure of the conversation to mesh in the ordinary way. Instead of being united by their common danger, these men are isolated—Lear by his struggle with true madness, Edgar by his feigned madness, the Fool by his strange figures and obscure rhymes, Kent by his sanity. It is true that in the early acts the evil characters, at least, seem to be able to "hit together." But in Acts IV and V even this changes, and in the final scene human insularity appears in extreme forms—absurd and pathetic, strangely comic and utterly tragic. It is, with the final scene of *Antony and Cleopatra,* Shakespeare's most daring tragic conclusion.

2

In the last two acts evil continues to confound good in the normal way. But now good begins to confound evil too—a hopeful sign. Moreover, evil now begins to confound itself, and this is also fine, though a commonplace in drama. But good finally cannot profit by evil's self-entanglement, for good too confounds itself in its own plottings. In *King Lear* it's not what the forces of evil accomplish that is so depressing—it's what the forces of good can't accomplish, what in fact they almost seem to refuse to accomplish.[2] In these scenes the good characters often seem perverse in refusing to "succeed" or to make contact with each other. This is the most striking thing about the characters in *King Lear.*

Actually, it is misleading to speak of "good" and "evil" characters in the facile way I have done so far, because one thing the odd structure of *King Lear* does is make these easy moral tags appear inadequate as descriptions of what the characters are really like. In fact, such tags are worse than inadequate: the play and the last scene in particular show the potential for cruelty and finally the danger in applying abstract notions like "good" and "evil" to specific human situations.

Edgar at one point makes a distinction between speaking what one feels and speaking what one "ought" to say, and he implies that normally one ought to say what one "ought" to say, rather than what one feels.[3] This may sound like a plea for hypocrisy, or for what we often call good manners, but it is clear from Edgar's behavior throughout the last two acts that by "ought" he must mean something quite different from good manners. "Ought" here is a matter of good morals, not of good manners. Just as there are certain things one ought to *do* on certain occasions, so there are certain things one ought to say. One "ought" to say, apparently, things which express the bonds and connections which form the system known as the Elizabethan World Picture, except that in *King Lear* the specifically Christian elements of this system are paganized. The bonds and connections may be between things at two points in time (as with crime and punishment, for instance) or between two things at the same time (as with the relation between a man and his family, or his king, or his gods). The system of bonds and connections, it need hardly be said, is orderly, just, and moral. The "ought" may even be ultimately religious. The relation between man and the gods is problematical and obscure in *King Lear*, specifically problematical and obscure. But it is clear that for Edgar (if not for others) doing, saying, and feeling have some kind of religious significance, and there would almost seem to be something like a doctrine of salvation operating—at least Edgar seems to think so. I will return to this point in a moment.

The odd thing is the contrast between this "ought" and one's feelings. Normally—and morally, one would suppose—a person should say what he feels. Since what one ought to say is prescribed, Edgar's contrast implies that people don't always feel the emotions they ought to feel in a given situation. And in that case what one ought to say is apparently supposed to bring the feelings into line. So the moralist will prescribe human emotions as well as human words and deeds. A feeling that does not correspond to the "ought" should be changed, got rid of, not expressed. There are some things one simply should not feel. (Or, as Edgar says in his capacity as mad Tom, "Keep thy hand out of plackets.")

The most extended example of this tension between "ought" and "feel," an example which helps prepare us for the experience of V.iii, is the long struggle between Edgar and Gloucester over the latter's desire to die. Gloucester wants to die because, since he has criminally cast off one son and been betrayed by the other, he feels he has nothing left to live for. Moreover, his experience has led him to the conclusion that the gods are capricious:

> As flies to wanton boys are we to th' gods;
> They kill us for their sport.
>
> (IV.i.36–37)

When Edgar perceives what Gloucester feels, he avoids the obvious remedy (that is, revealing himself to his father). He does not reveal himself to his father because, apparently, he does not approve of his father's attitude. One ought not desire to die, according to Edgar, nor should one doubt the justice of the gods, and as long as Gloucester does desire to die, he does not deserve to be blessed with knowledge of his son's presence. So Edgar sets out to bring Gloucester's feelings into line with his own moral presuppositions. This process involves dragging Gloucester through a long cyclical pattern of alternating wish for death and acquiescence in painful life. Edgar will momentarily convince Gloucester to live, and then Gloucester's feelings will surge up again to undo Edgar's good work.

Here we need look at only one point in this process. Gloucester has asked to be led to the cliff at Dover so he can jump to his death. For the real cliff, Edgar substitutes one he creates himself out of images. And he allows his father to fall off this cliff to a death that is really a swoon. Edgar tells us why he is playing this elaborate game with his father: "Why I do trifle thus with his despair / Is done to cure it" (IV.vi.33–34). In other words, Edgar's purpose is ultimately religious. Despair—Gloucester's belief that there is no point in living any longer in a world run according to whim and not according to justice—is a sin, and Edgar doesn't want his father to die in a state of sin. (Edgar is even more explicit about this later, when he says that he "saved him from despair" [V.iii.192].) Gloucester revives, much to his dismay ("Away, and let me die" [48]), and Edgar begins the second part of his lie about the cliff, telling Gloucester that he had fallen an enormous distance without being hurt in the least. And then the punch line:

Thy life's a miracle.

(55)

Edgar wishes to help his father spiritually, to cure him of despair, to bring him back to a belief in the justice of the gods, and what is his method? He fakes a miracle.

The world of *King Lear* is specifically not Christian; it is indeterminate pagan. This means that no doctrine can be assumed from outside the play. The play creates its own religion, or rather it gives us a sense of religion, a religious dimension, created by the religious values and opinions expressed here and there by the various characters. This allows Shakespeare (and his characters) a questioning of the universe that would have been harder, if not impossible, to accomplish in a poetic world into which Christian doctrine could more easily be imported whole (as in *Othello*, say, or *Measure for Measure*, which were written in roughly the same period). It allows Shakespeare, as it were, to *surround* the whole question of the relation of religion and human life, to examine the question from the outside instead of the inside. There is no "Christian context" to predetermine the answer. There is no necessity that order and justice ultimately prevail. There is no necessity that "the gods" turn out to be just powers instead of capricious powers who are to men as wanton boys are to flies.

On the other hand, Shakespeare builds much of our sense of the "religion" of *King Lear* out of analogies with Christianity— Edgar's notions of despair and salvation, or of miracles, for instance, or Tom's foul fiend, or the "redeeming" images associated with Cordelia, or, though less specifically, the notion of divine justice which occupies several of the characters. By using these analogies Shakespeare makes the religious problems in the play seem current, undated, urgent. Despite the mention of such figures as Apollo or Jupiter or Juno, one can't simply dismiss all this talk of "the gods" as merely residual paganism, as simply "Roman," say, and therefore obsolete anyway. By being both pagan and Christian in this way, the religion of *King Lear* has a kind of timelessness that makes the play a permanent poetic inquiry into the place of man in the universe. The play's impact is less softened by time than it might be with either a Christian or a "pure" pagan religion. One need make fewer adjustments.

Though *King Lear* is in this sense a religious play, it offers no definitive religious truth. It is simply about the confrontation with the mystery. By this means, Shakespeare throws more of a burden on Edgar. It is he who is making the moral demands, not the gods. And his moral demands prevent him from having full sympathy with his father's sorrow, prevent him indeed from making real contact with his father, the contact which they both seem so very much to want and Gloucester at least so very much to need. Their relationship is a particularly painful example of the human insularity in the play—Gloucester shut off in one sort of blindness, Edgar in another.

Edgar's moral demands prevent him from crossing the gap between them to comfort his father at the source of his pain. Instead he "trifles" with him. He tortures him, both by keeping him alive and by insisting on his blindness. When Gloucester asks whether he has "fall'n, or no" (IV.vi.56), Edgar assures him that he has:

> From the dread summit of this chalky bourn.
> Look up a-height. The shrill-gorged lark so far
> Cannot be seen or heard. Do but look up.
> (57–59)

"Do but look up." Edgar makes a physical exhortation which is a metaphor for a spiritual exhortation: "Look up to the gods with hope—cease your despair." Here Edgar would be working in the right direction—starting from a real physical problem rather than from a manufactured spiritual problem—except that "Do but look up" is both a lie and an impossibility: Gloucester has no eyes, but there is nothing to look at anyway. And *King Lear* does not offer a religious certainty which can make this lie a parable of the truth; it remains a lie. Edgar could avoid this torture by telling Gloucester the real truth. Instead, he drags him out until he hasn't even the strength to kill himself—he will just "rot." He drags him out until the old man's heart is too weak to survive the joy of recognition coupled with sorrow over past events (see V.iii.197–200).

We last see Gloucester in V.ii. He waits out the battle under a tree, and when Edgar returns with the news that Lear and Cordelia have lost and are prisoners, it finally looks as if Gloucester is finished. He will die simply by refusal to go on: "No further, sir. A man may rot even here" (8).

But Edgar will not give up:

> What, in ill thoughts again? Men must endure
> Their going hence, even as their coming hither;
> Ripeness is all. Come on.
>
> (9–11)

Edgar even turns Gloucester's metaphor against him. Gloucester feels he is ready to rot; Edgar implies he is not yet ripe. Gloucester is now past deciding, one way or the other. "And that's true too" (11), he replies, as he leaves once more with Edgar.[4] Anything might as well be true, for all he cares now. Poor old Gloucester, who became a hero through his human sympathy and stubborn defiance, has no will left, it seems, either to live or die. Edgar has killed his spirit.[5]

Characters who (like Edgar) claim to be acting on the basis of "ought," characters, that is, who speak what they ought to say, not what they feel, are really the ones who stir up the trouble in both Lear's family and Gloucester's. The hypocritical version appears in Edmund, who uses Gloucester's fondness for traditional bonds and connections to deceive him (compare, for instance, I.ii.101–14 and II.i.45–50). We find the at least equally dangerous honest version in Cordelia. She begins the tragic conflict of the play in I.i by her answer to her own question, "What shall Cordelia speak?" (62). When Lear makes the question public ("What can you say to draw / A third more opulent than your sisters? Speak" [85–86]), Cordelia decides to speak what she "ought" to speak, not what she feels. She is very precise about this:

> Unhappy that I am, I cannot heave
> My heart into my mouth. I love your Majesty
> According to my bond, no more nor less.
>
> (91–93)

This is as right as one can be, in theory. But should she have known better than to be so willfully right? Should she instead have spoken what she felt? The choice is hardly obvious, though in hindsight we can suggest that she might have made the best of the situation by compromising, by speaking part of what she felt.[6]

By the time she has returned from France in Act IV and found Lear again, she has changed. She does not see any reason to moralize their earlier experience. She sees that moral stances are of no importance in themselves. What counts is the relation, the emotional relation, between herself and her father. In fact, *King Lear* is about *relation*, that human association which offers the possibility, so often sought and so rarely realized in this play, that insularity might cease.

It's not that by IV.vii Cordelia ignores the claims of "ought," that is, the conventional bonds and ceremonies. She asks for her father's blessing:

> O look upon me, sir,
> And hold your hand in benediction o'er me.
> You must not kneel.
>
> (57–59)

Lear has learned something too; he was apparently beginning to kneel to her for forgiveness. And later, in V.iii, he sees their relation in ceremonial terms:

> When thou dost ask me blessing, I'll kneel down
> And ask of thee forgiveness.
>
> (10–11)

Conventions and ceremonies are important to human existence. The point is that they must be, as they are here, subservient to human needs and responses. "Ought" must express fact rather than dictate it.

The problem of the tension between "ought" and "feel" in human relations comes up early in the play, and keeps coming up in one aspect or another—Cordelia and Lear, Kent and Lear, Edmund and Gloucester, Kent and Oswald or Kent and Cornwall (where speaking what he feels gets Kent in trouble as usual), Cornwall and his servant. With Edgar and Gloucester, as with Cordelia and Lear, the problem comes up in a particularly acute, painful form: what, in the fullest sense, ought the child say to a father who is either morally or physically blind? Should one make the theoretical "ought" follow one's feelings or go ahead and "daub it further" in the interests of some moral purpose? Edgar chooses the latter course and thus in the last two acts we see, juxtaposed to the new relation of Cordelia and Lear, the great potential for cruelty in simply saying what one "ought" to say.

Now one may agree that Edgar should keep Gloucester from committing suicide yet still find his method somewhat perverse, as well as dishonest. Wouldn't it have been simpler, more honest, even more effective, to use as his miracle (in IV.vi) a real miracle, a miracle in the terms of this play, namely the fact that Gloucester had been found and cared for by the son who still loved him, after all? We see a miracle of this kind in the case of Lear, in the very next scene, and it is a miracle, and Cordelia is a "saint," though she would not see herself as one. She unselfconsciously performs what Edgar would like to perform, and can't, because he lies, because his love can't speak. He has an idea of what he "ought" to do, and that ruins him. We come to Lear and Cordelia with the pattern of Gloucester and Edgar fresh in our ears, and the judgment, if we were not too enthralled to make it, would likely rest heavily on Edgar.

And why have I spent so much time here criticizing Edgar and his moral principles, his sense of "ought"? After all, there are those characters who do consult their feelings, who begin from their feelings and base what they say and do on them— Goneril, Regan, Cornwall, Edmund, Lear himself. There's not much sympathy there, except in Lear from time to time. They only use "ought" when it suits them, suits what they feel. The problem of picking one's way between "ought" and "feel" is not easy to solve, not so easy as moralists, for instance, might believe. It's not so easy as amoralists might believe either. Morality is not unnecessary just because it's so often inadequate. Edmund's way is not preferable to Edgar's. In concentrating, in this essay, on the limitations of Edgar, Albany, and even Kent, I am by no means trying to excuse or justify the behavior of Edmund, Goneril, and Regan, which is destructive of human relationships in more obvious, though perhaps ultimately no less deadly, ways.

The impression Edgar makes is in many ways positive. His patience, his endurance, his resourcefulness, his courage—all these are admirable. He would even seem to be something of a hero, one of those who, like Albany, help restore order to Britain after a period of political, familial, and, yes, moral chaos. And like Albany, he is well intentioned and sympathizes with suffering human beings. But his sympathy, much like Albany's, is limited by its morality. He can't sympathize fully or finally, because he can't (at least until the very end) admit the validity of certain feelings that lie outside a morally prescribed order of the world.

The point is obviously not that one ought to endorse suicide. That might even be worse than what Edgar does, but in one way it's the same sort of thing—it involves "ought." It's not what Edgar wants to do (that is, to save Gloucester from suicide) that's so questionable; it's the way he goes about doing it. He insists on putting an abstract "ought" before the unique human realities he is faced with, and this sort of attitude towards life, which he shares with Albany, is at least as responsible as the activities of Edmund, Goneril, and Regan for the disaster of the final scene. It is to the details of that scene that I now turn.

3

As V.iii begins, Edmund is apparently fulfilling his promise (V.i.65–68) that Lear and Cordelia shall not receive the mercy Albany intends towards them, for he sends them off to prison and sends after them a captain bearing an ominous order. The exact order is not specified; but Edmund gives it with the admonition that "men / Are as the time is. To be tender-minded / Does not become a sword" (30–32), and we know well enough how Edmund thinks the time is. This is the point of suspense in the scene: Lear and Cordelia are in danger. Will Albany be able to get to them before the captain does his "man's work"? Our sense of the action that follows will be colored—for some time— by this suspense.

As the captain leaves, Albany, Goneril, and Regan enter with some of Albany's soldiers, and a little comedy of adultery, jealousy, and murderous intrigue begins. Albany is in charge of the proceedings in V.iii, and his character has a good deal to do with the shape of the scene and its outcome. Albany is a good man. Though perhaps not a man of keen intellect, he is hardly stupid and normally looks into things with a more balanced eye than do the other characters. He is the only one to feel a moral dilemma in the battle, because he is more able—or willing—than the other characters to consider things from another person's point of view. Nor, clearly, is he a coward, though Goneril doesn't care for his kind of courage—it's too moral and it doesn't unquestioningly serve her. Albany is extremely well intentioned and has ready sympathy for those who suffer injustice. Although he is finally too shallow (as Kent is not) to appreciate the terrible depths of Lear's suffering, he is always deeply affected by the sight of suffering—including his own, it must be noted—and would be eager to give aid and comfort except that under the pressures and passions of the moment he often becomes a bit inept and loses his sense of proportion. And here, while he is being sympathetically inept, Cordelia is hanged and Lear comes to disaster.

Albany begins efficiently enough by demanding that Lear and Cordelia be turned over to him. Edmund, posing as the voice of reason and common sense, stalls for time with some plausible arguments. From this point the conference between the victors proceeds, more and more clearly, by the interplay of simple self-interest. The scene is a little chaos of egos. It has, superficially, nothing to do with Lear or with "greater questions." Albany, Edmund, Goneril, and Regan are motivated by a normal, understandable preoccupation with their own insular desires and griefs. In V.i Albany had to join with Edmund to repel the invaders but could not do so wholeheartedly since he was too aware of the wrongs done Lear and of Edmund's treachery to his father. Now, however, since Albany has read the letter Edgar gave him, these causes seem insignificant beside his sense of the treachery of Goneril and Edmund *to him*. Edmund's assumption of responsibility, of authority, infuriates him. He wants to put Edmund in his rightful place—taking orders, not giving them:

> Sir, by your patience,
> I hold you but a subject of this war,
> Not as a brother.
>
> (59–61)

To this Regan objects. Besides resenting the slur on her beloved, she wishes to install Edmund in Cornwall's place and, by so doing, both win Edmund for herself and keep him from Goneril. Regan declares that as her general, Edmund may justly consider himself Albany's brother. Goneril, of course, equally wants Edmund raised to Albany's station, but not as his brother and not by Regan's means (see her letter, IV.vi.258–65). She uses an argument that Edmund himself had used earlier:

> Not so hot!
> In his own grace he doth exalt himself
> More than in your addition.
>
> (66–68)

And while Lear is forgotten, the private squabble proceeds:

> *Regan.*   In my rights
>   By me invested, he compeers the best.
> *Albany.* That were the most if he should husband you.
> *Regan.* Jesters do oft prove prophets.
> *Goneril.*   Holla, holla!
>   That eye that told you so looked but asquint.
>
> (68–72)

Is Albany's line here really a jest, or is it a taunt, or a trap for Goneril, or even a wish, a desire, like Regan's, to keep Edmund away from Goneril? Probably something of each. It is a dark and complex expression of his bitterness. He has clearly forgotten "the captives / Who were the opposites of this day's strife" (41–42). His mind now works on the subject of Goneril's letter to Edmund, with its "proposal."

We learn that Regan feels ill, and apparently her illness leads her to grow impatient with argument and sarcasm and to force the issue by simply declaring herself and her possessions Edmund's, a way of also declaring that he is hers, not Goneril's. It is interesting how the characters' separate desires overlap here: Albany and Regan want to keep Goneril and Edmund apart but can't agree on Edmund's status, while Regan and Goneril agree on Edmund's status but not on who should get him. Even Albany and Goneril seem to be together in that both are opposed by Regan. This overlapping only increases the sense of insularity, for there is no longer any way these people can work together. Reconciliation is out of the question. Edmund, for his part, is in a delicate position. He has promised too much to each sister and can say nothing as long as it is primarily Goneril and Regan who are arguing. Only when Albany attacks Goneril can he step in:

> *Regan.* . . . Witness the world that I create thee here
> My lord and master.
> *Goneril.*   Mean you to enjoy him?
> *Albany.* The let-alone lies not in your good will.
> [Albany is wrong here, as we soon learn.]
> *Edmund.* Nor in thine, lord.
> *Albany.*   Half-blooded fellow, yes.
> *Regan.* [*to Edmund*] Let the drum strike, and prove
> my title thine.
>
>   (77–81)

To Regan's attempt to make a decree, to formalize her relationship with Edmund, Albany opposes formal and ceremonial statements of his own. Showing his interest in order and propriety, he begins with "Stay yet; hear reason" (82), as if what he had to say were going to cool things off. But what follows is, first, a formal charge of treason against Edmund and Goneril, which he makes without producing his evidence, and then, as his anger and his wounded pride break forth in sarcasm, a parody of marriage negotiations which implies the evidence (we know now that he did read the letter):

>   Edmund, I arrest thee
> On capital treason; and, in thy attaint,
> This gilded serpent. For your claim, fair sister,
> I bar it in the interest of my wife.
> 'Tis she is subcontracted to this lord,
> And I, her husband, contradict your banes.

If you will marry, make your loves to me;
My lady is bespoke.

(82–89)

Albany is saying to Regan that, yes, he too would like to set
these personal relationships in order but that she doesn't realize
to what extent familial order has already been perverted, perverted to the extent of becoming not simply chaos, but chaos
appearing to be a new order.

To Albany's attempt to give the quarrel a clear and formal
basis, Goneril makes a belittling sarcastic remark of her own,
as she often does when her husband makes one of his reasonable,
moral statements: "An interlude!" (89). As with "Marry, your
manhood—mew!" (IV.ii.68), she is saying that she doesn't think
much of his threat and that she refuses to take seriously what
he feels so strongly about. What Albany thinks is an important
drama is really a trivial farce about adultery in which, as usual,
the husband is an incompetent fool and a cuckold. Moreover,
she implies, it is a farce which is a side issue, a mere interruption
in the really important dramatic structure, which is presumably
the union of Goneril and Edmund. Goneril is saying that something Albany is interested in could never be the true center of
interest. Actually what she says is more inclusively true than
she imagines. "An interlude" defines the nature of most of V.iii,
in particular the nature of the actions involving Albany, Edmund,
Regan, Goneril herself, and later Edgar.[7] All the action between
"If it be man's work, I'll do't" (39) and "Howl, howl, howl!"
(258) is an "interlude" in the tragedy of King Lear, a kind of
ghastly comic relief, in which what we laugh at (and there are
moments, I think, when one must laugh) is not comic.

Albany ignores Goneril's remark and tries to keep things
going according to "reason." He wishes to put the quarrel under
the rule of ceremony and so uses the device and the language of
a formal challenge:

Thou art armed, Gloucester. Let the trumpet sound.
If none appear to prove upon thy person
Thy heinous, manifest, and many treasons,

> There is my pledge. I'll make it on thy heart,
> Ere I taste bread, thou art in nothing less
> Than I have here proclaimed thee.
>
> (90–95)

Edmund answers in the same style, and they send for a herald.

In the middle of this exchange between Albany and Edmund, and to one side of it, so that neither of the men, engaged as they are in their own affairs, hears it, is an exchange between Regan and Goneril:

> *Regan.* Sick, O, sick!
> *Goneril.* [*aside*] If not, I'll ne'er trust medicine.
>
> (95–96)

We learn how far the division has already gone; our expectation that the quarrel was beyond reconciliation is answered by the event. Moreover, there are two separate actions going on here, as if everything is going to fall apart at once. The contrast between the two actions is also a contrast between Albany's (and, as we shall see, Edgar's) way of settling differences and Goneril's way. Albany wishes to proceed openly, according to ceremony, according to established rules, according to forms of justice. Goneril proceeds by means of the sly, vicious act.

As the herald is sent for, Albany tells Edmund that he is on his own—the only troops left around are Albany's. Shakespeare wants us to see how much in charge of the situation Albany should be, how much of the power is in his hands. (Later we will see what use he has made of this power.) Yet he allows Edmund a chivalric trial. Earlier Edmund had said that his "state / Stands on me to defend, not to debate" (V.i.68–69). Albany takes the opposite view and will engage in the debate.

Regan's "sickness" grows worse, and we see a flash of Albany's sympathy: "She is not well. Convey her to my tent" (V.iii.106). Again we see Albany's fairness, his unwillingness to take advantage of his opponents.

With the herald's proclamation and the sounding of the trumpet we seem to reach the opposite point in the play from the social disintegration, the storm, and the madness, the chaos of earlier scenes:

"If any man of quality or degree within the lists of the army will maintain upon Edmund, supposed Earl of Gloucester, that he is a manifold traitor, let him appear by the third sound of the trumpet. He is bold in his defense."

(110–14)

For a moment we seem to be back in a world where even conflict is governed by ceremony, where enmity proceeds according to accepted chivalric and hierarchical codes and standards, where disorder is made to look like order. It is as if we are back in the world of the opening scenes of *Richard II*, with their carefully measured insults and accusations. In *Richard II* we soon learn how superficial and unstable that controlling order really is. Here, we hardly need to be reminded. This trumpet signals the reassertion of ceremony, order, right, and justice after the chaos of the middle acts, the reassertion of the general good in place of the self, the reassertion of "ought" in place of "want" or "feel." And it is appropriate that what this trumpet summons is Edgar; for Edgar, like Albany, believes in justice and in the importance of doing the "right" thing. Also, like Albany, and unlike (so far as one can tell) Edmund, Goneril, and Regan, he feels sympathy for people he sees suffering. As we shall see, the insistence on "ought" and the feeling of sympathy come into conflict.

In the questions addressed to Edgar as challenger, in his answers, in his accusation, and in Edmund's reply we continue to hear the accents of *Richard II*, the formulas of trial by combat:

> Draw thy sword.
> That, if my speech offend a noble heart,
> Thy arm may do thee justice. Here is mine.
> Behold it is my privilege,
> The privilege of mine honors,
> My oath, and my profession. I protest—
> Maugre thy strength, place, youth, and eminence,
> Despite thy victor sword and fire-new fortune,
> Thy valor and thy heart—thou art a traitor,
> False to thy gods, thy brother, and thy father,
> Conspirant 'gainst this high illustrious prince,
> And from th' extremest upward of thy head
> To the descent and dust below thy foot
> A most toad-spotted traitor. Say thou "no,"

> This sword, this arm, and my best spirits are bent
> To prove upon thy heart, whereto I speak,
> Thou liest.
>
> (126–42)

With its formulaic words, its balanced syntax, and its several
series, the speech sounds as if it might have been delivered by
Bolingbroke, the champion of justice. The effect Shakespeare gets
by suddenly introducing the balanced, controlled, ceremonial
style at this point in *King Lear* is quite wonderful. How different
is this accusation, denunciation, and threat from Lear's:

> Life and death, I am ashamed
> That thou hast power to shake my manhood thus!
> That these hot tears, which break from me perforce,
> Should make thee worth them. Blasts and fogs upon thee!
> Th' untented woundings of a father's curse
> Pierce every sense about thee! Old fond eyes,
> Beweep this cause again I'll pluck ye out
> And cast you, with the waters that you loose,
> To temper clay. Yea, is it come to this?
> Ha! Let it be so. I have another daughter,
> Who I am sure is kind and comfortable.
> When she shall hear this of thee, with her nails
> She'll flay thy wolvish visage. Thou shalt find
> That I'll resume the shape which thou dost think
> I have cast off for ever.
>
> (I.iv.287–301)

> No, you unnatural hags!
> I will have such revenges on you both
> That all the world shall—I will do such things—
> What they are, yet I know not; but they shall be
> The terrors of the earth. You think I'll weep.
> No, I'll not weep.   *Storm and tempest.*
> I have full cause of weeping, but this heart
> Shall break into a hundred thousand flaws
> Or ere I'll weep. O fool, I shall go mad!
>
> (II.iv.273–81)

> Arraign her first. 'Tis Goneril, I here take my oath before this
> honorable assembly, kicked the poor King her father.
>
> (III.vi.46–48)

After all the uncontrolled violence in the poetry, as well as the action, of this play, Edgar's speech brings us, I think, a sudden sense of relief, a flood of hope—the good seem strong and assured again. The good are asserting themselves instead of lurking and raving and sneaking. We feel that finally what ought to happen is going to happen.

Except that Edgar leaves one thing out, something that he ought to have included: his name. Edmund realizes this, but since he has always believed more in himself than in social forms, he confidently engages in the fight:

> In wisdom I should ask thy name,
> But since thy outside looks so fair and warlike,
> And that thy tongue some say of breeding breathes,
> What safe and nicely I might well delay
> By rule of knighthood I disdain and spurn.
>
> (142–46)

Edmund, of course, does not win, and Goneril emphasizes the fact that for all its formulaic trappings, the fight was not conducted absolutely according to the rules:

> This is practice, Gloucester.
> By th' law of war thou wast not bound to answer
> An unknown opposite. Thou art not vanquished,
> But cozened and beguiled.
>
> (152–55)

We are likely to think this is merely sour grapes—she wouldn't have mentioned it if Edmund had won. But she may also make us realize the irony of ceremonial language at this point in the play. Things are not as much under control, under social rule, as the language would pretend.

As Edmund falls, Albany cries, "Save him, save him" (152). His motive here is more likely legalistic than humanitarian—he apparently wishes to confront Edmund with the evidence against him and Goneril. Albany produces the letter Edgar had given him which contains Goneril's suggestion that Edmund murder her husband. Goneril is defiant, though what she says amounts to a confession, and claims that she, not Albany, is the sovereign, the legal ruler. Albany, knowing perfectly well that she is guilty, nevertheless expresses his astonishment that anyone could be so immoral, expresses his shock at the enormity of her proposal:

> Most monstrous! O,
> Know'st thou this paper?
> (160–61)

Goneril realizes that the game is up, that Albany now has all the cards, and rushes out, refusing, rather in Iago's manner, to give any details of what she has done ("Ask me not what I know" [161]). "Go after her," says Albany. "She's desperate; govern her" (162). I hope I don't feel this way only from hindsight, but it seems to me that Albany's order here is like his previous order that the departing Regan be looked after. There seems to be some concern for Goneril herself in the order. After all, he doesn't say, "Don't let her escape." (Or maybe he simply wants to save her for the same reason he apparently wants to save Edmund—so that their guilt may be demonstrated unequivocally.)

For his part, Edmund, who knows he's dying, confesses:

> What you have charged me with, that have I done,
> And more, much more. The time will bring it out.
> 'Tis past, and so am I.
>
> (163–65)

The "more, much more" that he has done will presumably turn out to include what he ordered the captain to do to Lear and Cordelia. He does not seem to be in any haste to make a more specific confession, or to countermand the order, though whether the order is carried out or not can hardly be of any practical consequence to him any longer. He confesses to general villainy, but keeps a specimen unrevealed, almost as if it were a kind of guarantee that his name will be remembered after his death.

Edmund also wants to know who his nameless vanquisher is. Why has Edgar kept his name a secret? "Know my name is lost," he said, "By treason's tooth bare-gnawn and canker-bit" (121–22). He is rather like the revolutionaries who consider themselves as having no name until through their efforts the new, just society replaces the old, unjust society which keeps them

from being their true selves. Edgar cannot be "Edgar" while
Edmund is "Edmund Earl of Gloucester" (125). By defeating
Edmund, Edgar throws down the unjust society and can end his
series of disguises and reclaim his true name.

But I think that if we have been listening carefully to Edgar
from the moment he became Tom up until the fight, we can see
a further reason why he might keep his name secret, nor will his
manner of revealing it come as a surprise. There is always something theatrical about the return of a hero. "This is I, Hamlet the
Dane." The theatrical return is the key to Prince Hal's strategy.
Still, Edgar's announcement of his name before the fight would
be just as theatrical as his announcement after the fight ("theatrical" for the other characters, of course; we know who he is and
get some of the benefit of both versions). But Edgar is a believer
in the morality of the universe, and delaying his self-revelation
gives him an advantage in demonstrating this justice. For delaying his self-revelation until after the fight makes the fight a revelation of the justice of the universe, rather than simply an example.
And in this sort of quasi-religious context unexpected revelations
are more convincing than anticipated examples. Moreover, Edgar
can continue from the justice of his victory over Edmund to the
justice of his father's having been plunged into darkness for
having begot a bastard:

> I am no less in blood than thou art, Edmund;
> If more, the more th' hast wronged me.
> My name is Edgar and thy father's son.
> The gods are just, and of our pleasant vices
> Make instruments to plague us.
> The dark and vicious place where thee he got
> Cost him his eyes.
>
> (168–74)

To a modern reader, I think, this is likely to seem a terribly
cruel thing for Edgar to say to his brother at this point, whether
it is "just" or not. But I can easily imagine an argument that for
an Elizabethan audience what Edgar says would not be cruel.
It would be a truth that no one could deny, a truth that could
hardly be left unsaid. Edmund, this argument would continue,
does not seem to find Edgar's remark cruel—he admits its truth:

> Th' hast spoken right; 'tis true.
> The wheel is come full circle; I am here.
> (174–75)

He is back on the bottom, where he was born and where he belongs, and his rise was merely the occasion for punishing his father for begetting him in such a sinful way in the first place. In admitting this, Edmund would in effect repudiate his whole philosophy, for his beliefs, especially as stated in I.ii, imply a universe in which there are no moral connections between events: there are simply people and decisions and events—Nature.

Gloucester, on the other hand, begins by believing in the moral interconnectedness of all phenomena:

> These late eclipses in the sun and moon portend no good to us. Though the wisdom of nature can reason it thus and thus, yet nature finds itself scourged by the sequent effects. Love cools, friendship falls off, brothers divide. In cities, mutinies; in countries, discord; in palaces, treason; and the bond cracked 'twixt son and father. (I.ii.101–6)

Eclipses are moral events and have moral consequences. But after the horrible experiences of Act III it does not occur to him to see his suffering caused by Edmund as the proper wages of his sin in begetting him. He simply realizes that he was blind to the characters of his two sons. What he does say about the workings of the universe in his case is hardly a vision of the justice of all things:

> As flies to wanton boys are we to th' gods;
> They kill us for their sport.
> (IV.i.36–37)

Man's suffering is a result of the inscrutable powers' caprice, not of their laws. There is no grand purpose, no rational scheme, no justice to the events of the world. Suffering doesn't mean anything; it just exists, according to the whims of the gods. Gloucester does not therefore stop praying to them. But he is praying, not expecting. Some lines later, for instance, he pays "poor Tom" to lead him to Dover:

Here, take this purse, thou whom the heavens' plagues
Have humbled to all strokes. That I am wretched
Makes thee the happier. Heavens, deal so still!
Let the superfluous and lust-dieted man,
That slaves your ordinance, that will not see
Because he does not feel, feel your pow'r quickly;
So distribution should undo excess,
And each man have enough.

(64–71)

There is some softening of the "flies to wanton boys" attitude
here, for it seems that the gods do have some rules ("ordinance").
But this is precisely a wish that justice should prevail, not an assurance that it actually will. That it seems to have prevailed in
this instance (distribution from rich Gloucester to poor Tom) is
an accident, not evidence of universal justice. And it does not,
moreover, moralize Gloucester's fall in relation to his begetting
of Edmund; "superfluous and lust-dieted man" is a general term,
not a specific.

As I said earlier, a number of the characters in *King Lear*
are concerned, in one way or another, with the question of
whether or not the universe is run according to what we would
recognize as just principles. A world in which events are morally
connected is a more comfortable, reassuring place to live than
one in which the sequence of events is morally accidental. It has
been argued that the world of *King Lear* is one in which the
sequence of events is morally just. One can, for instance, take
some speeches which seem to deny a justly ordered universe and
show how these speeches are later "answered." There is, of
course, Gloucester's subversive utterance ("As flies to wanton
boys are we to th' gods . . ."), which is neatly put in its place
by Edgar's later affirmation: "The gods are just, and of our
pleasant vices / Make instruments to plague us. / The dark and
vicious place where thee he got / Cost him his eyes." Almost
equally convincing is a sequence of speeches by Albany. In the
first, he seems to see human immorality leading to the return of
chaos:

If that the heavens do not their visible spirits
Send quickly down to tame these vile offenses,

> It will come,
> Humanity must perforce prey on itself,
> Like monsters of the deep.
> (IV.ii.46–50)

But Albany has provided a way out, an "if" ("much virtue in If"), and a few moments later his hopes are answered when a villain is cut down in the midst of his villainies:

> This shows you are above,
> You justicers, that these our nether crimes
> So speedily can venge.
> (IV.ii.78–80)

The world is orderly, it is just; morality makes sense. *Lear* means that. The corrective statements of Edgar and Albany show it.

So the argument runs. But what their speeches really show is that Edgar and Albany want very badly to believe that events are connected morally as well as mechanically, that one event can explain another, as well as lead to it. They want to believe that the world is essentially orderly and just. But the play does not necessarily answer their desire or support their belief. Even if one says that speeches like those in question are "choric," it doesn't follow that the "chorus" of Edgar and Albany is not limited in its response to the world. Really one might as well say that because Lear in his madness "perceives" that morality and success are distinct, there is in fact no justice in the world. That Edmund finally agrees with Edgar that "the gods are just" is to me more telling than that Edgar says it in the first place. Still, it is hardly conclusive. The human desire to find the world just is strong, and Edmund too is human, never more than in this scene. Perhaps he feels more comfortable with the meaning Edgar gives his life than with an alternative like the meaninglessness Macbeth finds after the collapse of *his* ambitions. But perhaps he just wants to strike a "tragic" pose. He is in a mood for life's ironies (see "All three / Now marry in an instant" [229–30]) and maybe he sees Edgar's remark as an ironic joke—Edmund as *de casibus* hero. Or perhaps he doesn't care whether Edgar is right or not. One can only speculate on Edmund's motive, of course; he is not explicit. But the point is that one must look at the full range of human experience in the play, not just at some of the characters' theories about that experience or about what that experience ought to be. One can't reject certain feelings because they can't be moralized in a choric fashion, nor can one accept moralizations which don't do justice to the feelings.

We were considering Edgar's moralizing of Edmund's death (V.iii.171–74) and the possibility that it might seem crueler to us than to an Elizabethan. But it seems to me that Edgar's lines are unjustifiably cruel by the standards of the play, and that the structure of the play shows this. Let us examine Edgar's speech once more:

> Let's exchange charity.
> I am no less in blood than thou art, Edmund;
> If more, the more th' hast wronged me.
> My name is Edgar and thy father's son.
> The gods are just, and of our pleasant vices
> Make instruments to plague us.
> The dark and vicious place where thee he got
> Cost him his eyes.

We may compare this with another "exchange" of charity:

> *Lear.* . . . If you have poison for me, I will drink it.
> I know you do not love me; for your sisters
> Have, as I do remember, done me wrong.
> You have some cause, they have not.
> *Cordelia.*   No cause, no cause.
>
>   (IV.vii.72–75)

She does not say: "The gods are just. As you threw me out of your shelter into the world's storm, so my sisters threw you out." Not only does this set off the perverse relationship between father and son in IV.vi, with its faked miracle, but also it is a standard we have before us in V.iii when we come to Edgar and Edmund. Of course, Edmund has been villainous in a way Lear has not (though both initiate the destruction of their respective families). But the comparison does show that it was not necessary for a "good" character to insist on pointing out the moral; there are times when such activity is worse than useless. Moreover, Edgar does not moralize Edmund's defeat ("The gods are just; as you would have got me killed, so I have killed you"), but his conception. Edgar does not say: "Because of your crimes, you deserved this." He says: "Father deserved you. He should have known what would come from that dark and vicious place your mother's womb." (Notes on the passage usually interpret "dark and vicious place" as "the bed of adultery," or something similar. But Edgar is more vicious than that. He is saying, metaphorically, an eye for an eye.) And is not this a cruel thing to say, by any standard? It's what Tom's fiend might say, and Edmund is not really the "guilty" party: his principal crime was having existed at all.

It is true that to many of us the "flies to wanton boys" attitude seems more powerful in the play than the attitude that "the gods are just." It seems more adequate (though of course not wholly adequate) to the structure of the play in general, with its "gratuitous" last act, and to the final scene itself. To say "the gods are just" seems too optimistic as an interpretation of what happens in the play. But I don't think one's attitude here depends on the age one lives in. Johnson, as we saw, would have preferred a play in which "the gods are just" would be a true statement. But *King Lear* did not seem to him to be that kind of play. Johnson knew well enough what was going on in *King Lear*. He just didn't approve of it. Neither does Edgar.

4

When Edgar has revealed himself to Edmund and exchanged greetings with Albany, he gives his own version of his recent experience with his father, concluding with Gloucester's death " 'Twixt two extremes of passion, joy and grief" (199). As far as we can tell, Edgar's story is fairly accurate, but a couple of the parenthetical remarks are interesting:

> The bloody proclamation to escape
> That followed me so near (O, our lives' sweetness!
> That we the pain of death would hourly die
> Rather than die at once).
>
> (184–87)

What an incredible introduction to the story of Gloucester's last days! And yet, a few lines later, there is a hint that Edgar may be beginning to realize in an obscure way that there was something wrong with what he did to his father:

> [I] became his guide,
> Led him, begged for him, saved him from despair;
> Never—O fault!—revealed myself unto him
> Until some half hour past.
>
> (191–94)

He still thinks it important that he saved his father from despair (if he did—this is the doubtful point in Edgar's story; he did keep him from suicide); but "O fault!" suggests that Edgar may now question his method. He has still not arrived at Cordelia's method, but his recognition of some fault is a step in the right direction.

When Edgar finishes the first part of his speech both Edmund and Albany react. Edmund's reaction is enigmatic:

> This speech of yours hath moved me,
> And shall perchance do good.
>
> (200–201)

In what way good, we may ask? Is Edmund thinking of Lear and Cordelia? If he is, he is the only one who is. But there is no way of knowing for sure what Edmund is thinking; he doesn't explain but tells Edgar to continue. Albany's reaction, on the other hand, is not at all enigmatic:

> If there be more, more woeful, hold it in,
> For I am almost ready to dissolve,
> Hearing of this.
>
> (203–5)

Albany is in charge here. He is responsible for Lear and Cordelia, and he is ignoring his responsibility in order to listen to a sad story and come to the verge of tears. He shows sympathy, but his flaccid sympathy turns out to be at least as useless as Edgar's stern sympathy for Gloucester.

Edgar continues his story, telling how a man had appeared who "threw him on my father, / Told the most piteous tale of Lear and him / That ever ear received" (214–16). Finally someone mentions Lear, but Albany still does not recall the purpose he announced so boldly in his first speech of the scene—finding Lear and Cordelia. When Edgar tells how the man collapsed in grief, Albany merely wants to know who the man was. It was Kent, of course, who was "tranced" (219) as Albany, in a different way, is now.

At this point a Gentleman enters with a bloody knife, and the interlude nature of so much of V.iii becomes even more apparent, its grotesque resemblance to an interpolated farce more marked. In fact, the next thirty-five lines (223–57) almost insist on it, and in doing so epitomize the nature of human actions and human relations in the world of *King Lear:*

> Help, help! O help!
> (223)

But this is a gratuitous cry. It has no function, for neither in this particular case nor, it seems, in the play as a whole is any help possible. Edgar at least is practical: "What kind of help? . . . What means this bloody knife?" (223–24). We may wonder whether the Gentleman's hysteria announces the death of Lear or of Cordelia—certainly that is more a point of suspense for us, since we know at least that Regan is poisoned. But again it's a thought that, so far as we can tell, occurs to none of the characters on stage.

The Gentleman overcomes his frantic incoherence enough to make it clear that Goneril has poisoned Regan and stabbed herself; both are dead. Edmund's response, with its grim (and conscious) humor, is bracing in this context:

> I was contracted to them both. All three
> Now marry in an instant.
> (229–30)

Finally someone in this scene sees himself in an ironic light, and I think we admire him for it. (I am strangely reminded of

Antony's "Too late, good Diomed" as a response to the news of
Cleopatra's last trick on him.)

Kent enters. The pieces of this tragic world are beginning to
gather, though not to cohere. (One piece—the Fool—never does
show up.) Albany does not notice Kent at first and, ordering that
the bodies be produced, shows us that his sympathy does have
limits:

> This judgment of the heavens, that makes us tremble,
> Touches us not with pity.
>
> (232–33)

His kinship with Edgar is apparent in this. They both believe in
the justice of the gods.

Albany then can greet Kent, saying that the time does not
allow the observance of proper manners. Kent, for his part, is
in a mood which, though it is far less painful, is reminiscent of
Gloucester's:

> I am come
> To bid my king and master aye good night.
>
> (235–36)

Kent would have understood Gloucester. He, too, is weary of
the struggle of living, and he sees no reason to continue living
any longer now that the battle is over and Lear is safe.

But Lear is not safe, and Albany suddenly remembers what
he had come to do in the first place:

> Great thing of us forgot!
>
> (237)

It had slipped his mind. The line would be funny if it were not
so terrible in its consequences. It's so absurd that it's almost
funny anyway. In no other tragedy does Shakespeare allow his
central figure to be so ignored for so long in the final scene. By
giving the final scene of *King Lear* the form he does, Shakespeare
apparently wants us to see the death of Cordelia and thus the
death of Lear as finally the result of inattention, carelessness,
accident. True, Edmund gave the order, but that does not excuse

Edgar and above all Albany for acting as if everything were over when it's not. Shakespeare puts about two hundred lines between Albany's firm demand that Lear and Cordelia be turned over to him and his recollection, prompted by Kent, that that was his purpose. Shakespeare also makes it clear that Albany had the power to do as he wished, since only Albany had any soldiers under his command. As the well-meaning Edgar must share the blame with Edmund, Cornwall, and the rest for Gloucester's sad end, so the well-meaning Albany must share the blame for the tragedy of Cordelia and Lear. Shakespeare has built a final scene that would make the tragedy seem avoidable, not inevitable, the result not simply of human malice, but of human incompetence and human insularity.

For up to the final entrance of Lear that is what the last scene is, an absurd, "interlude" version of what has been going on all along. Albany gets involved in his private affairs and forgets his public responsibility. Edgar, after defeating Edmund, gets involved in his private story and Albany gets involved along with him. Even Edmund, who knows where Lear and Cordelia are, becomes strangely abstracted; he now seems to let them die through negligence rather than malice or self-interest. (If his statement that Edgar's speech "shall perchance do good" does refer to saving Lear and Cordelia, it shows this abstracted state of mind; for if good is to be done in that direction, it will have to be done quickly—not after Edgar has said all he may have to say.) Only Kent seems to have no other interest than Lear's welfare; but in the crisis, after all his efforts, he is prostrated by grief too long to be able to arrive in time to save Lear. Again with Kent, sympathy is finally useless.

All this is very natural, of course, all too natural in the world of this play. And it's not over yet. When he is reminded of Lear, Albany acts immediately to find out where they are:

> Speak, Edmund, where's the King? and where's Cordelia?
> (238)

But immediately he is distracted once again as the bodies of Goneril and Regan are brought out. And after Albany, Kent, and Edmund contemplate the sight for a few lines, it is Edmund who calls their attention away from the interlude and back to Lear and Cordelia:

> I pant for life. Some good I mean to do,
> Despite of mine own nature. Quickly send—
> Be brief in it—to the castle, for my writ
> Is on the life of Lear and on Cordelia.
>
> (244–47)

Apparently everyone is too stunned to move, for he must add: "Nay, send in time" (248). Now Albany issues an order, just the sort we might expect from him:

> Run, run, O, run!
> (248)

As usual, Edgar is more practical, cooler under the weight of fearful experience:

> To who, my lord? Who has the office? Send
> Thy token of reprieve.
>
> (249–50)

Even Edmund has not thought of that ("Well thought on. Take my sword" [251]). An officer is dispatched, Edmund explains what he has done, and he is carried off.

The officer, of course, is too late:

> Howl, howl, howl! O, you are men of stones.
> Had I your tongues and eyes, I'ld use them so
> That heaven's vault should crack.
>
> (258–60)

Men of stones? The much-abused, faithful Kent, the Edgar whose tears once sympathized with Lear so much they marred his counterfeiting (III.vi.59–60), and the Albany who just a few minutes ago was about to dissolve in tears at a mere narrative? Surely this is self-centered hyperbole on Lear's part, as usual. And yet in the rest of the scene they prove him to be in some ways right.

Lear has withdrawn into his own private world here; there is no doubt about that. With alternating despair and hope he keeps returning to Cordelia, unable to accept the fact of her death. He is barely aware that anything else exists. Kent attempts to intrude (268), to be recognized—as both Kent *and* Caius. But Lear seems to drift away again before he sees the connection clearly. If Kent wanted a more substantial reunion, he is disappointed; but if he is disappointed, he doesn't show it. Since, unlike Lear, he knows Cordelia is dead, he knows that nothing else can matter to Lear again. He understands, he sympathizes, in a way that Albany and Edgar do not, and he shows this by accepting the fact that Lear is beyond him and that neither he nor anyone else *can* fully sympathize with Lear.

At the beginning of the attempted recognition, Kent had joined himself with Lear in the fall from happiness to misery: "If fortune brag of two she loved and hated, / One of them we behold" (281–82). But when he sees that Lear is now past fully recognizing anything outside his misery, he sees that Lear is alone. For when Lear says to him, "You are welcome hither" (290), Kent replies: "Nor no man else. All's cheerless, dark, and deadly" (291). That is, no one can join you where you are.[8]

Yet even Kent has not been free of strange, insular concerns. In fact, in some ways Kent is remarkably like Edgar, though of course in others they are directly opposed; in the structure of the play they are foils to each other, and this appears nowhere more clearly than in the final scene. The most intriguing similarity between them is the attitude they share toward their disguises— their strange, perverse reluctance to reveal themselves, even when the original need for disguise is gone, to the men they are trying to serve. They begin to seem more interested in being finally recognized in a theatrically or morally effective way than in being simply helpful. They both have a "special purpose" in continuing to conceal their true identities. Edgar's special purpose becomes clear fairly soon, and we have discussed it earlier. He is rewarded for his reticence ("O fault!") by his father's death. Kent is rewarded, in the final scene, by virtual failure to be recognized as the man who was disguised. Before the final scene, despite his promise to the Gentleman (III.i.44–50; but there may be several of these functional "gentlemen" around), he seems to

have revealed himself only to Cordelia, and when she asks him
to reassume his true identity, he asks that she not insist on it:

> Pardon, dear madam.
> Yet to be known shortens my made intent.
> My boon I make it that you know me not
> Till time and I think meet.
> (IV.vii.8–11)

Again we may see, as with the Edgar who will not reveal his
identity before the duel with Edmund, something of the revolu-
tionary who will not assume a true name until the state is orga-
nized justly, that is, when Lear is once more on the throne. He
seems to have in mind a happy recognition and reunion, an
occasion on which Lear will recognize the man and his service
together and give him his name again. When it doesn't work out,
when Lear recognizes the man and the service separately, Kent
is not bitter—only sad, and more sad for Lear than for himself.
Kent's special purpose does no harm, so far as I can see, but it
is another sad manifestation of the prevailing insularity in the
play—the separateness that exists even when people care about
one another.

5

King Lear and *Antony and Cleopatra* are alike—and alone
among Shakespeare's tragedies—in having last scenes that as far
as plot is concerned are gratuitous. What we sense as the "inevitable" or foregone conclusions are virtually reached by the end of
Act IV; all that's required is a little tidying up. In the case of
King Lear the inevitable conclusion is the reunion of Lear and
Cordelia, in the case of *Antony and Cleopatra* the deaths of both
Antony and Cleopatra. However, the gratuitous final acts Shakespeare has constructed for these two plays are very different from
each other. In *Antony and Cleopatra,* Shakespeare presents the
final act as a single character's intentional creation: Cleopatra
merely *delays* the inevitable for her own purposes. Here in *King
Lear,* Shakespeare presents the final act as a group's accidental
creation: the inevitable is not merely delayed—it is, ironically,
avoided altogether and it is avoided contrary to the purpose of

the characters who are principally responsible for giving the last scene its shape. Albany is at the center of the group in *King Lear*, and when he enters in V.iii he thinks he is doing the necessary tidying up. He even begins to act as if, along with Edgar, he has done it. But, as we have seen, he has forgotten something, and this mistake costs the life of Cordelia.

Now, with Cordelia dead (and Edmund too, though to Albany "That's but a trifle here" [296]), he seems to feel that the action is concluded, and he makes a speech that belongs to the genre "final speech of a tragedy," the kind of speech we hear from a Richmond, a Prince of Verona, a Lodovico, a Malcolm, an Alcibiades, an Octavius Caesar. He makes the balanced assertion that everything can now be set right and order can return to the state:

> You lords and noble friends, know our intent.
> What comfort to this great decay may come
> Shall be applied. For us, we will resign,
> During the life of this old Majesty,
> To him our absolute power; you to your rights,
> With boot and such addition as your honors
> Have more than merited. All friends shall taste
> The wages of their virtue, and all foes
> The cup of their deservings.
>
> (297–305)

This shows all that is best in Albany, but also a good deal of what is most dangerous. Albany, like Edgar, very much wants the world to be a just place. He wants a world in which, to use the terms of the first part of this chapter, poetic justice is observed: the good win, the bad lose. He will do what he can to see that poetic justice prevails, but as we have seen, that's not much. And his distinction between "friends" and "foes" is inadequate to describe the action we have seen; the friends have done as much as the foes to cause the disaster. (Actually, we may wonder what "foes" are left. This may be another way in which Albany's speech fails to describe the situation. He is not looking at what is there; he is just making an abstract statement, a statement that is pointless as well as premature.) Like Edgar, Albany wants to believe that the gods are just, but are they, in any sense a human being can understand? Earlier in the scene, Albany was forgetful; now he is obtuse. He does not recognize, as Kent does, that no "comfort" of the sort he has in mind can ever be "applied" to Lear again.

However, no sooner has Albany declared that justice will prevail than he does seem to see that something extraordinary is happening to Lear: "O, see, see!" (305). And Lear asks the question that Albany's or Edgar's faith in a just world would have trouble answering:

> And my poor fool is hanged: no, no, no life?
> Why should a dog, a horse, a rat, have life,
> And thou no breath at all?
>
> (306–8)

Lear has once more accepted the fact of Cordelia's death, and yet once more he refuses to give up and thinks he sees some sign of life on her lips—and in this delusion he dies. In their response to this, Edgar and Kent are again foils:

> *Edgar.*   He faints. My lord, my lord—
> *Kent.* Break, heart, I prithee break!
> *Edgar.*   Look up, my lord.
> *Kent.* Vex not his ghost. O, let him pass! He hates him
>   That would upon the rack of this tough world
>   Stretch him out longer.
> *Edgar.*   He is gone indeed.
>
> (312–16)

"Do but look up," Edgar had said to Gloucester, as he tried to make him think his life a miracle instead of the misery it obviously was. Edgar believes that any life is better than none; Kent believes that there is a limit, that beyond a certain point death is a welcome end to the torture of living. Edgar had said that "Ripeness is all," and Kent does not dispute this. But as Gloucester at one time believed he was ready to rot, so here Kent suggests that Lear is more than ripe, that he has already lived longer than he should have:

> The wonder is, he hath endured so long.
> He but usurped his life.
>
> (317–18)

Albany has been silent all this while, and when he does speak, he is changed:

> Bear them from hence. Our present business
> Is general woe. Friends of my soul, you twain
> Rule in this realm, and the gored state sustain.
>   (319–21)

Now Albany does not simply resign his "absolute power" during Lear's lifetime—he gives it up altogether. He will no longer attempt to order things. He will leave that to others. But Kent also declines to rule. He has no active purpose now that Lear is dead, no reason to live:

> I have a journey, sir, shortly to go.
> My master calls me; I must not say no.
>   (322–23)

If Edgar accepts the responsibility, he does so very tenuously, with none of the positive sense of purpose that we find in other tragedies: [9]

> The weight of this sad time we must obey,
> Speak what we feel, not what we ought to say.
> The oldest hath borne most; we that are young
> Shall never see so much, nor live so long.
>   *Exeunt with a dead march.*
>   (324–27)

We find in these lines both the sadness and the sense of a diminished world that we find at the end of other tragedies, though I don't believe we find the latter expressed elsewhere so explicitly or with such a sense of permanence. But the speech also suggests that Edgar too may have changed because of what he has just experienced. The suggestion is, like his assumption of power, tenuous, but he seems to recognize that at least in some cases notions of "ought" are an inadequate response to human experience of the "tough world," that in certain circumstances it is necessary to express what one feels. He seems to imply that the experiences of Lear and Gloucester were of this extraordinary kind, that he will not endure the like, and that he will, to adopt his earlier term, ripen sooner.

The action of *King Lear* never does reach the kind of conclusion that Albany had in mind before Lear's death. The order the concluding couplets suggest is ironic because it involves a withdrawal, not a firm advance into the future. The disintegration of human associations we have been seeing since the first scene continues in the final speeches. Albany's "Friends of my soul" is generous and sincere, but, after the action of this play, ironic. It suggests a relationship which seems impossible in this world. There is no sense of an organic state here, and barely a sense of any new order at all. We may even wonder who is left for Edgar, if he does assume control, to govern. If there is harmony at the end of *King Lear,* it is the harmony of the lone survivor.

6

I have said that the disasters in *King Lear* are finally the result more of human insularity than of human malice. Certainly envy, lust, greed, and hate play an important part. But particularly at the beginning and at the end of the play, it is the less vicious but equally dangerous manifestations of selfishness that cause trouble—simple self-centeredness itself, forgetfulness, ineptitude, misunderstanding, perverse personal purpose, unfeeling morality, inadvertent or well-meant torture. All these prevent the characters who are not malicious from preventing the disasters when it is in their power to do so. Shakespeare has made this particularly clear in the Edgar-Gloucester relationship and in most of the action of V.iii. Division between people who like each other continues literally to the end of the play. Human insularity —in the world of *King Lear* it comes to seem inevitable.

But what about Lear and Cordelia? I have practically ignored them except as a contrast to Edgar and Gloucester. I have ignored them because they are ignored through most of the action in the final scene. Their relationship as established in IV.vii and glimpsed again at the beginning of V.iii is an example of what many of these characters would like to achieve but cannot. It is the only extended example in the play—and it is very short. (The teamwork of Goneril, Regan, Cornwall, and Edmund in

Acts II and III turns out not to be at all the same thing.) But
the other moments of contact are indeed moments—Lear and
the Fool in III.ii, Lear and Gloucester in IV.vi, and, almost, Lear
and Kent in V.iii. Edmund's *ménage à trois* (V.iii.229–30) is a
grim parody.

Lear and Cordelia are reunited in IV.vii, the scene of music,
harmony, healing, and, above all, the discovery and achievement
of *relation*. Lear loses his demands, his rage, his absolutes, his
abstractions, and in doing so finds what he wanted all along:

> *Lear.*   Do not laugh at me;
>   For, as I am a man, I think this lady
>   To be my child Cordelia.
> *Cordelia.*   And so I am! I am!
>   (68–70)

She is his *child,* not a monster, or "a soul in bliss" (46), or "a
spirit" (49)—or someone who must insist on her bond. He is "a
very foolish fond old man" (60), not a dictator of other people's
emotions. Neither needs to prove anything to the other. Cordelia
and Kent call him a king, too, but that is less important now,
as he shows in V.iii:

> Come, let's away to prison.
> We two alone will sing like birds i' th' cage.
> When thou dost ask me blessing, I'll kneel down
> And ask of thee forgiveness. So we'll live,
> And pray, and sing, and tell old tales, and laugh
> At gilded butterflies, and hear poor rogues
> Talk of court news; and we'll talk with them too—
> Who loses and who wins; who's in, who's out—
> And take upon 's the mystery of things
> As if we were God's spies; and we'll wear out,
> In a walled prison, packs and sects of great ones
> That ebb and flow by th' moon.
>   (8–19)

With his relation to Cordelia established he doesn't need the
hollow ceremony of the court, except as amusement. He needs
only the genuine ceremony of blessing and forgiveness, the ceremony of his relation to his daughter. In a way, the prison life he

foresees is what he originally dreamt of—escaping from the responsibility for making difficult decisions, and living with Cordelia—only now he can do without the empty name of king and the empty words of love. But it is still a dream, this translunary (and therefore immutable) togetherness that he envisions, a dream which the other characters will combine to destroy, as we have seen.

This brief reunion of Lear and Cordelia is our longest vision of what we want so much and apparently cannot have. It shows us for an all too brief time the possibility of not being so incessantly, insupportably, hopelessly alone. It also shows us how rare these moments are, how difficult to achieve, how tenuous at first, and finally how fragile. In III.vi Edgar speaks a few words on the subject of human contact:

> Who alone suffers suffers most i' th' mind,
> Leaving free things and happy shows behind;
> But then the mind much sufferance doth o'erskip
> When grief hath mates, and bearing fellowship.
> (102–5)

Edgar is talking about what he has just seen—other people suffering. In a sense, he doesn't take himself seriously enough; it seems to be sufficient that someone else is having a bad time of it (particularly if that someone else is a king). Real fellowship is beyond him. The neatness of the couplets, besides suggesting the moralist, makes Edgar's lines sound like a theory, stored wisdom, a priori truth. But unfortunately, when Edgar meets his father in Act IV, he forgets this theory in favor of his more deeply held theory of despair, which, as far as this play is concerned, contradicts the theory about fellowship in suffering. If he had to act according to a theory, he chose the wrong one. Edgar's treatment of his father is a version of the kind of insularity that (in the behavior of Edmund, Albany, Edgar, and the rest in V.iii. 26–257) destroys the reestablished relation of Lear and Cordelia. (They had of course broken their original relation themselves by insisting on abstractions.) Cordelia is hanged, and Lear is alone.

All tragic heroes are isolated in one way or another from their fellow men. This is one of the conditions of their greatness.

Is there anything special about Lear's case? We might try to answer this question by asking what happens to Lear in the final scene. Whatever else may happen to him, I don't think he reaches what we could call a perception or a recognition. If anything, the opposite happens, both in the sense that he forgets anything he may have learned and in the sense that he very pointedly does not recognize anything new, not even the mere fact that Cordelia is dead. Nor do I think he perceives that in this world no real perception is possible—that the universe is inscrutable, that the gods are capricious, that life makes no sense. I think that what happens to Lear, throughout the play but above all at the end of V.iii, is that he experiences extremes. Lear's advantage over a Timon, who also experiences extremes, is that he doesn't get stuck in one of them but keeps being pulled from one to another. But that is also his disadvantage, for the extremes tear him apart. Kent's metaphor—"the rack of this tough world"—is a perfect description of the form of Lear's experience.

The experiencing of these extremes involves a long series of "perceptions," from the perceptions that Goneril is neglecting him, and that he made a mistake with Cordelia, right on through to the end. Individually they are more part of the texture of the play than of its structure. We needn't examine them in detail. The important thing is the fact of the series, the continuing search, the refusal, or rather, the instinctive inability to come to rest. One might argue that in IV.vii and at the beginning of V.iii Lear himself does come to rest on a new perception of love, or, as I have put it, of relation, and that now it is the world, not Lear's instinct, that will not let him rest. But I think it would be more accurate to say that what he perceives here he has perceived before and that what makes these moments different is that now he *experiences* the relation. Moreover, he doesn't come to rest; he only looks forward to it. It is true that he isn't allowed to rest; but it is also true that we will never know what would have happened had Cordelia not been hanged, and I suppose that it is idle to ask what his life with her would have been like.

As things actually do happen, Lear is forced back to his old activity—the experience of extremes—and now in an extreme form, because the perceptions of the last scene are so absolutely and finally opposed: Cordelia is dead, Cordelia lives.

Lear in the final scene (that is, from the moment he enters with Cordelia dead in his arms) recapitulates the emotional responses to the world that he had exhibited throughout the earlier parts of the play. He is by turns imperious, accusing, hyperbolic, despairing, plain-spoken, revengeful, perceptive, accepting, deluded, hopeful. But the primary emotional pattern here is cyclic—despairing and hopeful according to whether Cordelia is dead or alive. He goes through the cycle three times. Again his experience is analogous to Gloucester's, but again there are important differences. In the first place, Lear's cycles are self-generated. He neither has nor needs an Edgar to bring him back from despair to hope. Like Gloucester he shows signs of weariness, but unlike Gloucester his energy always returns. Also, very unlike Gloucester, he never wishes for death. Kent welcomes for him something he doesn't welcome for himself, something, in fact, that he himself is not aware of. It is as if Lear can't quit living long enough to die. And again his decision to live is not forced upon him by an Edgar. More than that—he does not *decide* at all. His will to live is instinctive, not conscious. His isolation is different from Gloucester's. Gloucester does not particularly wish to be isolated, but Edgar refuses to make contact. Lear keeps plunging back from those brief moments of contact with others to his intense concentration on Cordelia.

This suggests a final comparison—for each man there is a redeeming miracle. If Gloucester and Lear are analogous, so are Edgar and Cordelia. Gloucester tells us what the miracle would be for him:

> O dear son Edgar,
> . . . Might I but live to see thee in my touch
> I'ld say I had eyes again!
>
> (IV.i.21–24)

The literal contact of father and son would be enough—a miracle. It happens immediately, but only with mocking irony, for Gloucester can't sense the touch and Edgar won't allow it to be recognized until it's too late. It was possible, but it didn't happen. For Lear, the miracle is more difficult:

> This feather stirs; she lives! If it be so,
> It is a chance which does redeem all sorrows
> That ever I have felt.
>
> (V.iii.266–68)

But she does not live. No virtue in If here. Edgar grants the touch, the human contact, too late, and Gloucester's heart " 'Twixt two extremes of passion, joy and grief, / Burst smilingly" (V.iii.199–200). Lear's heart also bursts smilingly, as he dies seeing some sign of life on Cordelia's lips:

> Do you see this? Look on her! Look her lips,
> Look there, look there—   *He dies.*
>
> (311–12)

There is irony here, too, but of a different kind. For whereas Edgar refused to grant the miracle until too late, the world has forced Lear to create his miracle out of his own imagination, to make something out of—nothing. Lear creates his own redeeming fake.

Just before he dies, Lear is granted another miracle, the most modest imaginable, but in the world of this play, a true one:

> Pray you undo this button. Thank you, sir.
>
> (310)

This trivial act is the final image of what has been too often missing, disastrously missing, from this world: a touch, a simple human contact, simply helping.

7

When Lear dies, he has no self-consciousness. He does not think of his role, his stance, his tragic heroism. Unlike Hamlet, Othello, or Antony, he does not set his life in order. There is no self-assertion like Cleopatra's, no defiance like Macbeth's. He does not think of his own death at all. He now directs all his attention to something outside himself. He concentrates on Cordelia, and finally on her life, not her death. He is hopeful, he will go on, he will continue to experience the world. He is deluded, too, but he does not perceive that.

What is great about Lear, what is tragic, what sets him above the other characters, is the *power* of his isolation and his suffering—the depth to which his feeling goes, its intensity, his tremendous energy, and its range, the extremes he encounters in his suffering and in his brief moment of joy. But at the same time, he is not the only character who is isolated and who suffers (and who is deluded); he is merely the extreme case. And just as his life is simply cut off, without the usual tragic shaping provided by some consciousness of death, so the community that survives him, the "new order," is fragmented, indecisive, shapeless, moving into the future with little sense of hope that things can be rebuilt. This makes Lear's dying delusion even more ironic—at least he had hope. Shakespeare produced this indeterminate ending by giving his play the odd structure we have examined, with its gratuitous last act, its lack of inevitability. The breakdown of traditional dramatic structure produces a breakdown of order in the final scene, and this breakdown of order, both in the "interlude" and at the very end, seems ultimately worse than the earlier, more violent "chaos" of madness, storm, and civil war. It is worse because it cannot easily be attributed to "evil" forces. It is worse because one does not see an end to it and because it is so trivial, so seemingly avoidable. Is man no more than this? Can men associate no more than this?

Thus *King Lear* is Shakespeare's most disturbing tragedy. *Macbeth* contains some utterances as black as any in *King Lear*, the "tomorrow" speech, for instance, where life "is a tale / Told by an idiot, full of sound and fury, / Signifying nothing" (V.v.26–28). But in *Macbeth* there is more to be set against the blackness. The "tomorrow" speech is answered by the structure of the play. At the end, "The time is free" (V.viii.55), and tomorrows can bring us something, even something good. But when Lear asks his last searching question, "Why should a dog, a horse, a rat, have life, / And thou no breath at all?" there is no answer, either from the characters or from the structure of the play.

This is not to say that Lear's question *has* no answer, only that in the play there is none. To say it has no answer would be to say life makes no sense. And that would really be to speak like Edgar or Albany—change places and, handy-dandy, which is the moralist, which is the nihilist? We do not know whether life makes sense or not, and we should not release ourselves too soon from the rack of this tough play. Ripeness is all.

5

▓ Othello and
▓ Antony & Cleopatra

Conclusions infinite of easy ways to die.

THE final scenes of *Antony and Cleopatra* and *King Lear* are Shakespeare's most unconventional and fascinating tragic conclusions, and *Antony and Cleopatra* V.ii is my principal interest in this chapter. But there are certain remarkable similarities and contrasts in the themes and structures of *Othello* and *Antony and Cleopatra* which make their juxtaposition especially revealing of Shakespeare's command and exploration of tragic form. In these two plays the final scenes, each about 370 lines long, contain a more crucial part of the essential tragic process than the final scenes of any other Shakespearean tragedies—in *Othello* because so much happens, in *Antony and Cleopatra* because so little.

Sexual passion is a primary motive in *Othello* and *Antony and Cleopatra* to a greater extent than in any other tragedies of the "tragic period." The sexual passion of both Antony and Othello becomes, to different degrees, a weakness, affecting their judgment and issuing in fits of jealousy. Both aim a savage justice at the supposed strumpet, though Antony ends in reconciliation. The manhood of each and accompanying pride (which centers around their function as generals) are called into question by their dependence on the objects of their passion.

There are obvious differences between the ways the passions work themselves out in the two plays, the principal difference being that between Desdemona and Cleopatra. When Othello turns against the innocent Desdemona, she merely persists in proclaiming her innocence. Cleopatra, with whom innocence and guilt seem to become irrelevant or hopelessly vague terms, sees that active defense and offense are safer. Moreover, she extends Charmian's merely practical suggestion into a grandly petty version of a Desdemona-like martyr-to-love role, commending herself, with her last breath, to her kind lord Antony. When this "death" has its undesired desired effect, she must give up the martyr role and strive for tragic heroism in "the high Roman fashion," though, by the time she achieves it, it is hardly "Roman." Thus in the final scene she makes *Antony and Cleopatra* a double tragedy, which *Othello* is not. This is the major structural distinction of *Antony and Cleopatra*.

It has frequently been noted that the world of *Othello* is closed, private, and domestic and that the world of *Antony and Cleopatra* is expansive, public, and cosmic. This difference corresponds to different methods of establishing the tragic hero. Othello has always been noble, a great man in the public world. This is a condition of the play and provides a basis from which, in the closed world, he can make his one great ignoble mistake and still salvage heroic stature. Moreover, the fact that the world of the tragic action is domestic is significant because it is in the inner, nonpublic part of his psyche, in the very core of his manhood, that he is vulnerable. Antony's nobility, on the other hand, is undermined from the first line of the play, at least provisionally, and, unlike Othello, he does not reverse this trend immediately upon his own appearance. Antony's "tragic mistake" is not a single action but a condition, a way of life. He knows he is not doing the noble Roman thing by returning to Cleopatra. Othello's character allows him to be driven into an ignoble act (which he performs thinking it to be just); but Antony's "ignoble dotage" is itself part of his character. Thus Shakespeare has a more difficult task in keeping Antony up to tragic stature. He does this primarily by creating an Antony who is able to absorb so much and such varied experience, to suffer so powerfully, to see himself ironically, and to end so without rancor. The other characters seem to agree that Antony could have beaten Caesar, that he is a better soldier, a more appealing leader. Caesar inspires respect and obedience; Antony inspires love. Caesar triumphs by his own lack of capacity for emotions, by luck and shrewdness, and by Antony's virtual abdication. The imperial and cosmic world of the play serves to keep alive the sense of Antony's greatness by reminding us of the grandeur of the scene he moves in even while he plays the strumpet's fool. His capacity is all the more emphasized. The "exotic" allusions in *Othello* merely emphasize the closedness of the play's world because they refer outside it. The Marlovian procession of Middle Eastern kings and countries in *Antony and Cleopatra* is *in* the world of the play (even if they do not appear on the stage). Antony has such a capacity for the experiences of mortal man that his fall is a fearsome, not a wretched affair. His potentially ignominious half-botched suicide is transformed to tragedy by his calm but full acceptance of the revelation of Cleopatra's deception ("Too late, good Diomed" [IV.xiv.128]), by the loyalty of his Guard, by his failure to question Cleopatra about her trick or about her loyalty, by his concern, incompetent as it is, about her future well-being, and by the simple dignity, expressed in the balanced phrasing with which he accepts the full range of his life, including the "miserable change," but pointing quietly and firmly at the basic noble Roman which the cosmic world supports.

By the last scene of *Antony and Cleopatra*, however, which is our particular concern here, Antony is already dead, if hardly forgotten, and it is with the death of Cleopatra in V.ii that comparisons of the two plays become most interesting. I will first examine some major points of comparison and then elaborate separately on each scene.

Among the tragic ends in Shakespeare, I think none is faster and more concentrated than Othello's, none more leisurely than Cleopatra's. In *Othello* the hero does not commit the fatal act until the last scene. The rest of the play builds to the moment of the murder and had Othello changed his mind there, tragic destiny could have been avoided. In *Antony and Cleopatra* one might well see tragic destiny in effect, at least for Antony, from the beginning, the return to Rome being only a brief and illusory respite like the murder of Banquo or Brutus's initial control of the mob. It is difficult to be certain in this tragedy of false starts, but probably the peripety for Antony and the play as a whole is no later than his decision in III.vii to fight at sea. In any case, Antony meets his fate in Act IV. In standard romantic tragedy the lovers die together. Dryden, who made a fine romantic tragedy out of Shakespeare's play (with reference to other sources, including Plutarch), cut out most of the material of Shakespeare's fifth act, so that his Cleopatra's suicide is essentially an immediate response to Antony's. But Shakespeare's Cleopatra chooses to play games with Caesar instead of promptly daggering herself, Juliet-like, over the just-expired body of her lover, and the result is a profound alteration of the tragic effect. *Romeo and Juliet* (like Dryden's play) is a single tragedy of two people. *Antony and Cleopatra* is a true double tragedy because Cleopatra must work out her own tragic end and join Antony only on its completion. The leisurely inconsequence of V.ii is the accomplishment of this end.

Though the final scenes of *Othello* and *Antony and Cleopatra* differ so much in pace, they may be unique in Shakespeare in holding back a peripety so long. The peripety of *Othello* is the murder of Desdemona and entrance of Emilia. One may, according to one's interpretation of Cleopatra, find the peripety of her tragedy (as opposed to Antony's) in V.ii when she sends Charmian out for an order of asps; or it may be that she has firmly decided on suicide by the beginning of V.ii and that her negotiations with Caesar are not a serious attempt to win but only a subtle though rather magnificent self-assertion. I suspect that Cleopatra is committed to suicide by the beginning of V.ii, but that partly out of necessity, partly out of instinct, and partly out of conscious self-assertion she goes through the dealings with Caesar and his henchmen. (The difficulty of "locating" the peripety is itself an indication of the peculiar nature of *Antony and Cleopatra*.)

The action of *Othello* V.ii, then, is fast and striking, that of *Antony and Cleopatra* V.ii leisurely and seemingly inconsequential. The former moves by violent stranglings and stabbings, the latter, with one moment excepted, by a process of going to bed. The former is structured in terms of religious judgment and ends in a vision of damnation; the latter is thoroughly secular and ends in a vision of ascent to a (secular) heaven. The former is a scene of division of love, the latter a scene of union. Both Othello and Cleopatra plan and carry out their own ritual deaths, and in both cases the form of the ritual significantly reflects the thematic structure of the whole play. The ritual of *Othello* shows justice striking down old life; Cleopatra ritualizes love enkindling new life. For these reasons, I think, the close of *Othello* is the most terrifying in Shakespearean tragedy and *Antony and Cleopatra* is as near to comedy, perhaps, as tragedy can come.

2

Justice is the main theme and the structuring principle of the final scene of *Othello*, particularly justice seen in the light of divine justice and the day of judgment. The two main actions are presented as the executions of justice on guilty parties, and the material that binds them together amounts to a trial—an examination of witnesses, a giving of evidence, a returning of verdicts, and a sentencing—a trial that ruthlessly sets out the irony of the justice of the first execution. Shakespeare presents this first execution, in which Othello kills Desdemona, as a perversion of justice expressing a perversion of love. A deluded Othello presumptuously sees himself as an agent of both civic and divine justice but performs an act that outrages both. The second execution, in which Othello kills himself, is an act by which Othello ritually punishes himself for his earlier abuse of justice.[1]

The scene built around this justice theme unfolds powerfully, almost unbearably. A good deal of its power comes from its lucidity, its simplicity. *Othello* V.ii is straightforward "drama" at its finest. But I discuss it here mainly in order to set off the much more daring final scene of *Antony and Cleopatra*, where ritual is so fascinating precisely because it lacks the clarity we find in *Othello* V.ii.

We are immediately set in a world of legal process by the iteration in the scene's first lines:

> It is the cause, it is the cause, my soul.
> Let me not name it to you, you chaste stars!
> It is the cause.
>
> (1–3)

In a passage in *King Lear* (IV.vi.108–10) the meaning of "cause" seems to be "theme of a legal process," not just "charge," or "accusation." "Cause" refers to the whole process, with respect to a specified charge, from the accusation to the manifestation of the verdict (which may be execution).[2] I believe Othello uses the word in the same way, saying, i.e., "It is the judicial procedure with respect to adultery which drives me to do this, to kill Desdemona." At any rate, the word is meant as a legal term.[3]

In V.ii.6 ("Yet she must die, else she'll betray more men") Othello is seeing himself as the impartial executor of public justice; he must kill Desdemona for the safety of society. In 16–17 ("O balmy breath, that dost almost persuade / Justice to break her sword!"), he explicitly presents his intended course of action as the impersonal deed of a "principle"—of Justice in the abstract. But also in these two lines (16–17) he explicitly indicates a tension between the duty of impersonal justice and the strong promptings of his sensual appreciation of Desdemona's beauty. Indeed this tension is apparent in the whole opening speech (1–22), in the style and the accompanying action, as well as in the semantic content. M. R. Ridley says that "nowhere in the play is [Othello] cooler and more coherent."[4] I believe that nowhere in the play would Othello more like to think himself so. The speech is calm, but calm as the eye of a hurricane, with dark violence all around. The repetition of the phrase at the beginning betrays the tension underlying this firm justice. The justicer must make his way against the lover. Many examples from the middle acts (III and IV) could be given to show Othello's violent and sudden alternation between rage against Desdemona and attraction to her. The most extended example begins at IV.i.175, where a long series of violent alternations comes to rest on a cruel parody of eye-for-an-eye justice:

Iago. Strangle her in her bed, even the bed she hath contaminated.
Othello. Good, good! The justice of it pleases. Very good!

(203–5)

The violence is veiled in V.ii.1–22, but the tension is there. After the insistence of the first two and a half lines, Othello lapses into sensual appreciation: "Yet I'll not shed her blood, / Nor

scar that whiter skin of hers than snow, / And smooth as monumental alabaster" (3–5). This verse indeed flows, but he must
bring himself back to duty: "Yet she must die . . ." (6). These
"yet's" are not the kind of "planned" balancing that a truly cool
Othello, as in Act I or in his last speech here in V.ii, would use.
For instance, in "Nothing extenuate, / Nor set down aught in
malice" (V.ii.343–44) the balance is the point of the utterance.
But the "yet's" in V.ii.3–6 imply vacillation.[5] With his resolution
renewed in line 6, Othello sets about his business, only to slip
by stages once more into the power of Desdemona's beauty,
ending on an elegiac vision of a rose. Then he kisses her and
expresses the conflict of sense and Justice in 16–17, quoted above.
Then he returns for another kiss.[6] Then he tries to combine killing and loving ("Be thus when thou art dead, and I will kill
thee / And love thee after" [18–19]), then goes back for another
kiss, the last.

After the last kiss the force of the conflicting emotions causes
him to break into "cruel tears." And finally we have what seems
to be Othello's arrogation to himself of the role of a just God:

> This sorrow's heavenly;
> It strikes where it doth love.
> (21–22)

The line is powerful for its union of sincere pity and gross, blind
presumption.

The indecision of action (first the hesitation over the light, a
physical object which turns his mind back to Desdemona, and
then the repeated kisses) and the successful struggle of the
impulse to justice against the impulse to love are set in a style
that cannot wholly sustain the firm, cool advance of Othello's
Act I verse, which flows "Like to the Pontic sea, / Whose icy
current and compulsive course / Ne'er feels retiring ebb, but
keeps due on" (III.iii.453–55). (I use Othello's own words ironically here, since with these words he had promised not to let
his passions ebb and flow as they do in the opening speech of
V.ii and, indeed, throughout Acts III and IV.) The interruptions
are not violent, but they indicate the conflict of passions which
Othello is determined to suppress.

Both of these passions, the urge to love and the urge to kill, are sexual. The former is Othello's powerful attraction towards Desdemona, under which he "hath devoted and given up himself to the contemplation, mark, and denotement of her parts and graces" (II.iii.302–3), as Iago puts it. The latter passion, the urge to kill, is the expression of Othello's outraged manhood, the loss of self-respect and self-confidence that he experiences when he thinks Desdemona has changed him for Cassio. This is the import of the "Othello's occupation's gone" (III.iii.357) motif. (With Othello's situation we may compare Antony's bitter outcry, "O, thy vile lady! / She has robbed me of my sword" [IV.xiv.22–23].) The general's honor is transformed under Iago's practice not only into dishonor but also into virtual helplessness, and Iago works through Othello's passion for Desdemona. Othello states the proper balance of duty and love in his assurance to the Venetian senate that though Desdemona be allowed to accompany him to the Cyprus wars, desire for her will not cause him to neglect the state's business (I.iii.261–74). Iago manages to destroy this balance, although, ironically, the state does not suffer. Iago believes that life is a reason-passion debate, and that he is one of the few in whom reason predominates. He is ready to think the worst about others' appetites. Accordingly he believes that Othello's "soul is so enfettered to [Desdemona's] love / That she may make, unmake, do what she list, / Even as her appetite shall play the god / With his weak function" (II.iii.328–31). At the moment he is not quite right, but he is near enough so that he can easily force Othello's mind to think the worst about Desdemona. Thus he perverts Othello's incautious love into jealous passion, as he plays on the virtues of Cassio, Othello, and Desdemona to "enmesh them all" (II.iii.345).[7]

In V.ii Othello begins the formal execution by stepping aside to allow the preparation of the condemned soul for death. He insists that this be a proper working out of justice. Of course, the crime he has in mind that she should confess cannot be confessed because it was never committed and she is not even sure what it is. The innocent Desdemona naturally does not and will not participate in the ritual, and as a consequence Othello's stern calm, which was achieved with difficulty in the opening lines, begins to give way visibly. Desdemona notes the passion in his appearance:

> . . . you are fatal then
> When your eyes roll so. . . .
> Alas, why gnaw you so your nether lip?
> Some bloody passion shakes your very frame.
> These are portents; but yet I hope, I hope,
> They do not point on me.
>
> (37–38, 43–46)

We may perhaps see in this astrological figure the signs of an angry heaven preparing to chastise sinful humanity, but of course it is only Othello's frame, not the frame of the earth that shakes. This image emphasizes Othello's actual separation from the powers he claims to represent, the society of man and the "chaste stars" who need to be protected from Desdemona's crime. Just after the execution of Desdemona the same image works another way to emphasize the same discrepancy, that the crime exists only in Othello's mind:

> O, insupportable! O heavy hour!
> Methinks it should be now a huge eclipse
> Of sun and moon, and that th' affrighted globe
> Should yawn at alteration.
>
> (99–102)

Truly, for Othello, "Chaos is come again" (III.iii.92), but the failure of the macrocosm to join in the disorder indicates the inwardness of the tragedy. Nor is the body politic disrupted; Cassio's appointment, for instance, has already been made. We may note further that when Othello was seen as directing a true public cause against infidels, the macrocosm did join in the war, and the "portents" descended on the Turks.

"Justice" is reluctant in V.ii to hear witnesses even under oath:

> . . . confess thee freely of thy sin;
> For to deny each article with oath
> Cannot remove nor choke the strong conception
> That I do groan withal.
>
> (53–56)

He refuses to hear her but offers Cassio's confession and Exhibit A, the handkerchief. At this point, with sentence passed, he may think the time for defense past, but he was never very impartial in taking evidence. In IV.ii, for instance, it is with great relief that we see him question Emilia and turn to Desdemona for what, were he explicit, might save all. But before Desdemona can enter, his conviction that she is a strumpet transforms the ritual and presents a perversion of justice (prejudging) in the form of a perversion of love (prostitution). At the end of the trial Othello and Desdemona are not judge and suspect but "procreants" who "have done [their] course." What Othello, in his bitter sarcasm, intends as an image of Desdemona's perversion, we recognize as an image of his own. The search for truth, as Othello makes it, is a sordid act, and of course it is Othello, under the influence of Iago, who comes to see love as whoring and whose imagination generates the goats, monkeys, foul toads, and summer flies whose business is love. And in the final scene, this combination of perverted love and perverted justice continues to characterize his relation to Desdemona, only now it is the perverted love (jealousy) that tries to make itself look like justice— and only succeeds in showing how far from justice it is.

Desdemona's refusal to go along with the ritual justice infuriates Othello to the point where he ironically states the real nature of his just act, though he is too blindfolded by rage to stop:

> O perjured woman! Thou dost stone my heart,
> And mak'st me call what I intend to do
> A murder, which I thought a sacrifice.
>
> (63–65)

Othello began the scene consenting to sacrifice the thing he loves to the demands of "the cause" in order to protect society and the "chaste stars" of heaven. This role allowed him the illusion of compassion, but her insistence hardens his heart as the destructive jealous passion seizes his whole being.[8] "Sacrifice" probably has a religious implication, in which case the ironically recognized (but unaccepted) distance between the ritual significance and the real is even greater. A few lines later the real motive appears in all the naked egotism of the phrase "my great revenge" (74).

At the very moment of the murder Othello's pretensions to the role of a chastising god are the most powerfully cut down. As he smothers Desdemona, she cries out to God:

> O Lord, Lord, Lord!
> (84)

Immediately there comes Emilia's call to Othello from the door:

> My lord, my lord! What, ho, my lord, my lord!
> (85)

The direct juxtaposition marks the turning point in the play, as it suggests the falsity of the whole structure which Othello has presumptuously built up in his mind and taken for eternal truth. The "lord's" continue to echo through the next forty lines ("good my lord"—91, 103, 107—is especially cutting), culminating in Emilia's return to "Lord" in "O Lord! what cry is that?" (118) and in Desdemona's divine "injustice":

> Commend me to my kind lord . . .
> (126)

which bestows forgiveness in a verbal form used to ask forgiveness.

The entrance of Emilia's common sense also starts the practical reversal. Shakespeare, whose ability to sustain both comic and tragic in a single moment is one of the major factors in his success with tragedy, has used Emilia to increase the tension by putting her on the track of the villain in Act IV. She has intuited the method but not the specific villain (see especially IV.ii.130–47). Whereas Desdemona is always half-awed by Othello, Emilia never flinches in proclaiming Desdemona's innocence. In a retrial she inverts the judicial proceedings and accuses Othello. There is no need to follow her investigation closely here. The reversal of the original verdict does not come at once. Shakespeare draws out new testimony to increase the tension. For instance in Emilia's "iterance" of "my husband?" we perhaps are meant to recall Othello's own iterance of "the handkerchief." Fate is catching up with Othello for his rash proceeding. (Emilia's "iterance" is a reluctance to believe guilt in her husband; Othello's was a haste to find it in his wife.) Emilia finally calls him what the audience has at several points been tempted to call him: "O gull! O dolt! / As ignorant as dirt!" (164–65). The matter appropriately comes down to the only "ocular proof," the handkerchief. This explains it all to Emilia:

> O God! O heavenly God!
> (219)

When Emilia explains the handkerchief and again calls Othello a fool ("O murd'rous coxcomb! What should such a fool / Do with so good a wife?" [234–35]), Othello, his passion having been violently wrenched in the other direction, attempts another divine execution, thinking heaven a little slow:

> Are there no stones in heaven
> But what serves for the thunder?
> (235–36)

Othello, left alone with the dying Emilia, laments his disarming but asks: "Why should honor outlive honesty? / Let it go all" (246–47). Yet the soldier's instinct is still strong in him, and, as Emilia dies, he procures another sword from his wardrobe. Exulting in former glory, he challenges Gratiano but retires immediately, admitting the impotence to which his ungoverned passion has reduced him. However, his sense of honor turns out not to be completely gone, for when the court returns from recess (with a new witness), Othello once more tries and fails to execute Iago. This time he does not seem really to care, and his assertion of honor is now unconcerned, even noncommittal:

> *Lodovico.* O thou Othello that wert once so good,
>   Fall'n in the practice of a damned slave,
>   What shall be said to thee?
> *Othello.*   Why, anything:
>   An honorable murderer, if you will;
>   For naught did I in hate, but all in honor.
>   (292–96)

If we compare this with "But why should honor outlive honesty? / Let it go all," we may feel that there is an inconsistency, in fact a regression here, an example of what Eliot calls "the desire to think well of oneself." [9] Othello's style in the second passage, however, suggests that he is beginning to plan his suicide (note his words to Iago: "I'ld have thee live; / For in my sense, 'tis happiness to die" [290–91]) and is paying only casual attention to Lodovico ("An honorable murderer, *if you will*"; in a few moments he will pay more attention to what Lodovico will call him). Moreover, the topic of the second of these passages shows him moving toward the balancing of good and evil he makes in his final long speech. He doesn't deny the murder, as he had wished to do at the beginning of the scene (63–65), and we should interpret "hate" as something like "malice," that is, the sort of feeling Iago would have: unlike Iago, Othello thought he was doing the honorable thing. But he was still a murderer.

The legal process is carried on to the end as material known to the theater audience is brought out and, as it were, made part of the public record. I believe this scene to be the most extended reexposition in the tragedies, and this is appropriate to the judicial theme. (*Romeo and Juliet* also has a fairly long recapitulation, though for a different reason. *Hamlet* is perhaps the opposite extreme.) Othello has a few spasms of passion left, but again the "ocular proof" ends all:

> *Othello.* . . . How came you, Cassio, by that handkerchief
>   That was my wife's?
> *Cassio.*   I found it in my chamber;
>   And he himself confessed but even now
>   That there he dropped it for a special purpose
>   Which wrought to his desire.
>
>   (320–24)

And, though the judicial process continues to the end under Lodovico, interrupted by Othello's speech, Othello here accepts Emilia's charge as the verdict:

> O fool, fool, fool!
>   (324)

171

References to heaven, hell, devils, angels, and God are extra-ordinarily numerous in this scene. These references, with the judicial nature of the action, bring the image of Doomsday and divine justice into the scene in ironic contrast to the presumptuous act of Othello. Thus throughout the scene the justice theme works on three variously interconnected levels—the personal, the civic, and the divine. I have already mentioned some of the more important connections, particularly Othello's confusion of personal justice (which is suspect) with civil and divine justice, and the operation of the play's climax by juxtaposition of the divine and the human "lord's." Here one need only note further the way the powerful emotion of the religious terms gradually takes the action under its domination. Lodovico's civil justice is very plain beside the divine justice which works in it and over it. Both kinds chastise the personal justice which had pretended to their authority.

As she dies, Desdemona declares that she has been wronged ("O, falsely, falsely murdered!" [118]; "A guiltless death I die" [123]), but unlike "wronged Othello" she does not seek personal justice:

> *Emilia.* O, who hath done this deed?
> *Desdemona.* Nobody—I myself. Farewell.
> Commend me to my kind lord. O, farewell!
> (124–26)

Othello wanted to make killing Desdemona a divine gesture, but it turned out to be a human lie; with Desdemona, what begins as a human lie really amounts to a divine gesture—an image of a grace that is as far above justice as Othello's crime is below it. Othello says of her merciful lie, "She's like a liar gone to burning hell" (130), to which Emilia replies, "O, the more angel she, / And you the blacker devil" (131–32). Later, when he knows the truth, he assents, in a vivid vision of damnation:

> Now, how dost thou look now? O ill-starred wench!
> Pale as thy smock! When we shall meet at compt,
> This look of thine will hurl my soul from heaven,
> And fiends will snatch at it. Cold, cold, my girl?

Even like thy chastity.
O cursed, cursed slave! Whip me, ye devils,
From the possession of this heavenly sight!
Blow me about in winds! roast me in sulphur!
Wash me in steep-down gulfs of liquid fire!
(273–81)

The point here is not Othello's inability to understand Desdemona's love. Whether or not she herself would accuse him at compt is irrelevant. Rather, her "look" will be the damning piece of evidence, and God, not Desdemona, will do the judging. This is an ironic and fitting end for the Othello of the scene's opening lines. Moreover, whether or not Desdemona or God would have mercy on him in the future, it is not in any case Othello's place to expect mercy for himself—from Desdemona's love or from God's. He must submit to justice. This he does by the ritual of his last act.

In discussing this final ritual, I don't think one need entertain the notion that Othello should have meekly submitted to state and God by taking no action, by leaving justice in their hands. Such a submission would have been false to Othello's character and false to the tragic form, and the play certainly does not condemn Othello for refusing to so submit himself. Moreover, Othello's act is seen as impersonal justice, not a removal of authority from where it belongs.

Othello's final speech does return to the steady, easily flowing style of Act I. It takes the form of a trial record, a summation of evidence, a careful weighing and balancing of facts, a temperate process of reaching truth. He asks that things be set down dispassionately, without prejudice of any kind.[10] The style itself gives the impression of balance and sanity, as it sets up the simple semantic oppositions and amasses ordered syntactic parallels:

Soft you! a word or two before you go.
I have done the state some service, and they know't.
No more of that. I pray you, in your letters,
When you shall these unlucky deeds relate,
Speak of me as I am. Nothing extenuate,
Nor set down aught in malice. Then must you speak
Of one that loved not wisely, but too well;

> Of one not easily jealous, but, being wrought,
> Perplexed in the extreme; of one whose hand,
> Like the base Indian, threw a pearl away
> Richer than all his tribe; of one whose subdued eyes,
> Albeit unused to the melting mood,
> Drop tears as fast as the Arabian trees
> Their med'cinable gum. Set you down this.
>
> $\qquad\qquad\qquad\qquad$ (339–52)

The syntactic framework here is very well ordered and thorough, in contrast to his rage-filled style in seeking justice earlier.[11] (His attempt at recreating the cool style of Act I in V.ii.1–22, and the ways it falters, strays, or breaks down were discussed above.) The ritual to this point consists of the temperate, reasonable weighing of truth that justice should involve and that was conspicuously absent from the ritual justice which began the scene. There Justice used her sword but not her balance. Now, having used the balance, she can justly turn to the sword.

The end of the ritual is the execution of Othello by Othello. It is partly an expression of pride by "the noble Moor"; but the specific terms show that this pride is perceptive and consciously ironic:

> And say besides that in Aleppo once,
> Where a malignant and a turbaned Turk
> Beat a Venetian and traduced the state,
> I took by th' throat the circumcised dog
> And smote him—thus.
> $\qquad\qquad\qquad$ *He stabs himself.*
> $\qquad\qquad\qquad\qquad$ (353–57)

Othello has turned the old truly noble Moor, the honorable Turk-conquering general, the legitimate champion of civil and religious justice, the Venetian and Christian Othello, against the Othello who has just murdered his wife. Othello decisively reduces himself to the level of an insignificant foreign infidel, a transgressor against state and God who performs a mean and savage crime. This ritual execution is thus the polar opposite to that performed by a man who saw himself as special minister of earth and heaven, even as God himself. This ritual is just.

Othello's final words express his own sense of the connection between the two rituals:

> I kissed thee ere I killed thee. No way but this,
> Killing myself, to die upon a kiss.
>
> *He dies.*
> (359–60)

The kisses in this scene become gestures of love associated with the two "executions," the two rituals of justice. Where earlier the murder had contradicted the kisses, now, at the end, the kiss extends the emotions of his self-murder. This final kiss, like the suicide speech, expresses not only his love for Desdemona and his renewed recognition of her value, but also the complete frustration to which his acts have brought him. Now all his acts and emotions can only turn back on himself. In redirecting his murderous energy towards himself, he admits that he is at once the good Othello and the vicious dog. In the suicide, killer and victim are one, as the hand that wields the knife turns it against the wielder. In the kiss the only living lips, the only truly kissing lips, are his own. Desdemona has the appearance of sleep both for the early kisses and for the last one, but where the first kisses have the power to wake her to invite Othello to "come to bed" (24), the last kiss cannot move her. The "balmy breath" has ceased, she is "cold," and the "Promethean heat" is not to be found. The impotence of the last kiss is the just result of the presumption of the earlier kisses and their betrayal of love. "To die upon a kiss"—this love-death is no metaphor. Dying upon a kiss here is a just and tragic mockery of sexual union, an image of love made impotent by its own failure.

3

Antony and Cleopatra closes with an even more carefully and elaborately staged ritual suicide, and as in *Othello* the ritual takes a form that reflects and illuminates the nature of the action it completes. That action is a double tragedy. The first tragedy, of Antony, was briefly discussed above (and in chapter 2), in terms perhaps too easy on Antony. After everything we might say about his capacity for emotion and his final acceptance and dignity, his end remains a little sordid, and if Cleopatra is really the petty creature that her last trick on him suggests she is, if he has directed his passion towards a hopelessly mean object, then his own tragic stature is much diminished. His decline would lack the significance that the excellence of Desdemona gives to Othello's. He needs a Cleopatra who herself has tragic stature. On the other hand, to be a tragic heroine she needs to borrow of the grandeur which, however tarnished now, is truly part of his being.

It may sound a little strange to be speaking of dramatic characters as if they themselves were consciously trying to become what their creator would have to make them, that is, "tragic figures." [12] But it is not essentially misleading to speak thus of Antony and Cleopatra even though Shakespeare and his age, and his creations, would not have used the term "tragic" as we do; it's appropriate to speak this way because the possibility for drama in the lives of Antony and Cleopatra is part of the subject matter of the final scene and because Shakespeare makes Cleopatra, in particular, aware of human life as dramatic structure, of dramatic structure as a human creation, and thus of the opportunity to create her own life by giving it a dramatic structure of her own choosing. She knows that her life is the material of which plays are made and she is disgusted by the thought of how her life and Antony's may be mimicked and degraded in the Roman theaters:

> The quick comedians
> Extemporally will stage us, and present
> Our Alexandrian revels: Antony
> Shall be brought drunken forth, and I shall see
> Some squeaking Cleopatra boy my greatness
> I' th' posture of a whore.
>
> (V.ii. 216–21)

She says this as part of her picture of what it will be like for the Egyptians in Rome, and her immediate problem is simply to avoid having to see in reality what she sees in her mind and conjures up verbally for Iras. But her ultimate problem is to make such parody inappropriate or at least to make sure it will be understood that such a play must be taken as parody and not as an image of the truth. And the way she does this is, in effect, to stage her own play in which she becomes the tragic heroine and Antony the tragic hero.

Cleopatra proceeds partly by associating herself with Antony the heroic, even superhuman, emperor, that is, by making herself *the* partner of the great man, by making "Cleopatra" go with "Antony" as a legendary pair. But it's perhaps even more important to note that the Antony with whom she associates herself is an Antony of her own creation, not the "complete" Antony (Shakespeare's creation) that we saw in the first four acts. She rescues Antony from his unheroic deeds and makes him simply what was grand in him. And as she does this she simplifies herself accordingly. She makes herself into what was "best" in her and seeks to associate this heroic Cleopatra with her heroic Antony.

She begins to align herself with the grand Antony—and at the same time to create him, to make this Antony *the* Antony— in the words she speaks at his death:

> The crown o' th' earth doth melt. My lord!
> O, withered is the garland of the war,
> The soldier's pole is fall'n: young boys and girls
> Are level now with men. The odds is gone,
> And there is nothing left remarkable
> Beneath the visiting moon.
>
> (IV.xv.63–68)

The idea behind these lines provides the basis for the structure of V.ii. She makes Antony the source of value in the world; since he is gone, nothing in the world has value. Having spoken these words, she faints, and then revives as "No more but e'en a woman, and commanded / By such poor passion as the maid that milks / And does the meanest chares" (73–75). To be a mere woman is not to be tragic; to be tragic, one must be a queen, an empress. And to faint is not to be tragic; to be tragic, one must commit suicide "after the high Roman fashion" (87). What Cleopatra will try to do is purge the woman and become the tragic heroine. And yet the faint is crucial, for it demonstrates the genuineness of her emotional (as opposed to convenient) attachment to Antony: she is not just "using" his stature to achieve her own. And the faint shows that she *is* a woman, and, as a woman, loves Antony: her suicide "after the high Roman fashion" will not be simply an adaptation of the male version (like Portia's in *Julius Caesar*) but a suicide that is thoroughly female, Egyptian, and her own. The final scene will show whether she can combine the best of all this—woman, empress, Roman, Egyptian, love, death, tragic heroine—in a single imaginative and physical act, an act that will unite the two ends, Antony's and Cleopatra's, in a double tragedy and make their story more than a costly affair between two over-the-hill hedonists.

Yet with this important matter to be decided, the last scene is full of seemingly irrelevant, gratuitous, even farcical material. It is an interlude which might be called "The Beguiling of Caesar" and which is at the same time "The True Tragedy of Cleopatra." The scene is certainly the least crushing final scene in Shakespearean tragedy; here sadness smiles. Indeed it has been often noted that this play is the most comic of Shakespeare's tragedies. There is of course episodic comedy and illuminative comedy (roughly comparable to that of the Porter in *Macbeth*). But *Antony and Cleopatra* has structural comedy as well. If we wish to view the play in terms of Susanne Langer's theories of dramatic form—and I think the terms will be useful—we can trace a comic rhythm of action as well as a tragic.[13] The principal motive force of the play, the force that structures the action, is, as in so many comedies, the passion of man and woman. (This is a modification of Plutarch, where Cleopatra's motivation until the death of Antony seems to be unadulterated ambition.) In *Othello*, sexual passion was the motive force, but it was the perverted destructive passion that structured the play, not, as here, the normal, "comic," life-creating force. The destructive passion appears only momentarily in *Antony and Cleopatra* and is also a very common momentary occurrence in regular comedy (for example, *The Comedy of Errors*, *Much Ado about Nothing*, and *Twelfth Night*, as well as *Cymbeline* and *The Winter's Tale*). The comic rhythm in *Antony and Cleopatra* is supported by the complex imagery of fertility, slime, the Nile, swords, horses, and serpents, and by the various allusions to Mars, Venus, and Isis. The name Eros was a handy derivation from Plutarch. Shakespeare's language is never richer in sexual resonance than in this play. Cleopatra's lines on the death of Antony, quoted above, are a good example of this; Antony's fall is a sexual catastrophe.

Of course, the play is not a comedy. Langer says, "The matrix of the [dramatic] work is always either tragic or comic; but within its frame the two often interplay." [14] The matrix of *Antony and Cleopatra* is tragic, because the deaths are real, but in no other Shakespearean tragedy do the two rhythms interplay so extensively and with such complexity. They cut directly across each other and effect an ironic reversal of each other's values. Antony and Cleopatra are protagonists in two actions, a tragedy and a comedy. Because they are part of a comic rhythm with comic values, their tragedy is made lighter without loss of stature and takes the form of a triumph; but because they are part of a tragic rhythm with tragic values, their comedy, their triumph, their attachment to comic values, begins to look fatuous, frivolous, and meanly self-indulgent. Antony and Cleopatra get the better of it because the dominant form of the play, the matrix, is tragic, and the comic rhythm and comic values come to play through it at the end, forcing an ironic reversal and gaining the triumph. Still, the other possibility is never quite forgotten.

The tragedy (or triumph) of Antony and Cleopatra is thus ironically achieved by the working of elements of a comic rhythm in the tragedy of the last scene. This rhythm generates two kinds of comic structure in the scene: (1) *a comic intrigue* reversing certain key values, an intrigue which overcomes a blocking figure who holds those values, like the heavy father of romantic comedy, and which thus achieves (2) *a ritual union* of the lovers amid images of birth and renewal.

Cleopatra's opening speech in V.ii, like Othello's in his last scene, introduces the themes of the scene and suggests the form the final ritual will take. Both are ironic—Othello's because he is mistaken about the direction of the ritual form, Cleopatra's because the ritual form of the tragedy is being provided by a comic rhythm of action. Cleopatra envisions a new life free from the restraints that Fortune and earth place on Caesar:

> My desolation does begin to make
> A better life. 'Tis paltry to be Caesar:
> Not being Fortune, he's but Fortune's knave,
> A minister of her will. And it is great
> To do that thing that ends all other deeds,
> Which shackles accidents and bolts up change;
> Which sleeps, and never palates more the dung,
> The beggar's nurse and Caesar's.
>
> (1–8)

According to Langer, comedy presents "destiny in the guise of Fortune," that is, man's struggle against and triumph over an indifferent, capricious, nonliving (and to that extent inimical) world. The basic force driving man is his complex life sense of which sex is an important part and which, because of his brain, is capable of symbolic expression. The same brain, however, realizes that life is ultimately time-bound, and so the tragic rhythm impels man to the height of his self-realization within "his unique, death-bound career. Tragedy is the image of Fate, as comedy is of Fortune." [15]

Cleopatra is transposing the values of the two rhythms. Her speech makes it clear that she intends to kill herself, but she sees this act as a move into a new life. Just as the comic hero triumphs over the capricious nonliving world, so Cleopatra will triumph over Fortune and the dungy earth (the world of accidents and change). On the other hand, Fortune and the dungy earth, the need to fight and to feed to preserve life, are precisely the subject matter of comedy; that is, to leave them is to leave the sphere of comic action. Cleopatra in going to her new life is about to reach the height of her powers in a death-bound career; yet in her vision it is Caesar who will be time-bound and thus death-bound: she will be free.

The earth-bound, time-bound nature of Caesar's "Roman" world has been a major theme of the play.[16] The comic movement has always fought time (life must do so)—thus the importance of sex in the comic rhythm. As Antony leaves for Rome he says, "The strong necessity of time commands / Our services awhile" (I.iii.42–43), and a few lines later he contrasts Egypt: "But that your royalty / Holds idleness your subject, I should take you / For idleness itself" (91–93). There is a connection

between Cleopatra's "idleness" and her supposed delay in committing suicide, for much of the material between Antony's death
and her own seems like idleness.[17] The delaying idleness takes
the form of an intrigue to make "Fortune's knave" an "ass
unpolicied." Just as Antony's "Let Rome in Tiber melt" appeared
self-indulgent in its context, so Cleopatra's "better life" risks
appearing to be sour grapes at having been turned off by Fortune. Her (and Antony's) diminishing of the reality of the dungy
earth must be "proved." The comic interlude, "The Beguiling
of Caesar," teaches Caesar a lesson, that he really is Fortune's
knave. The delay, or idleness, has the effect of putting Cleopatra
in control, so that the suicide is an act of her settled will, not of
her frightened impulse. It is an expression of defiance and of
victory, not of surrender.

The interlude begins with the entrance of Proculeius. He and
Cleopatra exchange words but nothing much is accomplished,
since neither really trusts the other. We may note, however, the
careful sarcasm in Cleopatra's "He gives me so much of mine
own" (20) and "I send him / The greatness he has got" (29–30),
lines which show Cleopatra's ability to flatter and to be insolent
simultaneously, an ability which will appear in her relation to
Caesar himself later in the scene. And of course Proculeius's
comfortable assurances of grace and good will are an extension
of his master's hypocritical spirit as we will see it in the later
face-to-face exchange with Cleopatra, an exchange she indicates
here (31–32) that she is ready for.

The kindness of Proculeius is quickly revealed as being mere
words in the only violent moment in what is (except for the close
of *Timon of Athens*) easily the least violent of Shakespeare's
tragic endings.[18] When Cleopatra is surprised by Proculeius's
men, she tries immediate, unritualized suicide and expresses her
will to die rather than be led through the streets of Rome in
Caesar's triumph. The attempt indicates that she means what she
says about doing the deed to end all deeds, though she would
prefer not to be rushed. According to Langer, "As comedy presents the vital rhythm of self-preservation, tragedy exhibits that
of self-consummation." [19] Cleopatra will cross these relationships,
for her tragedy (death) is actually accomplished by the impulse
toward self-preservation (escape), while her comedy (defeat of

181

Caesar) is achieved in self-consummation. Her recital of the horrors she would endure rather than be taken in shame to Rome suggests the power of her impulse toward self-preservation:

> Sir, I will eat no meat, I'll not drink, sir—
> If idle talk will once be necessary—
> I'll not sleep neither. This mortal house I'll ruin,
> Do Caesar what he can. Know, sir, that I
> Will not wait pinioned at your master's court
> Nor once be chastized with the sober eye
> Of dull Octavia. Shall they hoist me up
> And show me to the shouting varletry
> Of censuring Rome? Rather a ditch in Egypt
> Be gentle grave unto me! Rather on Nilus' mud
> Lay me stark-nak'd and let the waterflies
> Blow me into abhorring! Rather make
> My country's high pyramides my gibbet
> And hang me up in chains!
>
> (49–62)

Cleopatra imagines two futures here, one Roman and one Egyptian, each in its way an opposite to the Egyptian life of sensual pleasure she has led up to now. And she would prefer the Egyptian future, horrible as it would be, because in Egypt she would be submitting to Roman power but not to Roman vision, which is what she fears most of all—that she will be seen as through Roman eyes, eyes like those of Philo and Demetrius, through whose vision Shakespeare first presents the lovers to us. But there is another Egyptian alternative, one that will express Cleopatra's kind of power as well as her kind of vision.

Dolabella replaces Proculeius, and the action of the scene becomes even more inconsequential—or apparently inconsequential. As Dolabella tries to get her to notice him, Cleopatra shifts her imagination from worldly horrors back to the deed which "sleeps" and the things that transcend the earth:

> I dreamt there was an Emperor Antony.
> O, such another sleep, that I might see
> But such another man.
>
> (76–78)

These lines suggest the shape her ritual death will take, a going
to sleep to join once again the man of her dreams. She proceeds
to build up an elegiac portrait of the great superhuman Antony,
raising herself by imaginative association:

> His face was as the heav'ns, and therein stuck
> A sun and moon, which kept their course and lighted
> The little O, th' earth. . . .
> His legs bestrid the ocean: his reared arm
> Crested the world: his voice was propertied
> As all the tuned spheres, and that to friends;
> But when he meant to quail and shake the orb,
> He was as rattling thunder. For his bounty,
> There was no winter in't: an autumn 'twas
> That grew the more by reaping: his delights
> Were dolphin-like, they showed his back above
> The element they lived in: in his livery
> Walked crowns and crownets: realms and islands were
> As plates dropped from his pocket.
>
> (79–92)

Here is an Antony who is cosmic, colossal, epic in everything
including his pleasures, an Antony whose life is not the spring-
time of young lovers but the season of maturity, an Antony who
is eternally fruitful. But was this the Antony we saw? Partly, yes,
but partly, even mostly, no. This is the simplified Antony of Cleopatra's dream, and Dolabella, a kind of choric figure at this point,
kindly but firmly refuses to accept the dream, as if to say that
Cleopatra can't achieve tragic grandeur by rhetoric alone: [20]

> *Cleopatra.* Think you there was or might be such a man
> As this I dreamt of?
> *Dolabella.*   Gentle madam, no.
>
> (93–94)

But Cleopatra will not give up her dream, on the grounds that it
couldn't possibly be just a dream:

> You lie, up to the hearing of the gods.
> But if there be nor ever were one such,
> It's past the size of dreaming: nature wants stuff

> To vie strange forms with fancy, yet t' imagine
> An Antony were nature's piece 'gainst fancy,
> Condemning shadows quite.
>
> (95–100)

The effect of this is to reverse our sense of what is real and what is not, just as Cleopatra wants to see death as life and defeat as victory. Let us look at the logic behind what Cleopatra does with such grace. The human imagination, she says, is superior to nature in creating what is marvelous, because the human imagination ("fancy") is free to deal in shapes alone ("shadows") and thus will never run out of material ("stuff"), whereas nature can only create by embodying the shapes it imagines in substance. In fact, with nature it is wrong to speak of a separation between shape and substance. Nature "imagines" concretely, by producing unique things, which the human mind can then separate into shape and substance. But, whether he ever actually existed or not, a marvel like the "Antony" Cleopatra has been talking about is beyond the inventive powers of the human fancy ("past the size of dreaming"). Therefore, he cannot be merely her dream, and so if he exists at all he must be nature's creation and therefore substantial, making shadowy human dreams seem silly. And does he exist? Well, we've just heard the marvelous description of a shape that couldn't possibly be the invention of Cleopatra's human imagination; thus the Antony she described must be real, substantial, and Dolabella lies "up to the hearing of the gods" if he says otherwise.

If we see this as a logical argument, which I think it pretends to be, the weak point is simply the contention that such an Antony is "past the size of dreaming." Cleopatra seems to protect this from scrutiny by introducing it with a dependent clause that twists tenses in such a curious way: "But if there be nor ever were one such. . . ." By the time Dolabella and we have sorted this out, she has got the crucial assumption past us. But it is interesting to note in this combination of tenses how consistently her imagination is working toward the end she desires, the deed that achieves the better life, that sleeps the sleep in which she may once more see this dream Antony. In her previous speech Cleopatra had spoken of the possibility of this Antony's existence in the past or at any time ("Think you there was or might be such a man / As this I dreamt of?"). Now, by using present tense ("if there be") with the possibility of Antony's existence and past tense ("nor ever were") with the possibility of his nonexistence, Cleopatra implies that our two alternatives are that this dream Antony still exists or that he never existed. Thus, when Cleopatra proves that it can't be true that this Antony never existed, she is also proving not that he *did* exist but that he continues to exist, in that better life for which she longs.

We may further note that the verbs in this clause are subjunctive, so that the contrast of past and present tenses really refers *out of time*, that is, away from the time-bound Roman world to the world of the imagination. The subjunctive is, in a sense, Cleopatra's proper mood, and as we get farther into the scene, into the "play" she is putting on, her "subjunctive" will seem increasingly to be "indicative," which is like drama itself— the subjunctive pretending to be the indicative, an imaginary world presenting itself to us as if it were "real."

In the speech as a whole Cleopatra denies the power of her own imagination to create an Antony, and, if we extend this idea to the action of V.ii, the power of her imagination to give shape to the scene as a whole: the Antony she speaks of is not a character but a real man, and her words and actions are not a play, a staged scene, but a real life. And Cleopatra may be so splendid that we forget that this Antony in fact is her creation, her dream, not the "real" Antony who was so much more complex. But if we do remember this, we may also remember that the "real" Antony *and the "real" Cleopatra* are Shakespeare's dreams, as is the "real" life of the play, and that what Cleopatra does to the Romans and us, and even to herself, in V.ii—beguiles with words, with her poetic flights, with her dramatic strategies, with her marvelous characters—all this is what Shakespeare is always doing to us. And just as Cleopatra speaks no soliloquies to explain herself to us, so Shakespeare gives us no direct statements about his art. He has left us no prefaces or essays or notes, no soliloquies, as it were, about what he was trying to do. We have only this series of dreams which so tempt us to take them as life, tempt us to take shadows as substance, to believe in fairies, or to give Hamlet a past, and a future, or, yes, to speak of Cleopatra's intentions.

The magic of the witch Cleopatra—the dark lady, Shakespeare's malign double—is the magic of her creator. Her speech here is a description of what Shakespeare must do in every play. And in the *play* is the revelation—the art tells the truth about itself in a way that "soliloquies," whether Shakespeare's or critics', never can. It seems to me that among these plays that tell the truth about his art *Antony and Cleopatra* is the most profound because more than any other it contains and accepts the complexity of its own being. *The Tempest* explains itself and gives up the fight, but in *Antony and Cleopatra* Shakespeare shows but does not explain the nature of his art, its powers and its limitations, its triumph and its failure, its lies and its truth.

The "liar" Dolabella, even as he rejects the dream, succumbs to the dreamer and thus plays a part after all in the dream's realization, for he is not merely a choric figure or an efficient messenger for Caesar. He is obviously in love with Cleopatra himself and wants her to think of him, not of Antony. Thus he is concerned about whether she has heard of him. He keeps trying to interrupt her, to make her aware of his presence, but when he does, he has nothing of business to say, only that he feels her grief. Both are behaving idly (though for Cleopatra nothing is more serious than such idleness) until Cleopatra charms out of him a confirmation of her fears that Caesar means to lead her in triumph, at which point one droll conversation gives place to another even more amusing.

Caesar enters and one of the more mystifying of Shakespeare's scenes begins. (For convenience we may call lines 111–90 the "Seleucus scene." [21]) It is clear enough what happens, but what is the significance of it? Is Cleopatra really fooled by Seleucus? Did she really intend to "induce" the "mediation" of Octavius' wife and sister (the latter now Antony's widow)? In other words, are her negotiations serious, or is she just making a fool of Caesar?

The mystery probably cannot be cleared up, but if we consider the scene as part of the entire interlude, the function of the mystery itself may be clearer. The Seleucus scene culminates in the crisis of both "The Tragedy of Cleopatra" and "The Beguiling of Caesar." (We must bear in mind that the rhythm of the former is comic, because its end is new life and the union of lovers, and the rhythm of the latter is tragic, because its end is the achievement of death.)

The problem of "The Tragedy of Cleopatra" is whether or not Cleopatra and Antony will be able to join in a double tragedy. Can she achieve the necessary nobility? This is still in doubt at the beginning of V.ii. Her opening lines were noble enough but issued in no action. Her attempt at suicide when she was surprised would have been more anticlimactic than grand, an act of panic, not of noble "Roman" decision, like Antony's. At the end of the Seleucus scene she declares, with firmness: "He words me, girls, he words me, that I should not / Be noble to myself" (191–92). And this time her words are followed by action, as she for the first time in the scene takes the initiative from Caesar: "But hark thee, Charmian. . . . Go put it to the haste" (192, 196). This is the crisis, the fatal deed, since, like Othello's murder of Desdemona, it starts the machinery that brings death to the doer.

What happened in the Seleucus scene with respect to this structure? Did she gain time for suicide by cleverly fooling Caesar into thinking she intended to live? Perhaps this is what the action meant, but we certainly cannot prove it from the text. What the text does say is that Cleopatra tried to conceal some treasure from Caesar in order to buy the intercession of Livia and Octavia, that she was exposed by her treasurer, and that she does some undecorous cursing at him. Whether we think she was intentionally fooling Caesar or not, these actions are very much present, and they indicate rather untragic qualities. Just before the crisis of her tragedy the noble queen of V.ii.1–8 has again been made to look like a conniving bitch, the eternal "boggler" pictured by Antony in one of his rages (III.xiii.110). In fact, we do not know that this scene was not actually the crisis until "He words me, girls, he words me." Why did Shakespeare risk showing once more these untragic qualities if he wanted to make a tragedy? First, with respect to character it adds a little tension to Cleopatra's achievement of tragedy (though with respect to action not a great deal, since we know she knows already what Caesar really intends to do). Second, Shakespeare had been at pains up to the last scene to create a magnificently enigmatic woman. It is not an abdication of critical responsibility to declare Cleopatra finally an enigma; that is the point—and the beauty—of her.

We are not required to accept "her infinite variety" as a convention. Shakespeare shows it to us, and why should he undo all his fine work by making her a simple noble romantic queen in the last act? Her infinite variety of roles included tragic heroine, and that role she chose to die in. Finally, her untragic display in the Seleucus scene is funny.

The Seleucus scene is also part of "The Beguiling of Caesar." Of course, if Seleucus's betrayal is a hoax, then Caesar is thereby beguiled, but some other aspects of the scene are more interesting and, I think, more significant, especially since we will never know whether it is a hoax or the real thing. (For reasons suggested in the previous paragraph, the point is not that we *make* a choice, but that we *have* one, one I think we finally can't make.) The scene begins with Cleopatra kneeling to Caesar. He tells her to rise, obviously enjoying himself, and she addresses him with a submissiveness she can hardly feel. There is a sense of pointlessness in this scene because Caesar and Cleopatra never quite mean what they say. If there is any real communication, it is below the level of the semantic content of the words. Cleopatra reads Caesar beneath the words, but Caesar is apparently taken in. He may have been too self-controlled to be sexually attracted to her, but he seems to have been seduced by flattery into false security. If this is true, it is subtly portrayed. Caesar's modest, condescending answers ("Not so" [190] being the best because it could mean almost anything) could be part of his policy, but we notice that where before the interview he was careful to have a guard in Cleopatra's immediate presence at all times, after the interview she is left to herself. (Before, Dolabella replaces Proculeius like the changing of a watch; after, Dolabella specifically says he must leave [206].) Thence it comes that Caesar is beguiled by Cleopatra's suicide.

There is no doubt that Cleopatra's humility is counterfeit. In fact, she is asserting her superiority, for she is teaching him that he is Fortune's knave. This she must do to justify her "better life," and she begins by playing up to his new power, power given him by Fortune, of course. First, there is the veiled sarcasm of a line like "Sole sir o' th' world" (120), an effect achieved not only by our knowledge of Cleopatra's character, but also by the alliteration of a unique combination of epithet and term of address.

There is something almost insolent in her "flattering" answer to his "I'll take my leave" (133):

> And may, through all the world: 'tis yours, and we,
> Your scutcheons and your signs of conquest, shall
> Hang in what place you please.
>
> (134–36)

And her self-description as "one so meek" (162) is a fantastic assertion about this woman who has just caught at Seleucus's eyes. But more significant than her "wording" of Caesar is her direct instruction on the subject of Fortune and *de casibus* tragedy.[22] She plays the role of fallen prince and holds a mirror for Caesar:

> See, Caesar: O, behold,
> How pomp is followed! Mine will now be yours,
> And should we shift estates, yours would be mine.
>
> (150–52)

The traditional motif is given new dramatic life here because it is the death (the fall) of Cleopatra itself which will prove Caesar Fortune's knave; we do not have to wait for "The Tragedy of Octavius Caesar." In fact, he is being beguiled at the moment she says it, and in the unpolicying of Caesar they do shift estates, she up to tragic heroine, he down to ass.

Because Cleopatra makes such a point of teaching Caesar a lesson about Fortune, because she views (see 285 and 306–7) her negotiations with Caesar and their outcome as specific proof of his slavery, we are the more likely to give credit to her opening assertions about the "better life." More than once she gives him a lesson about the nature of worldly power, as shown by the Seleucus episode:

> Be it known that we, the greatest, are misthought
> For things that others do; and, when we fall,
> We answer others' merits in our name,
> Are therefore to be pitied.
>
> (176–79)

This moralizing of the episode, like Cleopatra's earlier proof that Antony could not be merely her dream, is outrageous, for Seleucus's crime was to tell the truth. Cleopatra is almost openly abusing Caesar by giving him this lesson.

I have tried to suggest how this enigmatic scene, where Cleopatra is at once the triumphant master of the situation and its gull, affects the overall structure of V.ii. I conclude that a "solution" to "the Seleucus Problem" would actually weaken that structure by interfering with the complex crossing of rhythms and forms. To accept a simple, explicable Cleopatra would be to fall into her trap. Cleopatra is, after all, not really her own creator; Shakespeare has created her, and the music of his close is more complex in its rhythms than the music of the close Cleopatra plans.

4

The interlude nature of V.ii continues: Dolabella walks through on a pointless mission (a reconfirmation of Caesar's plans—Dolabella just wants to see Cleopatra again, to serve her, like a courtly lover), and we hear yet another horrid description of a Roman triumph, this time one that includes a satirical dramatization of the "Antony and Cleopatra" story. As I suggested earlier, Cleopatra rejects this Roman drama for one of her own, which she takes care to have properly staged:

> Show me, my women, like a queen: go fetch
> My best attires. I am again for Cydnus,
> To meet Mark Antony.
>
> (227–29)

Cleopatra is ritualizing her coming suicide as another meeting with Antony, who may again pay "his heart / For what his eyes eat only" (II.ii.226–27). With this "comic" reunion in mind, she wants to look her seductive best again. But at the same time she declares that she has "nothing / Of woman in [her]" now (238–39), for the new life must throw out all changing, time-bound factors. Flesh is one, and to that extent the new "comic" life is ironic.[23] "Now the fleeting moon," she says, "No planet is of mine" (240–41), and indeed as Cleopatra dies Charmian will call her "Eastern star" (307), associating her no longer with patterns of ebb and flow, like the lunar cycle or the seasonal flood of the fertile Nile, but with the permanence of the "better life" created by the deed that "bolts up change."

At the entrance of the Clown, with his basket of figs and the worm "That kills and pains not" (244), this scene which has often been funny breaks out into open hilarity while nevertheless remaining (with its discussion of serpents, sexuality, feeding, enjoyment, death, immortality, and the nature of women) thematically coherent. The interlude quality of the scene becomes even more apparent as, to Cleopatra's impatience, the Clown keeps on babbling and refusing to leave, thus further delaying the tragic conclusion. His blunders, double entendres, and (presumably) innocent symbolism are a most appropriate introduction to the ritual death of Cleopatra—wedding jokes, as it were.

Cleopatra's death is a ritualization of enthronement, sexual union with Antony, and the bringing forth of new life. To this extent the rhythm which informs the tragic ending is thoroughly comic. When the Clown leaves, wishing Cleopatra "joy o' th' worm" whose "biting is immortal" (278, 246–47), Cleopatra begins the ritual, again with careful attention to staging (attention which Charmian will continue after her mistress's death [317–18]):

> Give me my robe, put on my crown, I have
> Immortal longings in me. Now no more
> The juice of Egypt's grape shall moist this lip.
> Yare, yare, good Iras; quick. Methinks I hear
> Antony call: I see him rouse himself
> To praise my noble act. I hear him mock
> The luck of Caesar, which the gods give men
> To excuse their after wrath. Husband, I come.
>
> (279–86)

Here and in the lines that follow, the various themes which have played through the scene from the opening lines are recapitulated. The promise of Cleopatra's first speech ("My desolation does begin to make / A better life") is being fulfilled. This play's version of "O death where is thy sting" is "The stroke of death is as a lover's pinch, / Which hurts, and is desired" (294–95). The sense of comedy is so strong here that we find unsardonic humor in a tragic death, as Cleopatra, when Iras has died "so gently" from her serpent-mistress's "aspic" kiss, expresses some jealous anxiety:

> This proves me base:
> If she first meet the curled Antony,
> He'll make demand of her, and spend that kiss
> Which is my heaven to have.
>
> (299–302)

In order to be a tragic heroine (not "base"), she must hasten to an Antony "Whom ne'er the word of 'no' woman heard speak" (II.ii.224), to an Antony who might not wait for his tragic partner if someone else should turn up first, and thus to a world where there are no "Roman" categories to curb passion or to define it as "lust," no "Roman" rules to prevent the union of an Antony and a Cleopatra or to insist that since they are "a pair so famous" they *must* stick to each other. Cleopatra's imagination (which is ultimately Shakespeare's) both embraces and explodes all standard notions of tragic romance: Antony-and-Cleopatra is marvelous, but Antony and Iras is possible.

With the asps she accomplishes what she had set out to do at the beginning of the scene. New life, death, sex, permanence, joining Antony, defeating Caesar, feeding, and sleep all finally come together here in both language and act:

> *Cleopatra.*   Come, thou mortal wretch,
>   With thy sharp teeth this knot intrinsicate
>   Of life at once untie. Poor venomous fool,
>   Be angry, and dispatch. O, couldst thou speak,
>   That I might hear thee call great Caesar ass
>   Unpolicied!
> *Charmian.*   O Eastern star!
> *Cleopatra.*   Peace, peace!
>   Dost thou not see my baby at my breast,
>   That sucks the nurse asleep?
> *Charmian.*   O, break! O, break!
> *Cleopatra.* As sweet as balm, as soft as air, as gentle—

O Antony! Nay, I will take thee too:
What should I stay—
                    Dies.
                    (302–12)

The comic rhythm in *Antony and Cleopatra* makes death a
better life. One can feel this even while realizing the ironies of it—
that death is still death, that Caesar has won, that the child is a
serpent, that visually Cleopatra dies alone, without her Antony,
that the marriage bed is finally a grave in the dungy earth Cleopatra claimed to despise even as she embodied it, that her "better
life" is at best simply a better death. But we must also recognize
that it is not only the "new" life of Antony and Cleopatra that
would be "better": the introduction of comic structure and comic
values in the final scene creates a world in which being a tragic
hero means not only having lived a greater life, but also having
lived a better life. Hamlet, Lear, Othello, Macbeth—these men
may be distinguished by their power to suffer. But Antony and
especially Cleopatra are distinguished by their power to enjoy.
Cleopatra even enjoys her death—she finds, as Caesar will say,
an "easy way to die."

When the deed is done and discovered, Caesar, to do him
justice, is not only cool but also appreciative, and his appreciation
plays its part in confirming the tragic stature of Antony and
Cleopatra:

> Bravest at the last,
> She levelled at our purposes, and being royal,
> Took her own way. . . .
>   . . . she looks like sleep,
> As she would catch another Antony
> In her strong toil of grace.
>   (333–35, 344–46)

What once he would have called a whore's enticements, a witch's
art, now, *seeing* her, he calls a "toil of grace." Responding to her
visual presence, to an image as carefully and craftily controlled
as her original self-presentation to Antony on the barge at
Cydnus, Caesar finds Cleopatra still indeed a net to catch the

viewer, but now a net characterized by beauty, dignity, power, and ease.

Caesar has stood in the way of the lovers' union like the heavy father in comedy and like the heavy father he has been made an ass. An interesting comparison might be made between the structures of *Antony and Cleopatra* and Congreve's *Love for Love*, particularly with respect to Angelica's "negotiations" with her lover's father (and rival). The significant contrast—and it illuminates the complex comitragic matrix of *Antony and Cleopatra*—lies in the relations between the ages of the characters. Unlike Valentine and Angelica, Antony and Cleopatra are not "young lovers" but old lovers, and while Sir Sampson is the literal father of Valentine, Octavius is "the young Roman boy" (IV.xii.48). The young Caesar is one of those heavy fathers who is reconciled to the marriage (since this is a tragedy, he can well afford to be). Sir Sampson may not join in the wedding dance at the end of the play, but Caesar in effect does, by accepting Cleopatra's drama rather than the Roman one, by confirming her dream rather than the daylight vision of a Philo, by making the union of Antony and Cleopatra as tragic lovers heroic and eternal, or, as heroic and eternal as it is in Caesar's power to do, mere fortunate landlord that he is:

> . . . her physician tells me
> She hath pursued conclusions infinite
> Of easy ways to die. Take up her bed,
> And bear her women from the monument.
> She shall be buried by her Antony.
> No grave upon the earth shall clip in it
> A pair so famous.
>
> (352–58)

In accepting in these terms the union and the fame of the lovers, Caesar evokes one more time a sense of that metaphoric relation which characterizes the deaths of both Antony and Cleopatra, that association of dying and sexual consummation in which either can be the metaphor for the other. Particularly in the context of the other images in this passage ("bed," "buried by her Antony," "grave," "earth," "clip," "pair"), Cleopatra's pursuit of "conclusions infinite / Of easy ways to die" suggests endless pursuit of sexual pleasure, infinite ways of intensifying life as well as of ending it.

Already in Act I Enobarbus had noted the ease with which Cleopatra could "die." He was predicting Cleopatra's response to the news of Antony's intent to return to Rome (following Fulvia's death, though Enobarbus didn't know that yet):

> Cleopatra, catching but the least noise of this, dies instantly: I have seen her die twenty times upon far poorer moment. I do think there is mettle in death, which commits some loving act upon her, she hath such a celerity in dying.
>
> (I.ii.137–41)

The words which punningly imply Cleopatra's sexual readiness are on the surface intended to point to her habit of *staging* her emotions, of making her life a series of dramatic scenes. Enobarbus, who is always an acute appreciator of Cleopatra's value, even though he becomes in some ways her principal antagonist, thus combines in his "light answer" (172) the ideas of quick sexuality, death, and one's life as a continuing work of art. But this mingling of sex, death, and art takes on structural importance in the ending of the play, in the deaths of the tragic figures, increasing in importance from death to death. Through the process of his play, Shakespeare accomplishes a remarkable transformation of Enobarbus's "light answer" into light high tragedy as a dirty joke in Act I becomes the mode of a tragic ending in Act V.

Oddly enough, the result of the prominence given to this combination of sex, death, art, and humor is that *Antony and Cleopatra* is the tragedy in which the structure of the end of the play is most an image of Shakespeare's own tragic art. At the end of chapter 2 we considered the paradox by which dying, the destruction of the human figure, can become a creative art, a creative art for the tragic figures as they shape their ends, or for Shakespeare as he shapes the tragic figures *and* their ends, which, artistically speaking, are his own. There is a series of three moments in *Antony and Cleopatra* where Shakespeare most clearly stages this paradox: Antony's suicide in IV.xiv, the scene of his actual death in IV.xv, and the scene of Cleopatra's death in V.ii. Each of these moments involves the mingling of sex, death, and art in a situation that is in some way funny, and the moments are progressively elaborate as images of Shakespeare's art.

The first of these moments of paradoxical creation, Antony's suicide, we considered in chaper 2, where we noted that Shakespeare presents Antony's rush toward death as a rush to create life:

> I will be
> A bridegroom in my death, and run into't
> As to a lover's bed.
>
> (IV.xiv.99–101)

But Antony, briefly an artist in the sense that he is choosing an appropriate metaphor by which to complete his life's shape, cannot live up to the demands of this marriage bed, and in his inadequacy lies the humor—albeit grotesque humor—of the scene:

> How? not dead? not dead?
> . . . I have done my work ill, friends. O, make an end
> Of what I have begun.
>
> (103, 105–6)

Nevertheless, however impotent his sword in IV.xiv, where indeed it is snatched from his wound by Decretas for presentation to Caesar, Antony the "sworder" (III.xiii.31) is carried in to Cleopatra in IV.xv bragging that "Not Caesar's valor hath o'erthrown Antony, / But Antony's hath triumphed on itself" (14–15). The incongruity between his sense of valor and triumph and his incompetence even in fighting himself is again a source of humor even as it is pitiable. Even more humorous is the language and action that joins him to Cleopatra for the last time. Shakespeare uses stage action and punning language to present the thrusting aloft of Antony into Cleopatra's monument as a sexual union which is "comic" in more ways than one:

> *Antony.* I am dying, Egypt, dying; only
> I here importune death awhile, until

>Of many thousand kisses the poor last
>I lay upon thy lips.
>*Cleopatra.*   I dare not, dear;
> Dear my lord, pardon: I dare not,
> Lest I be taken. . . . But come, come, Antony!
> Help me, my women, we must draw thee up:
> Assist, good friends.
>*Antony.*   O, quick, or I am gone.
>*Cleopatra.* Here's sport indeed! How heavy weighs my lord!
> . . . Yet come a little,
> Wishers were ever fools. O, come, come, come.
>   *They heave Antony aloft to Cleopatra.*
> And welcome, welcome! Die when thou hast lived,
> Quicken with kissing. Had my lips that power,
> Thus would I wear them out.
>   (IV.xv.18–23, 29–32, 36–40)

The Antony who had to ask for help with his sword now needs help to be united with Cleopatra, an ironic end for the great soldier-lover. A curious little comedy is played out here: the eagerness of the man, the initial reluctance of the woman, and so forth, ending with a consummation, an image of a "mutual death," as he dies and (after a moment) she faints. At the same time the scene is also very moving. Emotionally the scene is extremely complex because it plays on so many responses at once. Death, certainly, has become a more serious and literal concern than it was in Enobarbus's joke. But among the responses the scene plays on is a kind of laughter, for in transforming the emotionally simple joke into tragedy, Shakespeare does not cast away the humor that was Enobarbus's principal impulse. The humor has now become part of a complex whole.

It is clear enough where the sex, death, and humor lie in IV.xv. But where is the sense of art? The characters themselves are not aware of the shapes their acts and words give the scene. The explicit "art" here is Shakespeare's, made comically evident in any of the various means that have been used or proposed for getting Antony up to Cleopatra. In the peculiarity and awkwardness of this action Shakespeare makes us consciously aware of the physical properties of his stage in a way he doesn't normally do.

The way sex, death, humor, and art interplay in V.ii has been a major concern of this chapter. We have seen Cleopatra move through a series of scenes that are often vaguely, sometimes pointedly, perhaps increasingly, humorous—the first dialogue with Dolabella, the interview with Caesar and Seleucus, the encounter with the Clown, and, remarkably, the death of Iras. There is even something ludicrous in the incongruous notion that a serpent is a baby and that injecting venom is sucking milk, as well as in the fact that these asps can be both phallic and infantile in the same scene, or, indeed, at the same moment. But as with Antony's suicide and Cleopatra's death, the humor is part of an emotionally complex whole, a mingling of tragic and comic values. We see this mingling of values as an accomplishment of Cleopatra's art, for Shakespeare presents Cleopatra as someone artistically conscious, specifically stage-conscious, as Enobarbus observed in his joke in I.ii. She is here a creator of her own life, and, posthumously, in her dream, of Antony's. Through her most potent art she achieves, by dying, the lovers' triumph over the father and reclines, imperially crowned and robed, on a throne which is a bed (354), imaginatively involved in sexual union with Antony and in nursing a child.

In the three scenes I have just reviewed, Shakespeare, in presenting tragic death as a sexual act, presents it as a creative act. (This is one of the things he emphasizes by making the asp a baby at Cleopatra's breast.) The scenes are thus images of Shakespeare's art because, for Shakespeare as a tragic artist, death is the consummation of a creative process. Moreover, the three scenes are progressively elaborate as images of Shakespeare's art. For one thing, as we move from the first of these scenes to the last we move from the simple structure of Antony's suicide (a metaphor and a single act), through the more extended "marriage" (visual and verbal) of his last reunion with Cleopatra, to the complex process worked out by Cleopatra in V.ii, involving intricate verbal and visual patterns of imagery, metaphor, fantasy, dialogue, costuming, and practical maneuvering. There is a progression, too, in the way the scenes present the idea of the artist. Antony is an artist only by analogy, in that he gives his death a poetic significance in relation to his life. Artistry is explicit in the reunion scene, but this explicit artistry is Shakespeare's (in the unusual physical use of the stage); the characters themselves do not act out of an artistic impulse. In V.ii, Cleopatra herself is an artist consciously giving form to her final scene; she is, like Shakespeare, an actual artist, not simply an artist by analogy. Finally, there is a refinement and elaboration in the visual style of these three fusions of sexual union and death. Antony's suicide is violent and (because Antony "does his work ill") crude, the reunion with Cleopatra is awkward and clumsy (though Antony's death later in the scene is not), but the death of Cleopatra is graceful, "easy," "like sleep."

And yet, Cleopatra's death is not quite stylistically complete in itself: her "crown's awry" (317) and so she needs Charmian, working after her death, to make the picture perfect. In another way, too, the end of Cleopatra's play suggests the limitations of her art: Antony is present only in her fantasy, not in the visual tableau. It is to the credit of her art that we hardly notice this (especially when we read the words instead of seeing and hearing the play). Another thing we may hardly notice is the way Enobarbus's jesting vision of death as committing "some loving act" upon Cleopatra returns in the words of Charmian, words that suggest a further limitation of this "artist's death"— namely, that it is with death, not her dream of an Antony, that Cleopatra now lies:

> Now boast thee, death, in thy possession lies
> A lass unparalleled.
>
> (314–15)

Death's possession of Cleopatra is a metaphoric way of suggesting that when death ceases to be a metaphor but is finally itself, Cleopatra, like the rest of us, like the artist, must die alone.

These final scenes of *Antony and Cleopatra,* the suicide of Antony, the reunion of the lovers and the death of Antony, and especially the long, elaborate, graceful death of Cleopatra, are thus images of Shakespeare's art not only in their celebration of tragic drama as a creative process but also because they include a sense of their own limitation, or, in other words, because they are so comprehensive in their attitude toward the events they show us. Our responses are not restricted to awe or to disgust, to tears or to laughter, to desolation or to cynicism, to fear and pity, to woe, to wonder.

And here is where we come to the parting of the ways between Shakespeare and Cleopatra. Cleopatra uses all her considerable art to give a single shape to her world. She simplifies her world, she simplifies her Antony, she simplifies herself. Shakespeare remains true to the infinite variety of his creature and to the infinite variety of the art that made her. His world includes the irony as well as the triumph, the death as well as the intense life, the dungy earth as well as the bed. Shakespeare's play, unlike Cleopatra's, considers the fact that the triumph is only artistic: since what we see is in some ways different from what we hear, Cleopatra's triumph is partly a retreat into the verbal, into the merely metaphoric. Thus Shakespeare includes here the possibility of the artist's self-deception even as he shows the possibility of the artist's triumph. As *Antony and Cleopatra* extends tragic form by bringing comic rhythm into a tragic structure, so too it extends tragic form by criticizing as well as by celeLrating the power of its own creation. In its extension of tragic form the play puts in perspective both the tragic view of life and the role of art in life. Tragic art is clearly valuable for a creature who knows he must die but doesn't know why. But tragic art is not the only art, nor the art of a whole life, for life is mysterious in other ways than in its suffering and its end. *Antony and Cleopatra,* more than the other tragedies, sees life whole and sees the activity of living in terms of the activity of being an artist. In Cleopatra, the "serpent of old Nile," Shakespeare has given us an image of human creative energy dealing with a world that is constantly regenerating itself in new forms, an image, that is, of variety confronting variety. Cleopatra adapts her art to the changing conditions of her life, until finally, in an act that "bolts up change," she creates a masterpiece that will be her monument. Shakespeare himself, her creator and her critic, is even more comprehensive an image of the union of art and life. He seems to have been more interested in making plays than in publishing them, as if his art was not the attempt to establish lasting monuments but rather a way of facing the continuing challenge of existence in a mysterious, changing world. His art, in other words, was his way of living. It became, by happy accident and the lucky afterthought of other men, his monument after all.

"She hath pursued conclusions infinite of easy ways to die. . . ." A "conclusion" is both an *experiment* and an *end*. As Cleopatra experimented with ways of ending a life, Shakespeare experimented with ways of ending a play. For him, each end is an experiment. Cleopatra incorporates her experiments in a death that is a work of art. Shakespeare's experiments include her *and* her death. For Shakespeare, as a playwright, the conclusions may not have been infinite and the creative dying, from play to play, may not have been easy; but the conclusions were as many as the worlds he made and the dying was accomplished, if not with ease, certainly with grace. His dramatic structures are his "strong toils of grace," the nets in which we, an audience of Antonys, are caught. Shakespeare's experiments in the art of the play, his "conclusions," are a way of experiencing a world that, like the cloud Antony sees in the setting sun, is always blowing away from the shapes we attempt to impose on it. Clouds have various shapes, lives have various shapes, plays have various shapes, the world—dramatic or "real"—has various shapes, and to show this variety and evanescence of shape, this seemingly ever-shifting order of things, Shakespeare makes the music of the close different in each play, each deep harmony sounded by his art.

 **notes**

Chapter 1

1. See Walter Jackson Bate, *The Achievement of Samuel John-son* (New York: Oxford University Press, 1955), p. 161, and W. B. C. Watkins, *Perilous Balance: The Tragic Genius of Swift, Johnson, & Sterne* (Cambridge, Mass.: Walker-de Berry, 1960), p. 77. The original source is, according to Watkins, Arthur Murphy (*"Essay, Johnson's Works,* 1806, I, 124"*).

2. *Richard II* is a particularly interesting case. At first Boling-broke seems to be the center of disorder, but then we realize, by at least II.i, that it is really Richard who is the threat; then in the rest of Act II and in Act III it's Bolingbroke again, and yet by IV.i Richard is once more the energy which destroys order. This shifting in our feelings about where the energy of the play lies may be simply the result of Shakespeare's portrayal of Richard as a man of either-or tensions, but it may also be characteristic of "historical" disorder, which can be either tragic or comic but resolves dramatically into an order that is accompanied by a more or less precise threat that disorder lies ahead.

3. Some of the notions about comedy in this section are based on Susanne K. Langer, "The Great Dramatic Forms: The Comic Rhythm," in her *Feeling and Form: A Theory of Art* (New York: Scribner's, 1953), pp. 326–50, and Northrop Frye, *A Natural Per-spective: The Development of Shakespearean Comedy and Romance* (New York: Columbia University Press, 1965).

4. The problem of order has been discussed often in connection with Shakespeare's plays, and this is hardly surprising, given the intense interest his contemporaries in Tudor and Stuart England took in the problem. I suspect that most of us get our basic notion of the period's sense of order from E. M. W. Tillyard's well-known and convenient exposition of *The Elizabethan World Picture* (1943; re-print ed., New York: Vintage Books, 1961). Tillyard's book is of course a starting place, a modest *vade mecum* for a study of Shake-

speare's plays (and, perhaps even more, other literature of the period) and is not an explanation of what actually happens in the plays with respect to the "order" theme. Nor is it true that Elizabethans could not think about the world in other ways; many did. Nevertheless, taken for what it is, Tillyard's account is a useful place to start.

Among other ways Elizabethans could describe the world's order, Tillyard discusses the "planes" of order, "correspondences" in structure between various spheres of activity in the universe, analogies between microcosm, macrocosm, and body politic. When we come to the plays, it is probably more accurate to speak of "the planes of disorder" than of "the planes of order," since with drama as with news, order is normally more interesting in the breach than the observance. The set of planes I propose in the text is a bit different from Tillyard's, though consistent with it. I am trying to analyze the structure of the tragedies, not recreate a "normal" Elizabethan way of seeing the universe and its many parts. As a result, my categories are less distinct from one another than his are.

5. Again, because of the peculiar dramatic structure of *Richard II*, the final scenes show Bolingbroke not so much being an opportunist as facing the consequences of having been one.

6. Brutus is of course the central figure. But Cassius is the one who most appears to increase in complexity, because while it was still Caesar's tragedy Cassius looked more like one of the usual winners. None of the men I've been discussing the last few pages is as high-minded as Brutus. None of them makes a mistake like the one Brutus makes twice with Antony.

7. To say this is to take Hector as a tragic hero. But though his death, as the play's last "event," occupies the place in the dramatic structure normally given to the tragic figure's death, there are reasons for doubting that Hector is really of "tragic" stature. See below in this section.

8. Cf. Brian Morris, "The Tragic Structure of *Troilus and Cressida*," *SQ* 10 (1959): 481–91, who sees Troilus as a tragic hero. I treat Troilus as a tragic hero too—though not in Morris's way, since I see his heroism as ironic.

9. Though it is part of a large historical pattern, Octavius Caesar's *pax romana*—see *AC* IV.vi.5–7—is a very secular, administrative affair compared to the peace established by Richmond or Malcolm.

10. John Holloway, *The Story of the Night* (1961; reprint ed., Lincoln: University of Nebraska Press, [1963]), has explored this aspect of Shakespearean tragic structure and drawn an anthropolog-

ical analogy with scapegoat ritual—the tragic hero as repository of society's evils.

11. The one person we see him kill in Act V is specifically someone's son (Siward's) and one who is "born of woman." See V.vii.5–13. Actually, it might not be apparent on stage that the young man Macbeth kills is "Young Siward," since he is never so identified in the lines, only in the stage directions and speech prefixes. Perhaps we are supposed to see *what* he is (a young man) rather than who he is. Or perhaps we would see that his coat of arms identifies him with Old Siward. In V.vii, when Young Siward's death is reported, the point is made that in his death he became a *man* (39–43).

12. Edgar certainly means Lear and perhaps Gloucester. In the Folio, Edgar uses a singular verb ("the oldest hath borne most"), which might mean that he is referring only to Lear, though Shakespeare is not consistent, by modern standards, in his use of verb number. In Q1, where in fact, the lines are spoken by "Duke" (presumably Albany; see chap. 4, n. 9, for a discussion of *this* textual problem), there is a plural verb ("the oldest haue borne most"), which would refer to both Lear and Gloucester. But the point I am making is not really affected by which text we choose.

Chapter 2

1. For a different kind of discounting of "perception" as a defining characteristic of Shakespearean tragedy, see Maynard Mack, "The Jacobean Shakespeare," in *Jacobean Theatre*, ed. John Russell Brown and Bernard Harris (1960; reprint ed., New York: Capricorn, 1967), pp. 37–38.

2. *Samuel Johnson on Shakespeare*, ed. W. K. Wimsatt, Jr. (New York: Hill and Wang, 1960), p. 33. The passage is from Johnson's *Preface* to his edition of Shakespeare's plays (1765).

3. On Richard's forcing Bolingbroke to reveal his intent, see Brents Stirling, " 'Up, Cousin, Up; Your Heart Is Up, I Know,' " in *Unity in Shakespearian Tragedy: The Interplay of Theme and Character* (1956; reprint ed., New York: Gordian Press, 1966), pp. 26–39.

4. Eliot, "Shakespeare and the Stoicism of Seneca," in *Selected Essays 1917–1932* (New York: Harcourt, 1932), pp. 107–20.

5. Ibid., pp. 110–11. It was Eliot, of course, who said (in 1919) that he had "never, by the way, seen a cogent refutation of Thomas Rymer's objections to *Othello*" (see "Hamlet and His Problems," in *Selected Essays*, p. 121). This suggests that he and Rymer are alike in the kind of moral demand they make on art, or on tragic characters.

There is clearly a similarity in the demands they make on *Othello,* since they are apparently interested above all in what can (or should) be *learned* from the experience.

6. *The Business of Criticism* (Oxford: Clarendon Press, 1959), p. 39.

7. Even in *Romeo and Juliet* Shakespeare has not suggested as much union as the situation would allow. The crueler version of the story found in Gounod's opera, for instance, keeps Romeo alive until Juliet wakes up, so that he realizes his mistake and can join Juliet for a final duet—a final expression, that is, of a harmonious union. But Shakespeare, with no operatic requirements and for once finding the original version cruel enough, followed his source.

8. Gardner, *Business,* p. 48.

9. This is perhaps another indication of Shakespeare's interest in moral problems rather than in moral lessons.

10. This follows Maecenas's serious use of the "mirror" figure in describing the effect on Caesar of Antony's fall (see V.i.34–35).

11. The contradictory statements may be more a sign of Shakespeare's indecision or carelessness than of Timon's "oppositeness," his reflex to oppose whoever or whatever comes his way.

Timon, for his part, seems to take a good deal of care over his epitaph. As early as Act IV he starts planning both the epitaph and his death:

> I am sick of this false world, and will love naught
> But even the mere necessities upon't.
> Then, Timon, presently prepare thy grave.
> Lie where the light foam of the sea may beat
> Thy gravestone daily. Make thine epitaph,
> That death in me at others' lives may laugh.
> (IV.iii.372–77)

Later he tells the senators who have come to seek his aid against Alcibiades that his final statement is about to be published:

> Why, I was writing of my epitaph.
> It will be seen to-morrow. My long sickness
> Of health and living now begins to mend,
> And nothing brings me all things. Go, live still;
> Be Alcibiades your plague, you his,
> And last so long enough!
> (V.i.183–88)

Timon's opposition to all things human, which by now has grown almost mechanical, leads him into constant contradiction of motive.

He wants to be left alone, but he clearly enjoys an opportunity for
cursing men to their ears. He wants to be left alone in death as in
life, and yet he wants men to read his epitaph:

> Come not to me again; but say to Athens,
> Timon hath made his everlasting mansion
> Upon the beached verge of the salt flood,
> Who once a day with his embossed froth
> The turbulent surge shall cover. Thither come,
> And let my gravestone be your oracle.
>
> (V.i.212–17)

When the oracular epitaph finally appears, it takes three contradictory forms. First is the inscription, apparently in the vernacular,
read by the "Soldier . . . seeking Timon for Alcibiades":

> "Timon is dead, who hath outstretched his span.
> Some beast read this; there does not live a man."
>
> (V.iii.3–4)

But there are also the two couplets which must be carried to a scholar
(Alcibiades!) for translation:

> "Here lies a wretched corse, of wretched soul bereft;
> Seek not my name. A plague consume you wicked caitiffs left!
> Here lie I, Timon, who alive all living men did hate.
> Pass by and curse thy fill; but pass, and stay not here thy gait."
>
> (V.iv.70–73)

Does Timon want his name known or not? The easiest explanation is
that Shakespeare found two epitaphs in North's Plutarch, one attributed to Timon and the other to Callimachus, that he wrote down
both, intending to choose one later, and that either the text we have
is based on an early draft or Shakespeare never finished the play at
all. (See, e.g., the Arden note on the passage by H. J. Oliver, ed.,
Timon of Athens [London: Methuen, 1959], pp. 139–40.) However,
the epitaph as it stands—contradictory—is consistent enough with
Timon's attitudes and behavior in the last two acts, and it may be
that, whatever the basis of the Folio text, Shakespeare intended to
keep both versions as forming a fitting epitaph to the man we have
seen. Timon wants to be left alone, he wants to be forgotten; yet
he wants men to feel his hatred beyond his death, he wants to be
remembered for it. Timon would not be the only Shakespearean tragic

hero to die in self-contradiction; in their various ways, Othello, Lear, and Macbeth do the same.

12. For the life-sex-death metaphors, see M. M. Mahood, *Shakespeare's Wordplay* (1957; reprint ed., London: Methuen, 1968), pp. 58, 72.

13. Contrast Lear, whose manner of death is, as it were, chosen for him by death itself.

14. But cf. lines 21–22, where before learning of Cleopatra's "death" Antony is ready to die for "Roman" reasons: "Nay, weep not, gentle Eros, there is left us / Ourselves to end ourselves."

15. Again, note the difference between the moment of Antony's *suicide* and the moment of his *death*. And Cleopatra, in her suicide, speaks not of the past or of her future reputation in history but of what she is accomplishing at that very moment—the union with Antony and the nursing of the child and the fooling of Caesar.

16. For an analysis of this speech in a different context, see chapter 5.

17. I also find it interesting that Richard II does not ritualize his death. He reasserts his kingship for the last time; that is all. Of course, since he is murdered, he hasn't even the leisure Juliet has to select a happy metaphor. Nevertheless, I miss a final ritual in the man who earlier had so often experienced them, used them, or, more and more, as his power waned, created them—the ritual of his baptism (IV.i.255–57) and coronation (passim), the rituals of court arbitration and chivalric trial (I.i and I.iii), the ceremonious return to his country (III.ii.6–26), the ceremonies due to kingship which in Act III are either not there when they should be (iii.72–76) or there when they seem a mockery (ii.171–77 and iii.190–95), a ritual of exchange to turn himself from king to beggar to corpse (III.iii.143–59), a ritual of dis-coronation to mark officially his fall from office (IV.i.203–21). But perhaps the absence of ritual at his death is ironic and ultimately triumphant for the man who had invested so great a psychic stake in the power of ritual and who had come to grief because he had acted as if the bare ritual, divorced from the realities of daily political responsibility, could keep him king in spite of all. Now, at the end, it is after all Bolingbroke, as later it will be his son Henry V, who must face the problems of ruling a country where now ritual is ritual and reality is power.

18. On Brutus's use of ritual see Brents Stirling, "'Or Else Were This a Savage Spectacle,'" in *Unity in Shakespearian Tragedy*, pp. 40–54.

19. Revenge, like suicide, is an activity that invites ritualization,

and it is a prominent motive in the final scenes of a surprising number of the tragedies. But in only two of them, I think, do we feel that personal revenge is central in giving the final scenes their particular shape: *Titus Andronicus* and *Hamlet*. The common form in the final scenes of these two plays is the explosion of a social affair, a ceremonious meeting. In *Titus Andronicus* the affair is a banquet, in *Hamlet* a fencing match. In *Titus* the revenger (Titus) creates the form himself (having Tamora eat her own children, sacrificing Lavinia) but loses control of it and is killed in a flurry of less ritualized revenges. In *Hamlet* the form is created by others (one of them, Laertes, himself a revenger) and taken over in the middle by the principal revenger, though he has already received a fatal wound. The way in which the social affair explodes in *Hamlet* is unique in Shakespeare, though it appears elsewhere in Elizabethan revenge tragedies (in *The Spanish Tragedy* and *Women Beware Women*, for instance). It involves the contrived transformation of what appeared to be a "fiction" into a fact. A fencing match—murder in jest—is transformed by Laertes and the King into a deadly swordfight. Civilized play gives way to the old reality behind it. Since among Shakespeare's tragedies only *Hamlet* has this form, I will discuss it at length in the chapter on that play.

20. Kingship is taken from him in V.iii, but he finds that part of his identity to be the least important. I don't suggest that looking for an identity is all Lear is doing for four acts, or even that it is the most important thing.

21. It is perhaps also the attitude identified by Eliot as "this *bovarysme*, the human will to see things as they are not." Macbeth, of course, simply refers to "Roman fool[s]," who "die / On [their] own sword[s]" (V.viii.1–2).

22. Early in Act V, when Cassius asks him what he will do if they lose, Brutus seems to share Macbeth's opinion of Roman fools; he will not kill himself, as Cato did, "For fear of what might fall" (V.i.104). But when Cassius then asks him if he is willing to be led a captive through Rome, Brutus seems to contradict himself:

> No, Cassius, no. Think not, thou noble Roman,
> That ever Brutus will go bound to Rome.
> He bears too great a mind.
>
> (110–12)

He, too, will do "what's brave, what's noble, . . . after the high Roman fashion," and he, of all people, should. If Brutus is not contradicting himself here, he is apparently making the distinction between "might" and "will" which, ironically, he failed to make earlier. He killed Caesar "for fear of what might fall," but won't kill himself in the same circumstances; he will only kill himself when a shameful defeat and capture become a certainty.

23. For an extended study of "ultimate" things in Shakespeare, especially in *Hamlet, Othello, Macbeth, King Lear,* and *The Tempest,* see Robert H. West, *Shakespeare & the Outer Mystery* (Lexington: University of Kentucky Press, 1968).

24. I have seen productions of *Macbeth* in which the hero is killed offstage, but the Folio text says clearly that Macbeth is "slain" by Macduff in front of the audience. Troilus and Pandarus do go off the stage, but the play ends before they can die, which makes their situation the opposite of Timon's—their medium deserts them, instead of the other way around!

25. Of course, I don't entirely want to make Timon sound like a character who wandered backward in time out of some play by Pirandello and found a place for himself in the early seventeenth century. But there is certainly a stage-consciousness in Shakespearean drama and in Elizabethan-Jacobean drama generally that disappeared in the movement toward the "well-made" play and resurfaced in modern drama, above all in Pirandello. Shakespeare makes various of his characters conscious of their "dramatic" life in various ways. Cleopatra's way will be an important subject in chapter 5, below. For a discussion of Shakespearean tragedy in terms of its stage-consciousness, with a lot of well-deserved space given to Hamlet but none to Cleopatra, see Lionel Abel, *Metatheatre: A New View of Dramatic Form* (New York: Hill and Wang, 1963), pp. 2–11, 26–29, 40–72.

26. Literally, "one . . . of Lord Timon's frame" (I.i.69), but the intent is clear. As in *As You Like It* II.vii.70–87, Shakespeare is parodying the satirist's refusal to be specific and name names.

27. What I'm saying is not affected by the relative dates of *Timon* (1605–1608) and *Antony and Cleopatra* (1606–1607), which, as I noted earlier, come out of the same source in Plutarch. One may consider *Timon* nearer to *King Lear* on the basis of style and theme or nearer to *Pericles* on the basis of its use of an inadequate poet within the play, a poet who claims to tell the whole story but fails to do its complexities justice. (On the inadequacy of Gower as a narrator, see Kenneth J. Semon, "*Pericles:* An Order beyond Reason," *Essays in Literature* 1 [1974]: 17–27.)

Chapter 3

1. On plotting in *Hamlet,* see J. V. Cunningham, "Plots and Errors: *Hamlet* and *King Lear,*" in *Tradition and Poetic Structure: Essays in Literary History and Criticism* (Denver, Colo.: Alan Swallow, 1960), pp. 90–105.

2. See M. M. Mahood, *Shakespeare's Wordplay* (1957; reprint ed., London: Methuen, 1968), pp. 111–29.

3. On the poison theme in *Hamlet,* see Maynard Mack, "The World of *Hamlet," Yale Review* 51 (1952): 502–23.

4. See C. T. Onions, *A Shakespeare Glossary,* 2d ed. (Oxford: Clarendon Press, 1919), s.v. *absolute.*

5. Of course, the Grave-maker doesn't know that it is Prince Hamlet he's talking to. On the other hand, Hamlet and Horatio are obviously distinguished by their dress (and accent, presumably) as being upper-class types. Otherwise there would be no point to Hamlet's remark. And the Grave-maker addresses him as "sir."

6. See A. P. Rossiter, *English Drama from Early Times to the Elizabethans* (1950; reprint ed., New York: Barnes and Noble, 1967), pp. 100–101.

7. It is just possible that Osric is in on the plot to kill Hamlet. If he is, he is the ideal messenger to Hamlet, since because of his foppish triviality, Hamlet doesn't suspect him. Hamlet was more suspicious of his own friends. If *Der Bestrafte Brudermord* is any evidence, Osric's predecessor in the *Ur-Hamlet* was involved. As far as I have noticed, however, the only reason in *Hamlet* for suspecting Osric of being more than an ignorant, if useful, participant in the plot is that he seems to have been responsible for measuring the foils and getting them set up for the match (248, 254–55). But this is merely circumstantial evidence and it can easily be conjectured away. The main point, however, is that nobody in the play makes anything of Osric's supposed complicity. It doesn't seem likely in a play like this that a guilty party would go completely unnoticed. That would be carrying irony too far. (Again working from *Der Bestrafte Brudermord,* the Ur-Hamlet stabbed the Ur-Osric, who boasted of his part in the plot. I feel fairly certain that Osric is ignorant, and innocent, though ironically dangerous.)

8. I am not claiming, of course, that these sounds or this kind of pattern suggests weariness inherently. But given the content, and the context, I find that to be their effect. It is possible that Shakespeare associated such sounds and patterns with weariness; note the following lines from *Richard II:*

> But whate'er I be,
> Nor I, nor any man that but man is,
> With nothing shall be pleased till he be eased
> With being nothing.
>
> (V.v.38–41)

9. The strongest argument against this is the presence of the Ghost. But the Ghost has disappeared from the play just as Hamlet's demon has disappeared. He is no part of the final scenes.

Chapter 4

1. *Samuel Johnson on Shakespeare,* ed. W. K. Wimsatt, Jr. (New York: Hill and Wang, 1960), pp. 97–98. Johnson's remarks are part of his "General Observation" on *King Lear* in his edition of 1765.

2. D. G. James, *The Dream of Learning* (Oxford: Clarendon Press, 1951), pp. 106ff., makes a similar point; and yet his view of what the play's characters are like could hardly be more different from mine. He sees a "simplification" of characters taking place in *King Lear.* I see the opposite.

3. Edgar makes this distinction in the final speech of the play, where it seems to represent a change in his opinion:

> The weight of this sad time we must obey,
> Speak what we feel, not what we ought to say.
>
> (V.iii.324–25)

I will consider the speech in its context later. For the moment I am merely interested in the distinction between "ought" and "feel." (For the possibility that Albany speaks these lines, see below, n. 9.)

4. Gloucester's final line ("And that's true too") is in the Folio but not in Q1, so there is a chance that it is a non-Shakespearean addition.

5. For an analysis of the Edgar-Gloucester relationship based on the idea that what we see operating here is fear to be recognized, see Stanley Cavell, "The Avoidance of Love: A Reading of *King Lear,*" in *Must We Mean What We Say?: A Book of Essays* (1969; reprint ed., Cambridge, Eng.: Cambridge University Press, 1976), pp. 282–85. In his essay as a whole (pp. 267–353), Cavell deals with the subject of "insularity" in a more aesthetically and philosophically extensive way than I do here. He begins his analysis of the relationships between characters in *King Lear* with the well-known

"sight" images and eventually moves to the problem of *our* relationship with the characters we watch in a tragic drama and to the problem of human relationship generally.

6. As usual, it is Kent who speaks what he feels, not what he ought to say: "Be Kent unmannerly / When Lear is mad. What wouldst thou do, old man?" (145–46). This is hardly the language one "ought" to use to one's sovereign, but Kent says this and more ("Revoke thy gift, / Or, whilst I can vent clamor from my throat, / I'll tell thee thou dost evil" [164–66]). It is also true, and important, that Kent speaks what he feels *because* of his "bond" to Lear. Kent is explicit about this (139–42, 147–49, 155–57, and the fact that Kent stops arguing not when Lear threatens his life or swears by Apollo, but when he invokes Kent's allegiance). But Kent's bond, the "ought," is itself an expression of his emotional attachment to Lear. Cordelia's bond to Lear is of the same sort, but in Act I she doesn't know how to act and speak accordingly, or doesn't choose to do so.

7. That Goneril's line might have greater significance than she intended was first pointed out to me by Brents Stirling.

8. The meaning of Kent's lines here (i.e., 281–82, 291) are disputed. I accept, in essence if not in detail, John Dover Wilson's interpretation (in his edition of *King Lear* [Cambridge: Cambridge University Press, 1960], pp. 272–74). But if by "Nor no man else" Kent means that only he is capable of joining Lear, I would revise my interpretation of the scene only to this extent: Kent feels only he is welcome because only he is capable of seeing that for Lear life can now offer nothing. There is no "happy, bright, and lively" old age of the sort Edgar and Albany might envision for him. In any case, the difficulty of Kent's lines makes them expressive both of the distance that separates Lear and Kent and, more important, of the distance that separates these men from common, "easily understood" experience of the sort that Edgar and Albany still believe in.

9. There is just a chance that Shakespeare did not intend Edgar to speak the final lines of the play. The Folio gives them to Edgar; but Q1 gives them to *"Duke,"* i.e., Albany, and though Q1 is a sloppy text, it's hardly "bad" enough to be automatically ignored. We should decide the case on its own merits. As the highest-ranking survivor, Albany would ordinarily get the last lines, but we have seen, first, Albany's terrible incompetence as a leader, and, more recently (319–21), his complete collapse and abdication in the face of Lear's death: he offers power to Kent *and* Edgar. Kent gives his answer, and it is reasonable to assume that Edgar would give his, and that

it would be those final four lines. It is, of course, interesting to contemplate an Edgar struck dumb by Lear's end, but we are probably getting a lot to get the admission he does make in the last speech, if it is his. And he has been, since II.iii, stronger, more practical (once one gets past his ideals) than Albany. It would also seem appropriate to the continuing sense of disintegration at the end of the play that a character who is *not* formally of highest rank should speak the last lines. So I believe that the Folio is correct here.

Chapter 5

1. For discussions of the operation of justice in the final scene, see, for instance, A. C. Bradley, *Shakespearean Tragedy* (1904; reprint ed., Cleveland and New York: World Publishing Co., 1955), pp. 159–62; and, with special emphasis on the ritual, Brents Stirling, *Unity in Shakespearian Tragedy: The Interplay of Theme and Character* (1956; reprint ed., New York: Gordian Press, 1966), pp. 132–35.

2. The *OED* (s.v. *cause*) gives two meanings which probably include between them the use in *Othello:* (1) "A subject of litigation; a matter before a court for decision; an action, process, suit . . ."; (2) "Contextually, and in translation L. *causa* or Gr. αἰτία, it sometimes has or approaches the sense 'charge, accusation, blame.'" Under the latter, the *OED* cites the passage in *King Lear* ("What was thy cause? / Adultery? / Thou shalt not die. Die for Adultery? No." [IV.vi.108–10]) which is parallel in meaning to that in *Othello* and is clearly legal terminology. A guilty man ("When I do stare, see how the subject quakes. / I pardon that man's life." [IV.vi.107–8]) is brought before Lear (in his imagination) and pardoned. Lear then asks what the "cause" was. The answer is "adultery," as it would be in Desdemona's case too, according to Othello.

3. But cf. III.iv.158–61, which may destroy (or may not) this argument: "*Desdemona.* Alas the day! I never gave him cause. / *Emilia.* But jealous souls will not be answered so; / They are not ever jealous for the cause, / But jealous for they are jealous." Shakespeare need not be using the same meaning in both places. More lexicographical research is required. One might discover a drift in the meaning of "cause" comparable to the drift of "soon," "anon," and "presently" from meaning "right now" or "immediately" into meaning "a little later." If one found a drift from the first *OED* meaning of "cause" cited in the previous note to the second, the human habit involved would be that of prejudging—guilt by accusation. And that is the situation Desdemona finds herself in.

4. In his Arden edition of *Othello* (London: Methuen, 1958),
p. 177.

5. Cf. Othello's mimicry of Desdemona's modest vacillation,
I.iii.160–63; a mostly comic treatment of vacillatory "but yet's" in
Antony and Cleopatra II.v.49–53; and a fully comic treatment in
Two Gentlemen of Verona II.i.106–11.

6. The basic effect does not depend on which text one accepts
here. The Folio reading makes Othello the less cool.

7. As I said in chapter 2, when Othello later speaks of himself
as "one that loved not wisely but too well" and "one not easily
jealous, but, being wrought, / Perplexed in the extreme" (V.ii.345–
47), I think he is right.

8. The Quarto reading *"thy* heart" (63) would not essentially
change this interpretation; lines 64–65 are the significant ones.

9. T. S. Eliot, "Shakespeare and the Stoicism of Seneca," in
Selected Essays 1917–1932 (New York: Harcourt, 1932), p. 111.
Eliot's statement is discussed, in relation to Othello's final speech, in
chapter 2.

10. The final speech has the specific ritual form of a trial
because it comes at the end of a scene where "justice" has been
structurally so important. In more general terms, of course, Shakespeare is adapting the *apologia* described by Helen Gardner in *The
Business of Criticism* (Oxford: Clarendon Press, 1959), p. 39. For
additional discussion of Othello's speech, see chapter 2, pp. 43–46 and
53–55.

11. "Speak . . . Then must you speak"; "set down aught . . .
Set you down this"; "Nothing . . . Nor"; "Of one . . . Of one . . . of
one . . . of one"; "not . . . but . . . not . . . but"; "Albeit unused
. . . drop"; "eyes . . . as fast as . . . trees."

12. But for a clear demonstration that "tragic heroism" *is* a
conscious concern of the play and its characters, see Brents Stirling,
" 'The Nobleness of Life,' " in *Unity*, pp. 157–92. Stirling, who takes
as his point of departure Shaw's "technical objection" to Shakespeare's "making sexual infatuation a tragic theme," examines the
way Antony and Cleopatra throughout the play attempt to strike
"tragic" stances and the way other characters, and they themselves,
criticize or qualify or approve these attempts: "Shakespeare seems
to have anticipated the problem of sexual infatuation as a tragic
theme by actually posing the question as a theme within his play.
Conventional 'romantic' tragedy, with its concepts of stature-in-
degradation, flaw, and soulful catastrophe, becomes an issue among
the characters very early in the action" (p. 159). For example,

Stirling sees V.i as virtually an explicit discussion of the nature of tragic heroism and says that the trick that leads to Antony's suicide "stems directly from a desire of Cleopatra to create situation, to write her own tragedy" (p. 176). My own emphasis, below, is not so much on the "debate" within the play about the nature of the tragic heroism achieved as on the peculiar structure of V.ii and of the tragedy Cleopatra writes there for herself and Antony.

13. See Langer, *Feeling and Form: A Theory of Art* (New York: Scribner's, 1953), especially chapter 18 (on comedy) and chapter 19 (on tragedy). There is structural comedy in *Romeo and Juliet*, too, but the interplay of comic and tragic is far simpler than in *Antony and Cleopatra*. One could almost say that Romeo and Juliet are comic lovers who unfortunately become involved with a tragic Fate; but a simple formulation like this won't do even as a beginning for a discussion of the careers of Antony and Cleopatra.

14. Langer, *Feeling and Form*, p. 334.

15. Ibid., pp. 331, 333.

16. See, for example, I.i.33–40 ("Let Rome in Tiber melt," etc., including the phrase "dungy earth"), I.iii.42–43, II.ii.158, II.vii.99 (a parody), III.vi.82–85, IV.xv.60–62. Caesar's men actually call him approvingly "the universal landlord" (III.xiii.72; cf. *Richard II* II.i.113 for associations of the term "landlord").

17. Her idleness recalls that of another great comic character, Falstaff. And just as Cleopatra is defeated by the time-bound Octavius so Falstaff is cast off by the Hal who redeems time when men think least he will and who comes to weigh time even to the utmost grain. But whereas Caesar's only concession to idleness is the brief debauch which follows the peace with Pompey (a debauch to which he is ironically encouraged by Antony's invitation to "Be a child o' th' time" [II.vii.99]), Hal had more thoroughly experienced the attractions of the alternate way of life and is in some ways an Antony who has found life with Octavia acceptable. Again, just as it was Richard's idleness (his "wasting" of time) that led to the triumph of landlordism in England, so it is Antony's attraction to the queen of idleness that allows Caesar to become the universal landlord. The fertility of Falstaff's imagination cannot turn his defeat into victory, and he dies ill, broken-hearted, guilt-ridden, and offstage. Cleopatra will be able to make creative idleness triumph and will seem to die living as fully and guilt-free as she always has, still a queen in the center of the stage. Falstaff had been able to escape by counterfeiting death at Shrewsbury, but only Cleopatra, who had had so much practice (see I.ii.137–41) could escape by counterfeiting it forever.

18. In *Antony and Cleopatra* the nonviolence is the result of Cleopatra's love of ease and pleasure in all things. The nonviolence in *Timon* is a measure of Timon's absolute insistence on being at odds with the world, a world, in this case, that wants him to live. The exact manner of his death we never know. It "might" have been violent, but there is no violence *in the play* (and so there is no violence). The world will not harm him and wants him to rejoin it. Therefore Timon will go offstage, away from the dramatic world, and die. Cleopatra's death is nonviolent even though it is onstage. For further comparison of the endings of these plays, see chapter 2.

19. Langer, *Feeling and Form*, p. 351.

20. See Stirling, *Unity*, p. 180.

21. For an analysis of the "Seleucus scene" and its place in the whole play, see Brents Stirling, "Cleopatra's Scene with Seleucus: Plutarch, Daniel, and Shakespeare," *SQ* 15 (1964): 299–311. Stirling shows that the Seleucus scene is the last of three parallel episodes (the other two are IV.xv and V.ii.1–70) in which Cleopatra moves from her characteristic "equivocation" or "contradiction" to a new "resolution" in the decision to die; thus the first two episodes prepare us for the mode of the Seleucus scene. The structure I am describing, with its "comic" and "tragic" rhythms, is different from this but not, I think, inconsistent with it.

22. See Stirling, *Unity*, pp. 181–82. (See my chapter 2, pp. 49–50 above, for a comment on Shakespeare's general use of the *de casibus* stance at the end of his tragedies.)

23. Cf. lines 288–89: "I am fire, and air; my other elements / I give to baser life."

✳ Index